# Internet Marketing

# Internet Marketing

## A Practical Approach

### Alan Charlesworth

Fortis College
Cuyahoga Falls
Learning Resource Center

**ELSEVIER**

AMSTERDAM • BOSTON • HEIDELBERG • LONDON • NEW YORK • OXFORD
• PARIS • SAN DIEGO • SAN FRANCISCO • SYDNEY • TOKYO
Butterworth-Heinemann is an imprint of Elsevier

Butterworth-Heinemann is an imprint of Elsevier
Linacre House, Jordan Hill, Oxford OX2 8DP, UK
30 Corporate Drive, Suite 400, Burlington, MA 01803, USA

First edition 2009

Notice
No responsibility is assumed by the publisher for any injury and/or
damage to persons or property as a matter of products liability, negligence
or otherwise, or from any use or operation of any methods, products,
instructions or ideas contained in the material herein.

**British Library Cataloguing in Publication Data**
A catalogue record for this book is available from the British Library

**Library of Congress Cataloging-in-Publication Data**
A catalog record for this book is available from the Library of Congress

ISBN: 978-0-7506-8684-6

For information on all Butterworth-Heinemann publications
visit our web site at books.elsevier.com

Typeset by Charon Tec Ltd., A Macmillan Company.
(www.macmillansolutions.com)

Printed and bound in Slovenia
09 10 11 12 13 10   9 8 7 6 5 4 3 2 1

To my big sister, Sue.

# Preface

> *In theory, there is no difference between theory and practice.*
> *But in practice, there is*
>
> Yogi Berra

## INTRODUCTION

Before telling you anything about this book, I'll enlighten you about the aspect that caused me the most trouble – its title.

I'll come to the sub-title, 'a practical approach', in a moment, for it was the first two words that were undecided right up to the final manuscript being submitted. The problem was, What is the book about? Is it *Internet marketing*, *e-marketing*, *online marketing* or *digital marketing*? I must admit, in the classroom I tend to use 'e-marketing' – my modules have that title – but I think that is a combination of habit and laziness (of the options, it is quickest to say). The book I co-authored with Richard Gay and Rita Esen uses 'online marketing'. Despite this, I was drawn to what I eventually opted for – Internet marketing – because it actually tells potential readers what it is about, that is, marketing using the Internet. What the book is *actually* about was the problem I had with the term that eventually came second in the contest – digital marketing. When I asked them, many within the industry advised me that 'digital' was the term that was in vogue in the boardrooms and at conference discussions. However, I felt it might be rather 'faddish' – the term that is trendy when people talk about something they don't really know about. More important, however, is that

I do not think it is digital marketing in which I am an expert (if indeed I am an expert in anything).

My thinking is that 'digital' covers so much more than just the Internet. As we near the end of the first decade of the twenty-first century, all media use digital technology, those rotating adverts around the side of the pitch at major sporting venues, the advertisement on the bus or train, on the treadmill at a health club, in the lift, even those promotional messages in rest rooms – all digitally transmitted and part of what is being dubbed 'out-of-home advertising'. And that's before we consider *digital* TV and radio. Sadly, apart from the basics that any marketing lecturer should know, I have little specialist knowledge on any of these aspects of the discipline. Furthermore, I had no intention of covering such subjects in this book. This book is about marketing on the Internet – so it's called *Internet Marketing*. In reality, however, I don't suppose it really matters, and I am certainly not saying that everyone should adopt my way of thinking. Perhaps us Internet/e-/online/digital marketers should get our act in order? (To read my thoughts on the subject in more detail, follow the link on the website.)

> " this book is designed to be more practical in nature … in contrast to many other academic texts on the subject … which tend to concentrate on the strategy itself, rather than how that strategy is implemented "

The sub-title is, I think, self-explanatory. It was always my intention that the book's ethos would get down in the e-marketing trenches rather than standing back and taking a strategic point of view on the subject. Although strategic issues are included where appropriate, this book is designed to be more practical in nature – addressing tactics, operational and functional issues in detail. This is in contrast to many other academic texts on the subject of online marketing, which tend to concentrate on the strategy itself, rather than how that strategy is implemented at the virtual coalface.

After reading this book, and completing the exercises within it, the reader will be equipped to undertake any Internet marketing role within a variety of organizations. The practical case study exercises, based on theory and recognized good practice, will ensure that readers will be able to analyse situations within the work place, identify the most appropriate course of action and implement the strategies and tactics that will help the organization meet its online objectives, which leads me to the final point in this introduction. Although this book is primarily aimed at an academic market, the practical nature of the content and its presentation means that it will be equally useful in both training and self-learning scenarios.

> " Although this book is primarily aimed at an academic market, the practical nature of the content means that it will be equally useful in both training and self-learning scenarios "

## THE SUBJECT

This is a book on Internet marketing – it is not a book on marketing per se. To get the best from this book, the reader should be aware of – although not necessarily an expert in – common marketing theories, strategies and tactics. To spend time explaining aspects of marketing – segmentation, for example – within this book would be to diminish the focus on its titular subject area. The content is, therefore, driven by Internet-based marketing applications rather than elements of traditional marketing, although naturally there is some commonality.

Nevertheless, it is inevitable that each chapter will integrate elements of marketing within its subject area. For example, facets of the marketing mix are a constant throughout the book, as are issues associated with buyer behaviour, product/service, customer/consumer and market orientation. Other more strategic elements of marketing permeate the book. Relationship marketing, for example, is an inherent component – or objective – of many aspects of online marketing.

Any book that has pretensions as an academic text must have appropriate academic underpinnings, which this book has. There are, however, three addendums to this:

1. The practical nature of the content means that there are also significant 'practical' underpinnings – that is, there are also references to the work of practitioners who have proved themselves at the coalface of Internet marketing.
2. Many references are also made to statistics or research findings from commercial organizations. Although there may be an element of bias in some of these, they are up to date and represent real world issues.
3. The academic research in the subject area is limited, out-dated or, in some cases, of dubious quality.

Considering the third point in greater detail, a comment taken from one of the better pieces of academic work is worth noting, Doherty & Ellis-Chadwick (2006) make the comment that:

> *Much of the discussion of the internet's potential has been conducted at a conceptual level, and there have been rather fewer contributions that have empirically explored the actual benefits delivered via the Internet, or the wider organizational impacts that it might engender.*

Although this particular comment refers to literature about Internet *retailing*, I find it to be equally applicable to most Internet marketing-related academic articles. Other criticisms I would make of academic research include that:

• Although some findings pass the test of time, many conclusions do not. For example, any comments with regard to online buyer behaviour made in 2000 – a time when Google and Myspace did not exist – are not necessarily true for Internet users now.
• A continuation from the previous comment is that some later work uses the findings of earlier research without question, making subsequent conclusions potentially flawed.
• A surprising amount of the research is conducted only on university campuses, with respondents being either (a) academics, or (b) students.

Although this might be acceptable in *some* research, when looking at anything Internet related, this sample is not a reasonable representation of the population, as these two groups are experienced users of the web and in the case of students, representatives of the first Internet generation.

Also with regard to academic research, I find there is confusion in the crossover between computing and business subject areas, with examples of both disciplines making basic errors when they stray out of their own field. This includes marketers making 'technical' statements that are flawed as well as IT writers who – without the qualification or experience in the subject – make erroneous comments about business applications, or of specific relevance to this book, marketing. The language used by the two can also cause problems for students. For example, Maulana & Eckhardt (2007) make the point that in an IT environment, research into 'connectedness' concentrates on physical dimensions, whereas in a social setting the concentration is on the emotional interpretation. Naturally, there are exceptions to this edict. There are a number of subject specialists, academics and practitioners, in both business and IT who have successfully crossed over and can now be considered to be experts in both. These are however – in my experience – rare. And in case you are wondering, although I have a smattering of IT knowledge, any expertise I may have is firmly in the *marketing* side of Internet marketing.

Anything related to the Internet is bound to be a very dynamic subject. Online marketing is no different. For example, the book I co-wrote with Richard Gay and Rita Esen, *Online Marketing – a Customer-Led Approach*, was published in March 2007. In that book, I wrote the content that included 'social media marketing', and it warranted a small section within a chapter that also covered several other aspects of Internet marketing. In this book, not only does social media marketing get its own chapter, but it is one of the longest chapters. I have endeavoured to make this book as up to date as possible, but inevitably, between my writing these words and you reading them, some aspects of the book's content will have changed. To address this phenomenon I will use the accompanying website to keep things up to date.

I have decided not to include a glossary of terms in the book. In this regard, the key problem I faced was that once I started to list terms that might be new to readers I did not know where to stop. In an attempt to address this I have tried to explain terms within the text itself. Indeed, a number of online marketing-related descriptions used are based on, or adapted from, definitions from another of my books, *Key Concepts in e-Commerce*. When you consider that book has over 1200 definitions and is around 100 000 words long, you can perhaps appreciate my dilemma in trying to develop a two or three page glossary for this book. My decision was, therefore, that I would include a limited glossary on the book's website and suggest that if you are new to the discipline and find some of the terminology new – buy my Key Concepts book as a companion to this text!

## CHAPTER STRUCTURE

Each chapter is divided into a number of sections that address specific aspect of the chapter's subject area. Throughout the book you will come across a number of content 'boxes', each serving a specific function. They are as follows.

### RESEARCH SNAPSHOT

These are snippets of information taken from published research – sometimes academic, but more often the information has commercial origins.

### MINI CASE

As the name suggests, these are short examples that illustrate a concept or model. They are often examples of good practice in that concept.

### Practical Insight

These give readers an insight into how elements of Internet marketing are practiced in real life, with many serving as 'tips' for students when they might become practitioners.

### Go Online

From these inserts, readers are directed toward the book's website. There, links are provided that take them to information, articles or comments on the subject being discussed in that section, which will supplement the content of the book.

With the exception of the early part of Chapter 1, at the end of each section readers are presented with the challenge 'you decide', where a case study-based question is posed. The following sample is from section 4.4.

### You Decide

Advise Robert Terwilliger on the advantages and drawbacks of using a third-party website to sell the Modeller's Stand (case study 9).

Alternatively, conduct the same exercise for your organization or that of your employer.

The case studies are designed to make clear how the impact of each online application varies between organizations and markets. For each section, I have tried to select a case study that is pertinent to that section, although you are welcome to switch case studies for each question if you wish. Alternately, if you are employed or run your own business, you can ask that question to your – or your employers – organization. A similar format is followed at the end of each chapter, but at this time you are invited to advise one of the case study organizations on all aspects of Internet marketing covered in that chapter. The following sample is from Chapter 9.

## CHAPTER EXERCISE

Giving justifications for all your decisions, advise the board of the Matthew Humberstone Foundation Hospital (case study 6) on all aspects of social media marketing covered in this chapter. This includes taking a look at the 'dummy' blog that can be found by following the link from the chapter's web page.

Alternatively, conduct the same exercise for your organization or that of your employer.

## THE CASE STUDIES

Throughout the book, case studies are used as both examples of how theory might be practiced and as exercises for readers to complete. Although the case studies are fictional, they all characterize real life situations. The cases are not intended to be comprehensive or exhaustive – merely a snap shot of a particular state of affairs within what is normally a complex environment. The case studies have been compiled in such a way that all aspects of Internet marketing can be addressed, with each element of the chapters having its own case-related question, with one case being presented as an end of chapter exercise.

The case studies are as follows:

1. The Rockridge Museum – a not-for-profit organization with a mix of public and private funding.
2. Clough & Taylor Engineering – a small engineering company that makes bespoke products.
3. The Gilded Truffle Hotel – a new boutique hotel opening soon in a prime city centre location.
4. Cleethorpes Visitors Association – a publicly funded tourism centre.
5. BethSoft – a small business that sells a range of specialist software to the engineering industry.
6. Matthew Humberstone Foundation Hospital – a private medical facility with hospitals and clinics around the world.
7. 22 Catches Fish Products – a consumer packaged goods manufacturer.
8. Hill Street Motorist Shops – a chain of retail outlets with a limited online presence.
9. The Modeller's Stand – a single product sold in a niche market.
10. Huxley University – a small academic institution.

11. Two Cities Manufacturing Ltd – a medium-sized manufacturer and distributor of commercial and private grass-cutting appliances.
12. Lindsey Naegle Consulting – a sole trader who works as a consultant in Internet marketing.
13. Phelps Online Department Store – a pure play online retailer that sells women's clothes and accessories.

Note that all of the above are UK based, but their geographic location could be changed to suit readers' needs.

Note that the actual case studies are not included within the book – rather, online on the book's website where they can be printed off. Although I accept that might cause you a small inconvenience, I have made this decision for a very good reason. If the cases were within this text, I would not be able to change them – at least not until a second edition of the book is published! Online, however, it is relatively simple for me to change, add or delete any element of each case. This means that as the Internet, the way it is used by the public and how it is adopted by organizations' changes, I can adapt the scenarios to suit the environment in which those case study organizations operate. I have also made the conscious decision not to offer any answers to the case studies. The key reasons for this are fourfold:

1. As with all marketing, there is no single answer that can be considered to be unambiguously 'right'.
2. Such is the nature of not only the web's development, but also the global environment in which it exists, that the answers might actually change on a monthly basis (as I write this in November 2008, the last two months have seen the world's economy change in a way no one could have imagined – with all the resultant impacts on business).
3. As teaching staff may choose to use the case studies for summative assessment, I do not want sample answers in the public domain where misguided students might be able to get hold of them and present them as their own work.
4. The objective is that you should work to develop the answers yourself. If I put suggested answers in the book too many students would succumb to the temptations to read them rather than doing the work necessary to understand the subject.

## TERMS OF REFERENCE

Throughout the book I occasionally refer to *companies* or *firms*, but mainly I use *organization*. This is deliberately vague. Whenever you see the word organization feel free to replace it with any other term that you feel is relevant to the context or your own circumstances. As well as company and firm, other examples might include government department, university, hospital, foundation, school, society, not-for-profit business, association, college, religious body, charity, club or any other entity, including individual.

In a similar vein, it is common for marketers to use the term *customer* to describe anyone who uses or partakes in the service on offer – not just the person who pays for a tangible product. In some cases, the customers have their own descriptor – opticians have patients, universities have students, political parties have voters, sports teams have supporters, churches have members and so on. Likewise – and this is particularly relevant online – the objective is not always to have the target customer *buy* something. The objective could just as easily be to elicit a donation, a subscription, an order, an application or to have someone become a member. Again, please use whichever term you feel is relevant wherever you see the word *customer* or *buyer* within this text.

Wherever possible, I have avoided any promotion of specific brands or products within the text. This is particularly the case where Internet marketing tools, services or technologies are concerned – naming a particular website hosting company or software that helps with search engine optimization, for example. This is deliberate for two primary reasons: (1) I have not used all of the applications/companies and so am not in a position to rank one above another, and (2) to name one and omit another would appear to show favouritism which may be construed as prejudice. There are instances, however, when to not name names would be to the detriment of the content – for example, some aspects of the ubiquitous Google empire have become common terms to describe elements of online marketing and so are difficult to replace with a generic description. Indeed, to 'Google' something is now frequently used as a generic term for using a search engine. Note that it is also the case that for many of the tasks described within the text, there are software applications that *claim* to do the job for you. As I have used very few of these I am not in a position to either recommend them or otherwise. I am sure some work, just as I am certain that some do not. I have deliberately not mentioned the availability, or suppliers, of any such software – effectively, this book is about the *manual* way of doing online marketing. A slight deviation to this rule comes where I have used organizations as examples to illustrate a subject, concept or practice – often with an accompanying image. This is not to promote any organization, brand or product, it is simply that these are examples I have come across as I surf my way around the web.

## ONLINE SUPPORT

As well as the online elements of the case study exercises, this book makes extensive use of the Internet as source of information. This includes the book's own website, features of which include the following:

- Each chapter having its own page that includes references to websites that provide more details on subjects covered within the text and links to information that will enhance the book's content. For example, in section 9.6 reference is made to how Cadburys released clips of their 'drumming gorilla' advert as part of a viral campaign. Although it is expected that the majority of readers will have seen the advertisement, some may not be aware of it, so there is a link to a web page where the advertisement can be viewed. There are also links to
  - additional subject material
  - websites of organizations mentioned within the text.

- All case studies in pdf format.
- Tips and advice for lecturers and trainers – including 'what to look for' in the answers to the case study questions.

In addition, the dynamic nature of the subject is acknowledged by there being – where appropriate – chapter 'updates'. Although it is not feasible to produce complete re-writes of chapters, on occasion it might be prudent to add to or amend elements or sections in accordance with changes in contemporary practice. Although I cannot predict the future, before a second edition of this book might be published, it is pretty certain that there will be, for example, changes in how search engine algorithms work. Similarly, the Microsoft–Yahoo! merger failed to materialize (in May 2008), but any similar union in the future would have a significant impact on the Internet marketing environment.

In addition to the book's website, I also maintain my own website, which – amongst other things – has sections on Internet marketing-related articles, research papers and practical tips, hints and advice. Ultimately, I would like it to be a one-stop-shop for researching all aspects of Internet marketing. Judging by the visitor numbers around assignment time, this is already a popular site with students.

My website can be found on www.alancharlesworth.eu and blog on getoutsidethebottle.blogspot.com

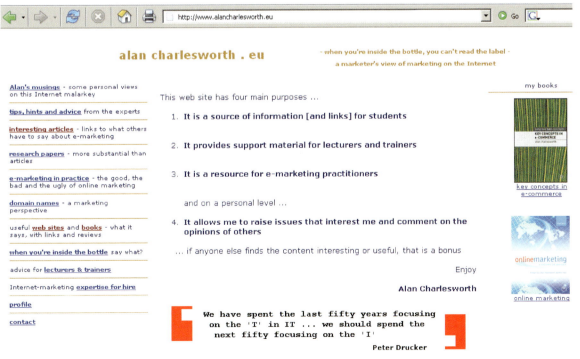

Finally, whether you are a student, trainee, lecturer, trainer or practitioner, I hope you find this book *useful*. Note that I have refrained from wishing that you *enjoy* reading it. Although I have tried to make it easily readable, you should *enjoy* a John Grisham mystery or Robert Ludlum adventure whilst relaxing in a comfy chair or sun lounger. I have written this book not to entertain – but to help you achieve a professional or educational objective. Of course, if you do get pleasure from it, that is a bonus.

Alan Charlesworth, Sunderland, UK.
alan.charlesworth@gmail.com

## REFERENCES

Doherty, N.F. & Ellis-Chadwick, F.E. (2006). New Perspectives in Internet retailing: A review and strategic critique of the field. *International Journal of Retail and Distribution Management.* Vol. 34, No. 4/5, pp. 411–428.

Maulana, A.E. & Eckhardt, G.M. (2007). Just friends, good axquaintances or soul mates? An exploration of website connectedness. *Qualitative Market Research: An International Journal.* Vol. 10, No. 3, pp. 227–242.

# Acknowledgements

To all at Butterworth-Heinemann who helped make this publication possible. In particular, Francessca – who from day one showed an enthusiasm for the project that sold BH to me – and Sarah who took up the reins when Francessca left for pastures new.

Karen Hadley – on whose 'old' laptop much of this book was written.

All the students, trainees and audiences at any event at which I have spoken – if you hadn't asked the questions, I would not have had to find out the answers.

All those practitioners, writers, bloggers and researchers who do the work that keeps people like me informed.

All those organizations that have asked me to monitor or participate in their online marketing efforts – you learn more in an hour at the sharp end than you do in days of reading the theory.

All those individuals and organizations that gave me permission to use content or images that are copyrighted to them. In particular, Elliance (www.elliance.com) who were kind enough to let me use a number of their 'infographics' throughout the book. Elliance is typical of organizations who recognize that all aspects of online marketing are inextricably linked (I particularly like their tag line of 'Art + Science of e-Marketing').

# The online environment

> *You'd better start swimmin'*
> *or you'll sink like a stone*
> *because the times they are a changin'*
>
> Bob Dylan

## CHAPTER AT A GLANCE

## 1.1 INTRODUCTION

>
>
> … we are still unsure of what the future will bring to Internet marketing.

In the early days of the commercialised Internet, an article in the *Journal of the Academy of Marketing Sciences* (Peterson et al, 1997) made the point that:

*'No one can predict with certainty what the ultimate impact of the Internet will be on consumer marketing. There is virtually no information on how, or to what extent, consumers will use the Internet in the context of marketing or what new marketing paradigms will prove viable.'*

Over a decade later we have some idea of that impact, but so dynamic are the technologies, the practitioners and the environment in which it is used that we are still unsure of what the future will bring to Internet marketing in both consumer (B2C) and industrial (B2B) trading as well as not–for–profit and public sector environments. Furthermore, we are equally unsure as to how much *more* the Internet will change society – for change it has. For marketers this is significant as it is society that makes up our customers. Back in the mid 1990s, predictions of how the Internet would change the way we do business were manifold – and they were largely ignored by those businesses that would be affected by that change. Opinions, however, have softened over the years and the Internet is now accepted by business leaders. Or is it? Speaking in an article in the *Sunday Times*, Google's president for Europe, Middle East and Africa, Nikesh Arora, commented that:

> *'The change in consumer behaviour is so fundamental that in the future one of the dividing lines between firms that succeed and those that don't will be the ones that have embraced the Internet.'*

This is the sort of comment that was commonplace towards the end of the last century – and so I find it quite disturbing that this quote comes from May 2008. Admittedly, there might be a bias from its author in that Mr Arora will be looking to increase business for his employers, but nevertheless it does suggest that acceptance of the Internet is far from accepted in board rooms around the world – more than 10 years after some of us saw the writing on the virtual wall.

## 1.2 A BACKGROUND TO THE INTERNET

Although it is not necessary for practitioners of online marketing to be given a full history lesson on the development of the Internet, a basic introduction to its history and how it works will help the new online marketer to implement an e-marketing plan. Contrary to common misconception, the Internet was born of military – not academic – parents. Although many universities took up use of the fledgling technology at the end of the 1960s, research into what became the Internet began a decade earlier when

Cold–War era American leaders, fearing that a limited nuclear attack on the USA would disable conventional communications systems, instigated the ARPANet (Advanced Research Projects Agency Network) project. The system's development as a simple medium of character–only communication continued throughout the 1970s until an Englishman, (now sir) Tim Berners–Lee, developed his 'rules for the World Wide Web' in 1980. Further technical advances were made in the 1980s including the development of the Transfer Control Protocol (TCP), Internet Protocol (IP) and the Domain Name System (DNS) – all of which are cornerstones of what we now know as the Internet. Still academia–centric throughout this period, it was not until the early 1990s that the technology moved into a more commercial environment – not least with the 1991 release of the World Wide Web – and some business leaders began to recognize the potential of the new medium of communications.

## Practical Insight

### The web, email and the Internet – misconceptions

In both technical and practical terms the Internet is the parent of the other two. In other words, the Internet is made up of the world wide web and email. The world wide web and the Internet are not the same thing. Email is not part of the world wide web. The Internet is not an element of either the world wide web or email.

The 1993 launch of the first web browser – Mosaic – meant that the general public now had easy access to the web. Although a number of commercial websites appeared during this time, few really appreciated the web – indeed, scepticism ruled the day, with many condemning the Internet simply as a fad that would go away. For many – myself included – the real birth of the commercial web was in October 1994 when 'Wired' magazine's online edition, Hotwired.com, featured the first online banner advertisement (for AT&T). While 1995 and 96 saw great commercial steps forward for the Internet in the USA (Amazon.com was launched in 1995), the rest of the world was slower in its uptake. Although the northern Europeans – including Scandinavia – were at the forefront of outside–USA adoption, it was 1997 before businesses – and significantly, governments and the EU – really took it seriously. Even then there was a long tail of uncertainty – with even some major brands and household names not even having a website until closer to the end of the 1990s. The end of the old century and the beginning of the new millennium saw a kind of 'Internet fever', with every news medium featuring web–related stories of some kind in every bulletin or edition. This culminated in the frenzy of ill–conceived investments in 'dot–com' businesses – and their inevitable failure, the so–called 'dot–bomb' era. But despite the highly publicized crashes of web–based ventures, the value of the Internet was obvious, and the doom mongers' predictions of its demise were well off the mark.

> ## Practical Insight
>
> ### The Internet was not the start of e–commerce
>
> Many assume that e–commerce began with the Internet – but they would be wrong. By the end of the last century, electronic data interchange (EDI) – which was responsible for revolutionizing procurement and distribution systems in the 1970s and 1980s – was estimated to account for $250 billion annually in business-to-business transactions (Merrill Lynch, 1999). What the Internet did do, however, was bring e–commerce within the reach of all businesses – and not just those that could afford a computer that was as big as (and far more expensive than) a house.

As with the history of the Internet, it is not necessary for the online marketer to know all the scientific and technical aspects of the medium. However – if only to prevent programmers and other techies baffling them with science – the marketer should at least have an inkling of how the thing works. What follows is a very rudimentary version of what happens when you go online.

1. The website is hosted on a computer (server) that holds it in the form of a program code until it is *requested* by a user.
2. When the user either types a URL into a browser or clicks on a hyperlink, a request is sent from their computer – via an Internet service provider (ISP) – for the files that make up that website to be delivered.
3. The elements that make up the website are sent – in 'packets' – to the requesting computer. Note that it is the 'packets' element of the communication system that satisfied the ARPENet military requirements. Essentially – and is still the reason why the Internet rarely fails and delivers quickly – the transmitted message is broken down into its component parts and each is tasked with finding its own way to the destination. The Cold War scenario was that standard single–line methods of communication could be easily broken by an atomic explosion. With the Internet there is no single–line, so if a packet hits a blockage it simply keeps looking until a clear route is found.
4. The packets arrive at the destination they are re–formed to make the complete message – which users see on their screens as a web page.

Of course – despite its complexity – online, this all happens in fractions of a second.

Throughout this book reference is made to 'techies'. This is meant as a term of endearment rather than insult. Although very rare exceptions exist, in general those involved in the technical (science) aspects of the Internet do not have marketing (art) experience or qualifications. Of course, the reverse is equally true.

Therefore, I use the term 'techies' as a non-abusive term bestowed on people whose work is primarily the development – or operation – of technical aspects of the Internet in particular or computing in general. I am happy to admit that although I know the *very* basics of how the Internet works I have no skills as a *techie* – indeed computer science is well beyond my comprehension. Techies would do well to return me the same compliment, however – having a rudimentary knowledge of the 4Ps does not constitute an understanding of marketing.[1]

---

*Go Online*    **Internet history**

A number of websites include 'a history of the Internet'– one of the best is Hobbes' *Internet Timeline*, which will give you a sound background to the Internet. For a view into how banner ads have developed since AT&T's first one, Toronto web designer, Tari Akpodiete, has a website chronicling their history. Follow the links from the chapter's web page for both sites.

---

In concluding this section, it is worth mentioning two web–delivery issues that may impact of online marketers in the future. Although both seem to frequently rise up the agenda only to drop back down again, both 'net neutrality' and 'Internet overload' do not seem to want to go away – and that they are both closely related is significant. Like any highway, the 'Information Superhighway' (a term made popular by the [then] US Vice–President Al Gore) has a limit to the amount of traffic it can carry. Despite advances in pertinent technology, the capacity of the Internet is finite – and that capacity is being severely tested by 'new media' such as streaming video. As more and more applications are moved online, so the system is struggling to cope – with some experts predicting the whole system will grind to a halt as we all try to watch the latest blockbuster movie or play video games online. To get around this impending gridlock, the service providers have – repeatedly – put forward a solution. This entails a split in website availability – effectively a fast and slow lane. In the fast–download–easily–available lane would be the websites of those organizations that can afford to pay for the faster service. The rest, it is feared, would disappear on the slow dirt–track–to–nowhere – essentially creating a situation that blocks (or at least hinders) free competition. Although at the time of writing congressional action (in the USA) has prevented the introduction of a two–tier Internet, many commentators feel the issue has not gone forever.

---

[1]If you are a techie seeking to advance your online marketing understanding and skills by reading this book, I applaud your endeavours – sadly, few marketers will take programming courses.

*You Decide* It is likely that the majority of people who use this book will be aged under 25 – meaning that they have grown up as part of the first 'Internet generation'. For those readers the following question will require some imagination, for the others (like me) it is a test of memory.

In the following sections of this chapter we look at the impact that the Internet has had on both society and business – but before doing that consider how different your lives would be if the Internet did not exist. I'll start you off by saying that doing assignments at college or university would be a lot harder!

## 1.3 THE IMPACT OF THE INTERNET ON SOCIETY

While a book of this nature cannot ignore the impact of the Internet on society in general, that could be the subject of a social–science focused book in its own right. For example, how in traditional societies where the elders are revered and respected for their accumulated knowledge the availability of knowledge online has usurped their prestige and caused breakdowns within those societies, or can online gambling sites increase addiction. In this section, therefore, we will concentrate only on where societal issues interact with the organization – in particular the commercial organization. It is difficult, however, to differentiate between the socially relevant and the not–relevant. The influence on buyer behaviour, for example, is pretty straightforward. But whilst the impact on society might not be overtly commercial, it is rare that there is none. Political parties could be described as commercial in that they practice marketing, or if the 'societal' aspect is the content of a news item then the medium carrying the news might be doing so as a business model.

*Go Online* **Social networks and regime change**

For an example of how the Internet has impacted on society, follow the link on the chapter's web page to the excellent article on the role the Internet played in the worldwide reporting of demonstrations against their government by Burmese monks in October 2007.

Although the Internet can be described as a substitute for traditional business channels in three ways: distribution, transaction, and communication (Butler & Peppard, 1998), the first two have only limited application. Distribution is restricted to products that can be digitalized (music, word files and computer software, for example) and despite the hype, online is far from the preferred option for making purchases (see section 4.7). Essentially, for most users, the Internet is a medium of communication. Certainly it has unique characteristics and facilitates types of communication – particularly

>  the Internet has one significant function – it is a provider of information

interactive – that other media lack, but it is first and foremost a medium of communication, full stop. As such, the Internet has one significant function – it is a provider of information. This is the reason for search engines being so powerful – they help people find information. That information could be commercial (how much is product X and where can I buy it?), non–commercial (when was the Battle of the River Plate?) or a mix of the two (what is killing my tomato plants, and what can I buy to stop it?).

## Practical Insight

### You can't have the good and not the bad

Because this book is primarily about commercial use of the web, I have chosen not to include a section on the misuse of the Internet for illegal or nefarious purposes. In societal terms this mainly entails the use of the Internet for the dissemination of material deemed unacceptable by society – and in much the same way as the web is lauded for its ability to spread the *good* word, so it is efficient in spreading the *bad*. That said, the same media is used to combat negative online aspects of our society. For example, the charity 'Crimestoppers' *Most Wanted* system on its website (www.crimestoppers-UK.org/wanted) helped locate nine of the UK's highest risk child sex offenders in the 12 months to November 2007.

Note however, I do appreciate that there is an *adult* industry that is legal – and so can benefit from the legitimate marketing practices covered in this book. Indeed, because it was one of a very few industries that made a profit from online activities in the early days of the web, the adult industry is responsible for many of the marketing-related technical innovations that are now common place on websites.

>  … in the information-rich Internet age the power is switching to the buyer

In commercial terms, it is the provision of high quality, well–developed, relevant, product–related information in a manner that is easy to access so that it best meets the needs of the customer that is the primary use of the Internet. Commenting on their research into the uptake of the Internet, Papacharissi & Rubin (2000) suggested that people will only use media because of the utility they derive from the medium – the subsequent success of the web would indicate that users do indeed derive a benefit. I – and others – would contend that the benefit gained is the availability of information – and that information is changing the way that customers shop (Markillie, 2005). Sir Francis Bacon's axiom that 'knowledge is power' holds true in business – and in the information–rich Internet age the power is switching to the buyer. As Kamarulzamam (2007) comments, one of the attractions of e–shopping is the customer's perceived control over purchase decisions. The concept that marketers are losing control of their brand is covered in more detail in chapter 9.

In previous eras of business, a marketing text would concentrate on how the organization might use a medium to interact with its market.

Any social interaction would be either beyond its control or be so informal as to be insignificant in any strategic planning. Certainly in some industries – entertainment, for example – word of mouth (the so–called 'water cooler' effect) might have played a part in a product's promotion, but for most any such benefits were ad hoc rather than formal and – importantly – not accountable. However, the Internet has brought a way for society to interact with itself. No longer is the public media governed by an elite few that may limit its views to that of its owners, a particular political persuasion or the demands of its advertisers. We now have the *social* media – which is open to anyone with the ability to access the Internet. Although we cover marketing in the social media in chapter 9, the social phenomenon is worth consider-ing within the context of the impact of the Internet on society.

## Practical Insight

### Online, privacy might not mean private

Although social media sites offer guides on the etiquette of how to use them – respecting the community, for example – other issues can be more troublesome. Online bullying, for example, is an offline problem that has moved seamlessly online. However, perhaps the biggest societal issue is that of privacy. Offline, it is (relatively) easy to make a judgement on all the people to whom you give personal information. Online, however, it is impossible to tell whether or not someone is who they say they are, or totally restrict who has access to your personal data. For this reason, all users should think carefully before giving out any information that might be used for unethical, immoral – or even criminal – activities.

Although there are a myriad of reasons why someone might visit a social media website, there are four primary purposes, they are:

1. As part of their *social* life – that is, chatting with friends or acquaintances in much the same way as their ancestors might have passed time by gos-siping about nothing specific. Essentially, this is the social conversation that has always existed – and marketers should be aware that the tech-nology driven communication medium that is the Internet can spread an opinion – or rumour – in a way only imagined previously. Twelve years ago the early adopter who was the first to see a new movie might pass a glowing review to only a few close friends and work mates. Now – with the power of social networks''friends' facilities – hundreds might read that review, and in turn pass it on to hundreds of their 'friends'.
2. Using the web as a medium to engage in an existing and/or offline pastime or hobby. This can range from supporting a particular football team, though arts and culture via cult TV shows or pop stars to grow-ing particular types of flower. As is the case with (1) above, such chat can be monitored by marketers as research into how products might be perceived by the public.
3. Joining a particular social group to gain benefit from their combined knowledge – self–help and support groups linked to illness and/or

disease, for example. Although there may be an element of chatting to like–minded individuals, this interaction is information based – 'can anyone help with this problem' to 'where can I buy this product?' Once again, this can have commercial implications and so is pertinent to the online marketer.

4. Employment, career or industry related. As with the previous listings, there will be an element of gossip about these sites, but they are primarily about networking with individuals or groups that may help further an individual's work or income stream. Though such sites might be considered as *commercial* media (rather than *social*), they differ in that they are inhabited by individuals rather than organizations – with commercial media sites more likely to be the industry portals or marketplaces that are covered in section 5.5.

## MINI CASE

### It can be hard to keep secrets in an online society

When her husband insisted on disconnecting their phone and keeping their television turned off Miami housewife Donna Campbell was confused – and when a postcard offering congratulations on a new house purchase arrived she moved to being suspicious. Turning to the web to satisfy her curiosity she entered her husband's name into Google – and discovered he had recently won $600,000 on a local lottery. She was soon looking for him again – for a divorce.

Given the *why* of people going online, let's now consider *who* is going online? Although the USA cannot be held as an absolute exemplar of Internet use – it is a reasonable benchmark for 'mature' Internet adoption. Research from the Pew Internet & American Life Project (2005) suggested that around two-thirds of Americans went online, and this figure seems to have remained fairly static since then (only wider access to lower-income groups may increase the online percentage). Americans online are also an experienced group, with 79 per cent of users having access for four years or more – and only six per cent having access for a year or less – so there are fewer 'newbies' around.

## RESEARCH SNAPSHOT

### The Internet: It's a way of life

Results of a survey – published in 2007 – from Nielsen/NetRatings (www.nielsen-netratings.com) and SEM firm Webvisible (www.webvisible.com) into consumer behaviour and attitudes with regard to online advertising found that 81 per cent said the Internet was *vital* to their lifestyle.

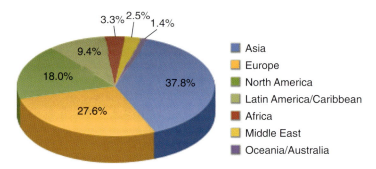

**Figure 1.1** World Internet users, March 2008.
*Source*: www.internetworldstats.com. Copyright © 2001–2008, Miniwatts Marketing Group. All rights reserved worldwide.

| WORLD INTERNET USAGE AND POPULATION STATISTICS | | | | | | |
|---|---|---|---|---|---|---|
| World Regions | Population (2008 Est.) | Population % of World | Internet Usage, Latest Data | % Population Penetration | Usage % of World | Usage Growth 2000–2008 |
| Africa | 955,206,348 | 14.3 % | 45,321,040 | 4.7 % | 3.3 % | 903.9 % |
| Asia | 3,776,181,949 | 56.6 % | 512,251,104 | 13.6 % | 37.8 % | 348.1 % |
| Europe | 800,401,065 | 12.0 % | 374,244,342 | 46.8 % | 27.6 % | 256.1 % |
| Middle East | 197,090,443 | 3.0 % | 33,625,200 | 17.1 % | 2.5 % | 923.7 % |
| North America | 337,167,248 | 5.1 % | 243,399,574 | 72.2 % | 18.0 % | 125.2 % |
| Latin America/ Caribbean | 576,091,673 | 8.6 % | 127,093,209 | 22.1 % | 9.4 % | 603.4 % |
| Oceania/Australia | 33,981,562 | 0.5 % | 19,176,162 | 56.4 % | 1.4 % | 151.6 % |
| WORLD TOTAL | 6,676,120,288 | 100.0 % | 1,355,110,631 | 20.3 % | 100.0 % | 275.4 % |

**Figure 1.2** World Internet usage and population statistics for March 31, 2008.
*Source*: www.internetworldstats.com. Copyright © 2001–2008, Miniwatts Marketing Group. All rights reserved worldwide.

Statistics from Internet-mature countries (e.g. the Northern Europe, Scandinavia) would suggest the American figures will be mirrored in these areas. Other regions of the world lag behind – China being the obvious example – and web marketers should take this into account if they are seeking to appeal to a global market. Figures 1.1, 1.2 and 1.3 give a snapshot of Internet usage statistics. Go to the website (www.internetworldstats.com) for regional breakdowns for these figures, there is some very interesting reading – and the information is regularly updated.

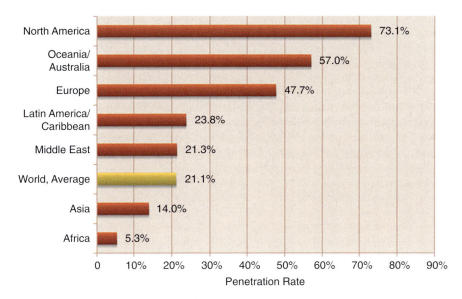

**Figure 1.3** World Internet penetration rates for March, 2008.
*Source*: www.internetworldstats.com. Copyright © 2001–2008, Miniwatts Marketing Group. All rights reserved worldwide.

## RESEARCH SNAPSHOT

I can assure you that it has nothing to do with me, nor is it the reason for my living and working here, but Sunderland is the UK's digital capital. According to Ofcom's *The Nations & Regions Communications Market 2008*, the city has the highest percentage of homes with broadband connection – 66 per cent compared with the national average of 57 per cent.

In concluding this section it is necessary to point out that not all people have access to the Internet. Although a small number have deliberately eschewed the medium, the majority of those who do not use the web do so because it is not readily available to them – essentially, they cannot afford it. This creates something of a haves and have-nots scenario, often referred to as the digital divide. If the Internet can provide information that will improve your life – be that through access to education or simply cheaper products – than the have–nots will fall still further behind the haves. It is this notion that has seen many Western governments heavily subsidise public Internet access in the more deprived areas of their countries – in schools and libraries, for example.

## Practical Insight

**I got it for free – do you want it too?**

Not part of commercial marketing on the web (in that no organization is involved and no money changes hands) but important to note in the impact the Internet has had on society is the phenomenon of peer to peer (P2P) 'trading'. Its significant impact was on the music industry, where once music was made available in a digital format it could be copied and the music files then passed on to others via the web. Originally vigorously fought by most of the music industry, it is now accepted – with some bands giving away free online downloads of their latest recordings.

## DECISION TIME

Right up to the end of the last century, many organizations refused to accept that the Internet was anything more than a fad that would appeal to only the computer geeks in society. Similarly, a percentage of the public also thought that the Internet was not for them – with computer–phobia the most common reason. However, it is now the case that the majority of organizations and public not only accept its presence, but have access to it and, indeed, now depend on it as a way of life. Significant, however, are the figures from the United States where the public's web access seems to have levelled out at around 70 per cent. This means that there is a significant minority that will not use the Internet in (1) any buying decision or actual purchase, or (2) seeking any information that might better their quality of life. For the business, it is likely that their product will appeal to either a segment that *does* or *does not* use the web – and so that can be taken into account in any marketing expenditure. However, non–commercial organizations – particularly those in the public sector – must continue to cater for any segment of their public that cannot, or will not, access the Internet.

*You Decide*    Consider the (continuing) impact of the Internet on society – and in particular, on those who cannot afford access.

1   How might continuing non–access have a significant negative impact on their lives?
2   Does the government have an obligation to deliver free or subsidised access, or is the Internet simply another commodity that people can take or leave?

## 1.4   THE IMPACT OF THE INTERNET ON BUSINESS

> " not all businesses
> will benefit from
> the Internet "

Although it may seem to the reader as puzzling for an online marketer to admit it – but not all businesses will benefit from having a presence on the Internet. Some will continue on as they have done for centuries before. The independent local greengrocer, for example, does not need a website. Nor will they ever sell online – and their procurement will be conducted locally, and in person.

However, I do have three caveats to this declaration.

1  If the web is a source of information to those who have access to it (see previous section), then a customer of the aforementioned greengrocer may have been online to research the nutritional values of certain fruit, for example. However, that information is unlikely to drive a customer away from their *local* fruit shop.

2  Things change. For example, if ever we get to the stage that people go online before they reach for the printed Yellow Pages (or similar), then a basic website – or at least an entry in an online local business directory – will be necessary for most businesses (though don't forget that not all of the population is online).

3  I accept that a manufacturer's Internet-based promotion for a consumer packaged good (CPG) may drive a customer to the small store – but it has always been the case that various media beyond the control of the shopkeeper has been used by manufacturers.

## MINI CASE

### Selling and sold

One thing that I find causes a problem for students is something that is basic to all marketing – the word *sell*. The problem comes from its two main meanings, namely: (1) to sell – exchange goods for money, and (2) to sell – promote the benefits of something. In the second, an *exchange* may take place some time after I have *sold* you on product. For the Internet marketer, the issue is that we normally refer to *online sales* as being when a credit card is used to make a purchase online. However, this is a narrow definition – a customer might, for example, read about a product on a company's website and be *sold* on the product, then jump in her car, drive to one of the same firm's outlets and purchase it. If this is the case, where did the *sale* take place? And which element of the organization's marketing should take the credit – the website or the physical store? The answer is important when the allocation of budgets is considered. Add to this scenario that the content of company A's website might *sell* the product, but the customer buys it from company B, and the problem becomes a significant issue for online sellers.

This interpretation of 'sell' is a constant throughout both off– and online marketing – and it is also a recurring issue in this book.

- Open-minded shoppers (40 per cent) – open minded to new things, 97 per cent of this group has shopped online and the majority do so regularly.
- Reserved information seekers (45 per cent) – this group is typically careful and reserved, and although open to purchasing on the web they use the Internet mainly for information searching and pre-product evaluation.

More pragmatic is practitioner and writer Gerry McGovern (2002), who suggests that there are four types of user that might arrive on a website. McGovern presents his list of users in the context of web designers needing to cater for each – and it reflects his commercial outlook (rather than Barnes' more academic appraisal) that he considers all but one of the groups to be potential customers – prospects. The first are *perfect prospects* – people who know what they want and so may well take an action that helps the site meet its objectives (a purchase, for example). The second group of *prospects* 'sort of' know what they want, but are not sure. Third are the *prospects* that aren't even sure if they want anything, but would buy something if the right product came along. The fourth group is the only one not made up of prospects – and that is because its members have arrived on your website by mistake. It is the latter that is the only group that can be ignored when developing a website.

Also of concern to the e-marketer are issues of how and why Internet users behave as they do when they are online. As with offline buyer behaviour – on which much is written – the key elements revolve around psychological and social factors, though the concept of *benefits sought* is also a key consideration, particularly for e-tailers looking to make online sales.

Research into the purpose behind peoples' visits to the web strongly suggests that it is a search for information that drives them online. As we covered in the earlier sections of this chapter, that information need not be commercial in nature – but it would appear that even with commercial intent the web is used primarily to gather information. Furthermore, the product–related information gathering is not limited to high–value items. In a survey into consumer packaged goods, for example, DoubleClick Performics (2007) found that American 'moms' – of whom 89 per cent used the web daily – reported using search engines to find sites to compare prices (72 per cent), find retail locations (71 per cent) and gather product information (71 per cent). To put these figures in perspective, only a small percentage of US retail shopping is conducted online – so emphasizing to the online marketer the importance of the Internet in the contemporary customers' buyer behaviour.

Although facilities to easily compare selling prices for products is something the web has brought to the homes of users, price is not the single driver of online sales. As we will see in this and subsequent chapters – although the web is used to find low prices, it is for an *offline* purchase. Indeed, when considering online purchases, price is not a key determinant – convenience having the most positive impact on their purchase behaviour

(Kotler 2000, Skyrme 2001, Alreck and Settle 2002, Bhatnger et al 2000 and Constantinides 2004). Researchers at Massachusetts Institute of Technology's Sloan School of Management (Brynjolfsson, E. & Smith, M. 2001) even found that providing it came from a well-known vendor, more than half of the consumers actually paid more for a product online. Other buyers might consider that the cost in their time of travelling to buy a product in a physical store far outweighs any higher price they may pay online (Athiyaman 2002).

## MINI CASE

### At four pounds an hour, it's a bargain

In 1997, I worked on a project to develop a website selling a series of 'past times' books that featured photo-histories of UK towns and cities. Books featuring specific towns or cities were readily available in local bookshops, but our target market was ex-pats who wanted to revisit their past, but could not physically return to their hometowns. The first subject city was our own – Sunderland. The office sweepstake for the country of origin for the first order had Canada and Australia as joint favourites. So it was something of a disappointment when the first online order came in from the village of Whitburn, a couple of miles up the coast from Sunderland's city centre. Contact was made with the buyer. Why had he paid full retail price plus postage for a book he could have purchased at a discounted price in a city centre shop?

On reflection, his reason was obvious – and many others in the still emerging practice of e–commerce were soon to realise it too. Our customer – who ran his own business – worked 7am until 7pm, Monday to Friday. On Saturdays he played golf. Sunday was his family day. To travel to the city centre on a weekend, park his car, walk to the shop, buy the book and return home would take at least an hour, nearer two on busy days. To this gentleman, ordering online during the evening and paying an extra £4 or so to have the book delivered to his house was a bargain. He valued his leisure time at well over £4 an hour.

A further consideration is that segment of the market for which visiting bricks–and–mortar shops is physically problematic. This applies not only to those who are disabled, but those who might have family obligations that tie them to their homes – caring for elderly or infirm family members, for example. For others, shopping is simply seen as being a chore – something to be avoided if at all possible. Zinkhan (2005) makes the point that many online buyers revel in the fact that they can complete a transaction without having to go through a third party – in other words, by completing their buying cycle online the hassle of dealing with pushy, ill-informed – or just poor – sales staff is eliminated.

# DECISION TIME

In their efforts to develop a marketing mix that best meets the needs of their customers, marketers have long used the science of psychology to address why buyers behave the way they do in relation to the purchase of their products. Not only has the Internet added to the *why* aspect of buyer behaviour, but it has also intensified the issue of *how* they practice that behaviour. Although the issue of *why* raises new problems – and solutions – for the marketing, it is the aspect of *how* that impacts most on marketers. Most significant is customers' use of the web to seek information on which they base their buying decision. For the contemporary marketer, simply putting product instructions and information on the packaging is not enough, they need to find out where the customer expects to find information – and then make sure it is there for them to access.

*You Decide*    Advise Frank and his management team at Hill Street Motorist Shops (case study 8) on how they should adapt their communications mix so as to best suit their potential market.

Alternatively, conduct the same exercise on your organization or that of your employer.

## 1.7    ONLINE MARKETING OBJECTIVES

> *there is a lack of joined-up thinking between off- and online marketing efforts*

Without specific objectives the likelihood of any venture succeeding diminishes greatly – and this is equally true for Internet marketing – and yet perhaps the biggest failing when organizations go online is that they fail to determine their objectives for doing so. The reasons for this are many, though the IT departments 'ownership' of the web presence was certainly a significant factor in the mid to late 1990s. So too was a lack in understanding in what the new medium of communication had to offer. While these reasons are (sadly) still in evidence today, another problem has moved to the fore – a lack of joined–up thinking between off– and online marketing efforts.

Too often *online* is considered to be separate from other marketing activities – and so is treated as such in strategic planning. In chapter 10 we consider in some detail how online marketing operates as an element of an integrated marketing strategy, in this section, however, we will look at specific online *marketing* objectives.

In marketing terms, there are three objectives to any Internet presence or activity. They are:

1. Brand development – where the online presence compliments and enhances the offline branding efforts of the organization.

2. Revenue generation – where the online presence increases revenue into the organization by sales, lead generation or direct marketing.
3. Customer service/support – the web is used to enhance the service and support offered to customers – and potential customers – at significantly reduced costs.

However, such is the nature of the web that: (1) it is possible for a single website to address one, two or all three of these objectives, and (2) it is rare that a website addresses only one. Given this second point, perhaps it would be more accurate to describe the site's *leading* or *primary* objective, expressed as a percentage. For example, Amazon might be considered to be 80 per cent revenue generation, 10 per cent brand development and 10 per cent after sales service. Note that I developed the 'three objectives' concept around 1997, and it was first published in a book I co–authored – Gay et al. (2007) *Online Marketing – a Customer–Led Approach*.

Although specific objectives are necessary in order to develop effective strategies, having distinct objectives are also essential to the Internet marketer in (1) determining whether or not the site – or online activity – has been successful, and (2) assessing any return on investment (ROI) for any online operations. As is true for much of marketing – strategic and operational – establishing ROI for Internet marketing is problematic and despite there being a plethora of metrics with which to track online activity (see section 2.5) as Welling and White (2006) observe, little information exists on qualitative or quantitative measures of website ROI. Certainly some objectives can be tangible – sales, for example – and so total costs can be calculated against direct income (i.e. cost of sales), but as Welling and White (ibid) also point out, many e-business benefits – such as better customer service, increased responsiveness and faster deliveries – are intangibles that are difficult to translate into monetary benefits. It is also the case that some quantitative metrics do not reflect overall marketing objectives. For example, in the same way that the best restaurants might promote exclusivity by making it difficult to get a table, so website visitor numbers are not everything – with strategies for building online volume being potentially counterproductive in building customer relationships. In contrast, setting requirements to be a customer may raise a firm's perceived exclusivity, so making existing customers proud (Pitta et al, 2006).

Worth mentioning at this point – though it is a theme throughout the entirety of this book – is that the market or industry in which the organization operates will have a profound influence in how that organization might use the Internet in its marketing. As you will find in the chapters to come, the key factors of Internet adoption are whether (1) the organization trades only from bricks and mortar locations – i.e. it does not facilitate online sales, (2) it trades both off – and online – clicks and mortar – i.e. it facilitates online sales/orders, or (3) it trades online only – so called *pure play*. For the pure play online business the online strategy is, in effect, *the* strategy – and although we will return to pure play marketing throughout the book, the objectives of such an organization are worth considering in isolation from the other two models.

## Using social media

Throughout the book the point is made that – as is the case in all marketing – different organizations can use the Internet in ways that will suit them best. This 'infographic' demonstrates how different elements of social media can be used to meet the objectives of different departments within the organization. Social media marketing is covered in detail in chapter 9.

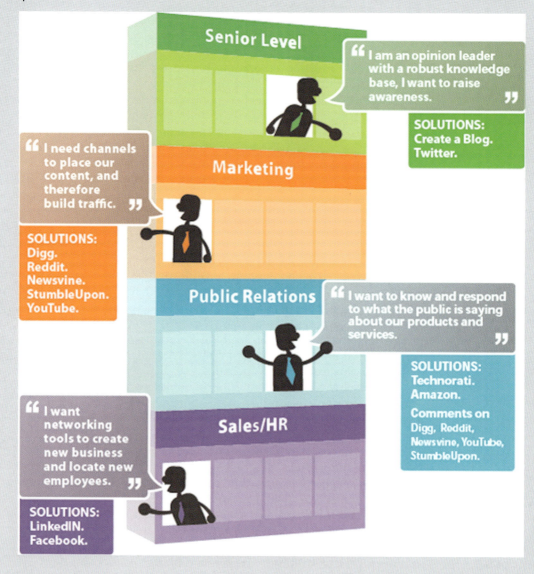

## The pure–online organization

Whist it is a popular pastime to list *types* of website, less common are attempts to identify the business models of pure-online businesses. One concept that has stood the test of time comes from David Rappa. His 1998 list of *online trading business models* does not attempt to describe types of websites, but what income models are available to the online-only business. Rappa's models are:

- The Brokerage Model – buyers and sellers are brought together in an online environment. Income is from fees charged for each transaction.
- The Advertising Model – the website provides content that attracts readers. Income is from the sale of ads on the site.
- The Infomediary Model – the website is used to collect data on visitors. Income is from the sale of that data to third parties.
- The Merchant Model – the website is a retail or wholesale outlet. Income is from the sale of goods or services.
- The Manufacturer Model – income is generated by selling goods direct to the end user, so reducing the dependence on channels of distribution.
- The Affiliate Model – visitors are encouraged to purchase goods or services from businesses to which the website is affiliated. Income is from fixed fees or a percentage of each sale.
- The Subscription Model – income is generated by charging for access to the site. This model requires high value-added content to attract subscribers.
- The Utility Model – online services that are accessed from the site are offered for a fee.
- The Community Model – a model that relies on income generated through affiliates, ads or subscription, but where the content is community oriented. Because of the visitor's investment in both time and emotion in the site's subject, community sites are ideal for targeted marketing.

Such is the nature of the web that whilst a model can be used in isolation, it is common practice for several to be employed within one website.

It is worth noting that – like all aspects of online marketing – all of these models existed in other media or industries prior to the development of the Internet.

## DECISION TIME

Although many would consider it to be an essential element of any organization's strategic planning, setting objectives for any Internet–based endeavours is not something that all organizations practice. Indeed, research by Lesjak & Vehovar (2005) found that only 20 per cent of companies that have significant e-business projects (on which at least 48,000 Euros per year was spent) use some kind of formal evaluation – with half of the surveyed companies stating that the benefits of e-business are so obvious that they do not need to be measured. A complete lack of evaluation strongly suggests that there was no explicit objective to be measured in the first place.

For the pure play business, determining key objectives for the online presence is pretty straightforward – in essence, whatever it is that generates income. For example, in (Rappa's) advertising model the strategy must be built around driving the maximum number of visitors to the website, or for the merchant model generating online sales is the goal.

For both the bricks and mortar and clicks and mortar organizations, the marketing objectives must go beyond online sales generation – and should compliment, enhance or be integrated with, the organization's overall strategic marketing and business aims. Ultimately, of course, the marketing objective of any Internet presence must be to meet the needs of the target visitor. If you do not do achieve that goal no organizational objectives will ever be met.

*You Decide*

Advise the marketers at the Matthew Humberstone Foundation Hospital (case study 6) on what their key online objective might be.

Alternatively, conduct the same exercise for your organization or that of your employer.

## CHAPTER EXERCISE

Giving justifications for all your decisions, advise Quincy Adams Wagstaff and his staff at Huxley University (case study 10) on all aspects of Internet marketing covered in this chapter.

Alternatively, conduct the same exercise on your own organization or that of your employer.

## REFERENCES

Alreck, P. & Settle, R. (2002). The hurried consumer: time-saving perceptions of Internet and catalogue shopping. *Journal of Database Marketing*. Vol. 10, No. 1, pp. 25–35.

Arora, N (2008) Online revolution, adapt or die. Sunday Times, May 18 2008.

Athiyaman, A. (2002). Internet users' intention to purchase air travel online: an empirical investigation. *Marketing Intelligence & Planning*. Vol. 20, No. 4, pp. 234–242. , 2002

Barnes, S.J., Bauer, H.H., Neumann, M.M. & Huber, H. (2007). Segmenting cyberspace: a customer typology for the internet. *European Journal of Marketing*. Vol. 41, No. 1/2, pp. 71–93.

Bendoly, E. & Schoenherr, T. (2005). ERP system and implementation-process benefits. *International Journal of Operations Management*. Vol. 25, No. 4, pp. 3014–3319.

Bhatnagar, A., Misra, S. & Rao, H.R. (2000). On risk, convenience and Internet shopping behavior. *Communications of the ACM*. Vol. 43, No. 11, pp. 98–105.

Brynjolfsson, E. & Smith, M. (2001). The Great Equalizer? Customer Choice Behavior at Internet Shopbots. *MIT Sloan Management Review.* Vol. 42, No. 2, pp. 9.

Butler, P. & Peppard, J. (1998). Consumer purchasing on the Internet: process and prospects. *European Management Journal.* Vol. 16, No. 5, pp. 600–610.

Center for the Digital Future (2008). Surveying the Digital Future. The University of Southern California's Annenberg School for Communication.

ComScore (2007) *comScore Segment Matrix.* Available on http://www.centerformediaresearch.com/cfmr_brief.cfm?fnl = 071023

Constantinides, E. (2004). Influencing the online consumer's behavior: the web experience. *Internet Research: Electronic Networking Applications and Policy.* Vol. 14, No. 2, .

Day, G.S. & Bens, K.J. (2005). Capitalizing on the Internet opportunity. *Journal of Business & Industrial Marketing.* Vol. 20/4/5, pp. 160–168.

DoubleClick Performics (2007) *Searcher Moms – A Search Behavior and Usage Study.* www.performics.com

Enquiro (2007) *Business to Business Survey 2007.* pp 27. Available on www.enquiro.com/Downloads/b2b-research-2007.aspx

Garrido Samaniego, M.J., Gutiérrez Arranz, M. & San José Cabezudo, R. (2006). Determinants of Internet use in the purchasing process. *Journal of Business & Industrial Marketing.* Vol. 21, No. 3, pp. 164–174.

Gay, R. Charlesworth, A. & Esen, R. (2007). *Online Marketing – A Customer-Led Approach.* Oxford University Press.

Hughes, T. (2007). Regaining a seat at the table: marketing management and the e-service opportunity. *Journal of Services Marketing.* Vol. 21, No. 4, pp. 270–280.

Kamarulzamam, Y. (2007). Adoption of travel e-shopping in the UK. *International Journal of Retail and Distribution Management.* Vol. 35, No. 9, pp. 703–719.

Kotler, P. (2000). Marketing Management. Prentice Hall.

Lesjak, D. & Vehovar, V. (2005). Factors affecting evaluation of e-business projects. *Industrial Management & Data Systems.* Vol. 105, No. 4, pp. 409–428.

Markillie, P. (2005) Crowned at last. *The Economist.* April 2005, pp. 3–16.

McGovern, G. (2002) *Information Architecture Versus Graphic Design* Available online at www.clickz.com/design/site_design/article.php/945631

Merrill Lynch (1999) E-commerce: virtually here. Accessed 1999 on www.ml.com, but no longer available on that URL.

Papacharissi, Z. & Rubin, A.M. (2000). Predictors of Internet use. *Journal of Broadcasting & Electronic media.* Vol. 44, No. 2, pp. 175–197.

Peterson, R.A., Balasubramanian, S. & Bronnenberg, B.J. (1997). Exploring the implications of the Internet for consumer marketing. *Journal of the Academy of Marketing Sciences.* Vol. 24, No. 4, pp. 329–346.

Pew Internet & American Life Project (2005) *Digital Divisions.* Available on www.pewinternet.org

Pew Internet & American Life Project (2008) Online Shopping. Available on www.pewinternet.org.

Pitta, D., Franzak, F. & Fower, D. (2006). A strategic approach to building online customer loyalty: integrating customer profitability tiers. *Journal of Consumer marketing.* Vol. 23, No. 7, pp. 421–429.

Rappa, D. (1998) *Managing the Digital Enterprise.* Available online at www.digitalenterprise.org

Skyrme, D.J. (2001). *Capitalizing on Knowledge from E-commerce to K-business.* Butterworth-Heinemann.

Thomas Industrial Network Inc (2003) *Supplier Survival in the Information Age.* Available online at www.thomasnet.com

TNS, TRU & Marketing Evolution (2007). Never Ending Friending – a Journey into Social Networking. Fox Interactive Media Inc.

Welling, R. & White, L. (2006). website performance measurement: promise and reality. *Managing Service Quality.* Vol. 16, No. 6, pp. 654–670.

Zinkhan, G.M. (2005). The marketplace, emerging technology and marketing theory. *Marketing Theory.* Vol. 5 pp. 105–115.

# Getting started online

*Oh, so they have Internet on computers now!*

Homer Simpson

## CHAPTER AT A GLANCE

## 2.1   INTRODUCTION

> **"** So why is business-commonsense so absent in many aspects of Internet marketing? **"**

Where the Internet is concerned there is a strange phenomenon that is pretty much unique in a business environment – and it is this. In all other aspects of business – be it commercial or not–for–profit – any expenditure is assessed on its potential benefit to the organization, what the return on investment (ROI) is likely to be and what might be the negative impact of not committing to that spending. On the subject of websites, however, that reasoning seems to leave by the nearest window. Things are getting better, but we are far from being anywhere close to perfect. For example – in my personal experience – I have come across businesses that have paid thousands of pounds on a sign for the building's reception area (that will be seen by only a few customers), but have the website (that is available 24/7/365 throughout the world) developed by the owner's daughter's boyfriend for 50 pounds cash. Similarly, the purchase or lease of a van would involve careful consideration of how many miles it would be expected to travel, its payload, maintenance downtime and a whole host of other issues before any decision on a specific vehicle from a particular supplier was made. Yet the company's web presence is barely discussed before its development is given the OK.

So why is business–commonsense so absent in many aspects of Internet marketing? My own opinion is that the key issues are a balance between managers (a) being *scared* of computers, and (b) not realising the importance of the Internet in contemporary business. In this chapter – as its title suggests – you will be introduced to the key elements in getting started in the online environment. If it is not the case already, by the end of it you will know that the Internet is not scary and that it *is* important in contemporary marketing. You will also know that it is not the exclusive domain of the folks from the IT department.

## 2.2   DOMAIN NAMES

First impressions can be crucial. In an online environment, the organization's domain name may well be the first point of contact between it and a potential customer. First impressions are all about perception, and a 'good' domain name can influence how a potential customer might perceive the organization – that is: poor domain name equals poor company, good domain name equals good company to do business with. Although this notion is far from absolute – and may even be nonsense – given the price of a domain name, it costs little to pamper to a customer's perception.

### Practical Insight

**It's pronounced 'dot'. Period**

Although spelt using the full stop (or 'period' in the USA) character to satisfy Internet protocol, the full stops in domain name suffixes are always pronounced as 'dot' – dot com, dot co, dot uk and so on.

Choosing an effective domain name – often referred to as the organization's address on the Internet – is a crucial decision for any organization. It is primarily a marketing decision and not one to be taken by 'technical' staff who do not appreciate the value of a domain name in marketing terms.

To have a web presence, an organization must have a domain name, and if they must have a domain name, then they should give some thought to not just having a *good* domain name, but the *right* domain name. Before the online marketer can select the *right* domain name, they must first understand a little about domain names.

## What is a Domain name?

Every presence on the Internet is identified by a series of numbers (142.56.89.43 for example) – called the Internet Protocol, or IP, address. To make these IP addresses easier to remember, the early proponents of the Internet decided to allocate a *word* (or series of characters) to each IP number. As no two sets of IP numbers are the same, no two domain names can be the same.

Domain names are, and always have been, allocated on a first come – first served basis. The majority of generic, one-word domain names were registered in the early to mid 1990s – and as registration was free at the time, many were registered by IT students (who were amongst the first to use the Internet on a regular basis). It is the generic .com domains that many consider to be the *best*. It is also difficult to trademark a generic word. By definition that means that generic .coms are the most valuable domain names.

---

### MINI CASE

**High price names**

Domain names that demand the highest value when offered for sale are generic dot coms. Loans.com, for example, was purchased by the Bank of America for $3M. Note, however, the majority of domain names that sell for high sums have with them 'related assets' – normally functioning, profit-making websites complete with customer details – which is where the *actual* value lies. For example, a group of domain names including dictionary.com, reference.com, and thesaurus.com were bought by Answers.com for $100 Million – but the websites hosted on those three domains attracted 11.5 million unique visitors in June 2007 alone.

---

The domain name system is run by the Internet Corporation for Assigned Names and Numbers (ICANN) and is responsible for a range of technical aspects of the Internet, including the Domain Name System (DNS), which allows for the registration of domain names within a number of registries known as 'top level domains' (TLDs). TLDs fall into two broad categories:

- Generic Top-Level Domains (gTLDs), e.g. dot com
- Country Code Top-Level Domains (ccTLDs), such as dot uk for the United Kingdom.

Each country has its own *naming* authority that runs the domain name system for that country – referred to as *sponsoring organizations*. To register a name you must apply to that authority for 'permission' to use that name. Effectively, those who register the name are the *owners* of that name and as such are the only ones who can use that name. There are organizations that act as intermediaries between the customer and the naming agencies. It is with these *registration agents* (or registrars) that the vast majority of people or entities register their domain name.

## Practical Insight

**Navigation by search**

More common in the USA – where .com is the dominant suffix – is the practice of bypassing search engines and typing keywords as domain names directly into their Internet browser – hence the value placed on generic words. If I wanted to borrow some money, for example, I might simply type 'loans.com' into my browser. According to a 2007 survey conducted by Opinion Research Corp (www.opinionresearch.com), 64% of those surveyed had used this kind of search. The fast-developing .eu and newly introduced .asia may see the practice spread to those geographic areas. An extension of the activity is to type the generic word plus the .com suffix into a search engine. It is rare for search engines not to return the website that is hosted on that domain at the top of the results page.

## Domain name construction

When a name is registered it takes the suffix of the registered naming authority. There are a number of suffixes to choose from (more of this later) but to illustrate how domain names are constructed this example will use the best-known suffix – .com (dot com). The domain used as an illustration is yagahit.com.

As the suffix is considered to be the *primary*, or *top level* domain, combining the 'name' with the suffix creates a *second* level domain:

e.g. yagahit.com

When indicating their use as the URL (Uniform Resource Locator) of a world wide website, it has become accepted protocol to use the prefix 'www' on the primary domain name:

e.g. www.yagahit.com

As the dot com suffix now has two distinct *words* before it, this is now a *third* level domain name.

Any subsequent *words* placed in front of the primary name, but divided by a full stop, make the URL a fourth/fifth level domain name. Theoretically, there is no limit to the number of *words* that can be placed prior to the domain, in practice, however, three or four is really the limit.

e.g. www.sunderland.yagahit.com

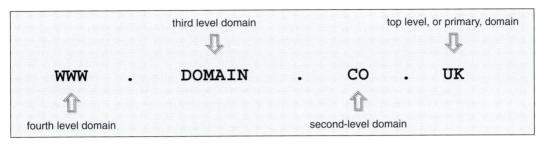

**Figure 2.1** How a domain name is constructed.

When used as a Country Code Top Level Domain (ccTLD) the domain name takes on an extra level to donate their country of origin. Figure 2.1 shows the make up of a domain on the .uk ccTLD.

There is a very unambiguous limit to the characters that can be used in a domain name. They are: all the letters of the Latin alphabet (A to Z) plus any number (0 to 9) and a dash/hyphen (-). NB these *rules* apply to domain names that use the English language – others, known as Internationalised Domain Names, are available in different languages. A domain name must begin and end with a letter or a number, no spaces or other characters are allowed. Any amount of dashes can be used, but must not be placed together. Domain names must be at least three and less than 63 characters in length (excluding suffixes). Although two letter domains do exist, they are only allocated to organizations that can prove that they are universally recognised by a two-character name. Communications giant O2 for example, use O2.co.uk and Hewlett Packard, HP.com – realistically, however, unless an organization is in the same league as these examples, they can forget two character domains.

## Practical Insight

### Just having fun dot com

Given their low price, domain names are ripe for funsters to amuse themselves. For example, the imaginatively named 'the longest list of the longest stuff at the longest domain name at long last' website – can be found (of course) on www.thelongestlistofthelongest stuffatthelongestdomainnameatlonglast.com.

Also registered are aaa.com (three x A), aaaa.com (four x A) through to sixty three x A dot com – yes, that's aaaaaaaaaaaaaaaaaaaaaaaaaaaaaaaaaaaaaaaaaaaaaaaaaaaaaaaaaaaaaaa.com

Finally – and this is important for marketing reasons – domain names are NOT case sensitive. From a technical standpoint, it is possible to set up a website's host server so that it recognizes upper and lower case characters in a domain name (so making a domain case sensitive) – however, this is (virtually) never practiced, it being the standard operating procedure to set them up as being non-case sensitive.

## Suffixes

The most common domain name suffix is the .com (dot com). This is the suffix for the USA and is considered to be the *global* name as it has no country identification (such as uk for the UK) – in reality, it has no country identification because it was the first suffix made available (there is a rarely used .us domain that is normally linked to state abbreviations, eg .fl.us for Florida).

There are over 250 countries with a country-specific domain, for example: .de for Germany .jp for Japan .fr for France and .gr for Greece. The need for 'global regions' to have their own identity in a domain name has been addressed – the first of what is expected to be a number of regional names, .eu for Europe is already established, with .asia going live in 2008.

---

*Go Online*  For a full list of the suffixes available from around the globe and tips on the legal aspects of domain names, follow the links on the chapter's web page.

---

Whilst some countries impose restrictions on who can register their names, more than 80 countries are *unrestricted* meaning anyone anywhere can register any names. Some of these unrestricted names have been heavily promoted, but they are still considered as *novelties* in the majority of business fields – these include: .tv (Tuvalu) and .cc (Cocos Islands).

As well as country specific suffixes that use Latin characters, there are also a growing number of Internationalised Domain Names (IDNs) – also referred to as multi-lingual domain names – which use characters outside a-z, 0-9 and the hyphen. At the time of writing around 39 additional character sets are available, supporting over 350 languages including Arabic, Hebrew, Korean, Russian and Greek. Applications of IDNs for the marketer are limited. The most obvious issue is that if the domain uses non-Latin characters only the keyboards of users in countries where those characters are used can type the domain names into a browser.

---

## RESEARCH SNAPSHOT

### Domain names add to email credibility

Having your own domain name means that you can use it for your email address. Research by Microsoft UK, published in 2008, found that almost half of respondents said that they would rather not use a company which had a personal email account – e.g. hotmail or googlemail – rather than a company email address.

Choosing the right suffix is dependent on the use to which the website is to be put, and the essential question to be addressed is what is the nature of the organization and where it trades – or hopes to trade. If the organization is a business then the main choice is between the local suffix and .com. Using .co.uk as an example; if the business trades only in the UK then .co.uk is the suffix to choose – if the business trades globally, then .com. That is, of course, rather simplistic and other options exist in the grey areas that sit between the black and white – a hotel, for example, might seek to attract customers from around the globe but using the country code of its home country will identify where it is located geographically. For example, nicehotel.com could be located anywhere in the world, but nicehotel.co.uk is in the UK.

> *Go Online*    The link on the chapter's web page will take you to more advice on choosing a domain name.

## Creating the right domain name

Although there are guides for creating domain names for specific purposes, each having different criteria for the selection process, there are some issues that are generic to all purposes. They are:

- Length – in general, when picking a name, less is more
- How easy is it to recall the name?
- How will it be communicated? (e.g. verbally or in print)

Other general considerations include:

- Is the domain name a representation of the organization and/or business?
- What is it to be used for? (e.g. website, email address, company name)

## RESEARCH SNAPSHOT

**Coffee is more important than a domain name, apparently**

In a survey, released in November 2007, FastHosts Internet (www.fasthosts.co.uk) revealed that the UK's small businesses are rushing their choice of web address, with 41 per cent taking less than an hour to make the decision – around the same time they took to source their coffee making machine. This was despite most of them recognised that their domain name could have a lasting effect on their business, with one third of businesses believing that their revenue would improve as a direct result of having a better web address, and 1 in 4 businesses admitting they had 'concerns' about the effectiveness of their domain name. More than 60 per cent of respondents did not seek a second opinion, and only 10 per cent of businesses considered the long term effect of their domain name on their business image. Little surprise then, that many British businesses believe that their choice of domain name could have been better.

For those new to domain names it is worth reiterating that all (useful) generic words have long since been registered, so a toy company wanting to register www.toys.co.uk or www.toys.com (owned by Toys"R"Us and eToys respectively) it is too late. So assuming that a suitable generic word that represents the product or service being marketed is not an option, how does the organization choose a suitable domain name? Options include:

- Take the company name, and add a suitable suffix. If I were a consultant, alancharlesworth.eu would be an example of this – although businesses often use the possessive 's' in the name, e.g. charlesworth's which might be problematic for the domain name.
- Although the company might be known by the owner's name, surnames are rarely still available to register – a simple solution is to add the product or service offered to the company name. A business known as Alan's Ltd that makes toys might use alanstoys.co.uk.
- Along the same lines – add the location to either the company name or location – alansofyork.co.uk or yorktoys.co.uk, for example.
- Register the name by which the company is commonly known – such nicknames are common where the organization's name is particularly cumbersome or formal.
- Use the abbreviation of the organization's initials – Alan's Toys of York Ltd using aty.co.uk or atoy.co.uk, for example. This option is severely limited as most 3 and 4 character domain names have been registered.
- Abbreviate some of all of the words in the company name – an engineering company from Philadelphia, for example, could easily shorten that to phillyengineering.com.

It is worth noting that in the USA the use of the dash (-) in domain names is shunned, 'all one word' being the norm. However, this is not so much the case in Europe, with there being three significant examples of when it should be considered. Firstly is where your 'first choice' name has been registered – simply split any words with a dash. Secondly, where the dash makes the domain 'read' better (perhaps because the term would be grammatically correct if a dash is used) and thirdly, there will be occasions when two words run together to create an unfortunate term. For example, a company that provided expert consultancy service called Experts Exchange registered those two words as its domain name – unfortunately, the subsequent term read ExpertSexChange.com.

## Practical Insight

### Capital practice

Earlier in this section it was mentioned that domain names are not case sensitive. This can be very important aesthetically when the name is presented in print. The following are all the names suggested as examples in the previous section – but all are presented using upper case characters where pertinent. Not only do they look better, they sometimes make more sense grammatically.

| | |
|---|---|
| alancharlesworth.eu | AlanCharlesworth.eu |
| alanstoys.co.uk | AlansToys.co.uk |
| alansofyork.co.uk | AlansofYork.co.uk |
| yorktoys.co.uk | YorkToys.co.uk |
| phillyengineering.com | PhillyEngineering.com |

Note that the suffix is always presented in lower case.

## Registering a domain name

The process is relatively easy – and conducted online. There are two main choices:

1. Register it yourself using any one of the hundreds of online domain name 'registrars'.
2. If professional services have been employed to develop a web presence that organization will normally register the domain name as part of the package – though they should not choose it without discussion with the customer (you).

Whichever is chosen, there is one vital issue to note. Part of the registration process includes a section that requires details of the registrants – effectively who is the *owner*. It is not unknown for unscrupulous operators – both registrars and service providers – to list themselves in this section and not their clients, so make sure you or your organization is listed as the owner.

## MINI CASE

### Renew it or lose it

Although you may 'own' the registration of a domain name – you must renew the registration periodically, if you don't, you will lose the name and it goes back on the open market. Over the years there have been a number of embarrassing examples of major organizations and brands – Microsoft and Amazon have both been guilty in the past – forgetting to renew, but being able to recover their domain name as there were trademark issues.

However, October 2007 saw the International Federation of the Phonographic Industry mysteriously 'lose' its domain name (ifpi.com) – presumably through not renewing the registering. But that's not the embarrassing bit for the IFPI. That organization – the lobby group for the record industry – has been engaged in a long–standing battle with The Pirate Bay, a Sweden–based website that has links to sites where users can download illicit music. So who is behind the International Federation of Pirates Interests – the organization that now has a website hosted on ifpi.com? You guessed it – none other than Pirate Bay. Ouch.

3 The majority of B2B websites concentrate on lead generation (see section 5.4), and so when the potential customer contacts the firm – by whatever means – it is to the sales team that their inquiry should be directed. If they have had a hand in the development of the site then the sales staff will be better prepared to respond effectively to that initial communication.

## Practical Insight

### It's a balancing act

A great Website needs to do many different things. It needs to be user-friendly, aesthetically pleasing, and easy to find. Focusing too closely on just one aspect will inevitably create a less-than-desirable site. A site that overemphasizes SEO will likely lack design flair and have poor copy flow. Conversely, a site designed purely for aesthetics will be a feast for the eyes but won't likely satisfy the needs of the users or the search engines.

Julie Batten, The ClickZ Network, Feb 4, 2008.

As with most elements of running a contemporary organization, the manager must decide whether tasks are undertaken in-house or whether they are out-sourced. Website development is no exception. Given the list of skills described above, it seems doubtful if all, or even any, of the necessary talent can be found within the organization – and it is worth noting that *unskilled* staff who are either co-opted to, or volunteer for, the task rarely produce effective websites.

## DECISION TIME

The well-used phrase 'you get what you pay for' and 'if you pay peanuts you get monkeys' are pertinent in this scenario. Much depends on the marketing objectives for the web presence. For the successful offline business that has traded locally for many years through word of mouth referrals, then a fairly basic web page – containing little more than the company name, contact details and what they are good at – developed by an amateur *might* be sufficient. However, the higher the stakes of what is expected from the site – its objectives – then the higher the gamble in not paying for a professional job. Conversely, any expenditure must give return on investment – paying tens of thousands of pounds to a big-city web design company for a website that generates little income, does nothing to develop the brand or provides no customer support is not a sound business investment.

However, the prime consideration must be given to the visitor to the proposed site and what they expect. Although we consider website development in detail in chapter three, it is worth noting that Schlosser et al (2006) suggest that 'investment' in site design can enhance trust – and so increase purchase intentions. Whilst it should be appreciated that the 'monkey-peanuts' argument is valid, and that Schlosser et al have a point, (a) highest cost does not necessarily equal highest quality, and (b) can a surfer really tell how much 'investment' has been made in order to make a judgement?

> *You Decide*  Advise Quincy Adams Wagstaff and his executive at Huxley University (case study 10) on the most suitable web development solution for them. What internal issues might arise?
>
> Alternatively, conduct the same exercise for your organization or that of your employer.

## 2.5  WEBSITE ANALYTICS AND E-METRICS

Marketing is the aspect of business that is hardest to determine if a return on any investment (ROI) has been made from any costs incurred. Brand advertising, for example, *may* or *may not* influence *some* buyers at an undetermined point *sometime* in the future. The nature of online marketing has, however, gone some way towards addressing this marketing Achilles' heel – with web analytics not only telling us *what* happened, but helping us determine *why* it happened, and so make predictions for the future. This is because any visitor to a website, or recipient of any email, leaves a digital footprint from which marketers can glean data. Sadly, not everything in the e-metrics garden is rosy. The digital footprint, for example, can give details of the (potential) customer's activity on the website, but as there is rarely any correlation between online activity and offline sales it is difficult to measure the impact of a website on company performance (Welling & White, 2006). Not only is the ability to collect data an issue, so too is the will of organizations to conduct any online analysis and the importance they might place on it. A study by the Aberdeen Group (Creese and Kahlow, 2003) suggest how little value was given to web analytics by revealing it was common for multiple departments to take a hand, with it being rare for any individual to be responsible for assessing online performance. The result of this was a lack of direction to the task in hand, and a lessening of perceived importance. Furthermore, research by the FMI Group in 2001 found that only 3 per cent of respondents stated that website analysis was used strategically – the others used any data for reporting purposes. Hopefully, the intervening years will have seen changes as e-metric value has been better appreciated – particularly in pure-online traders.

> " The nature of online digital marketing has, however, gone some way towards addressing this marketing Achilles' heel "

**Go Online**

Although the technical aspects of the Internet are not part of the brief for this book, it is important for marketers to know that e-metrics are gathered can be gathered in two distinct ways – (1) server-side, or (2) browser-based. Follow the web page links for more information on the two.

E-metrics is a perfect example of how IT and marketing staff must work together in order to be effective. Without the marketer's input the techies do not know which data is worth collecting and which is useless – even if it is easy to collect. Conversely, without IT's help, the marketer has no way of implementing the technology to gather the data that they can then turn into valuable marketing intelligence.

As with other elements of the online presence covered earlier in this chapter, there is the question of performing e–metrics in-house or out-sourcing the job. The answer lies in the objectives determined for the website. For the offline business which has a lead-generation website that might attract a dozen visitors a month, one of the many DIY tools offered by web hosting companies will be quite sufficient. At the other end of the spectrum, for the pure online operation analysis of their web operations is an essential element of their business – and one that requires significant expertise. Key issues in online analytics include:

- What metrics are needed to help make both strategic and operational decisions?
- How should that data be collated?
- How should that data be collected – technically?
- How should that data be stored and mined?
- How is the data to be converted into information and then analysed so as to produce intelligence that is beneficial to the organization.

Although all of these issues should be addressed in equal measure, in practice that is rarely the case – one particular problem is the scarcity of qualified analysts (Weischedel et al, 2005).

**Go Online**

With new technologies being constantly developed and practices evolving, the terms used in website analytics are dynamic – even the phrases *website analytics* and *e-metrics* can mean different things to different people. There are also problems with some of the terms themselves, with different phrases being used to describe the same thing. For a full list of definitions of terms used in e-metrics – and a comment on what a 'web page' is in e-metric terms – follow the link on the chapter's web page.

## What to measure?

Digital communications offer the marketer something never before available – the ability to gather statistics on every aspect of the marketing that is related to the online environment. In the early days – and still today to a limited extent – the ability to gather an almost infinite amount of data was seen as opportunity not to be ignored. As a result – and this was more often than not driven by technology-providers – vast mountains of data were collected. This was then stored until it went out of date (sometimes a matter of days) and then destroyed before any analysis was conducted on it. Best practice is to gather only that data that (a) can be analysed, and (b) as a result of that analysis provides information on which decisions can be made. Although resources may impact on the decision, the primary issue is to determine the purpose of any analytical efforts – with the objectives of the online presence underpinning that decision.

### Practical Insight

**Hits are a miss**

Used in reference to the Internet, a *hit* means a request from a web browser for a single file from a web server. Therefore, a browser displaying a web page made up of three graphic images and a paragraph of text would generate five hits at the server – one for the HTML page itself, one for the file of text and one for each of the three graphics. In the early days of the web (and occasionally still today) hits were *the* way of expressing how popular a website was. In contemporary e-commerce, however, a hit is a next-to-useless term of reference. Saying a website has a thousand hits a day, for example, is an almost pointless statement. It could mean ten visitors went to a website that has a hundred files, one visitor who downloaded a thousand files, or anything in between. The chances are, however, that the first is most accurate. The use of hits (in a press release for example) to indicate the success of a website would suggest that the organization is (a) using hits as a metric in order to inflate numbers as the visitor count is relatively low, or (b) out of touch with contemporary practice.
Note that this is taken from my book, *Key Concepts in e-Commerce* (2007).

As discussed in section 1.7, online marketing objectives can include such things as income generation, brand development and after sales service. However, just as each of these strategic objectives can be sub-divided, so too can the purposes of the e-metrics that might be used to assess the success or failure of those objectives. In addition to assessing *strategic* issues, e-metrics can be used to assess individual tactics that are employed to achieve those strategic aims. For example, a website's strategic objective might be to sell $x$ thousand pounds worth of goods per annum – a metric that is easily measured. However, individual sales can be broken down by customers, value, items per customer or a myriad of other components.

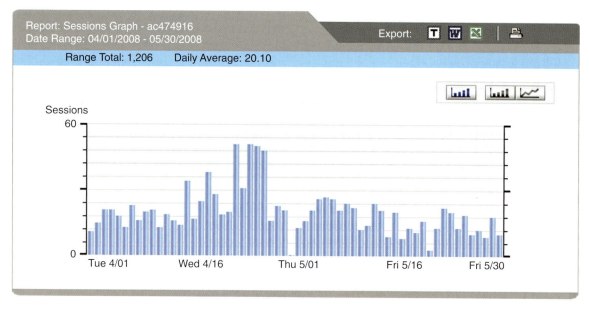

**Figure 2.4** A sample of the site analysis for alancharlesworth.eu provided by the site's host.

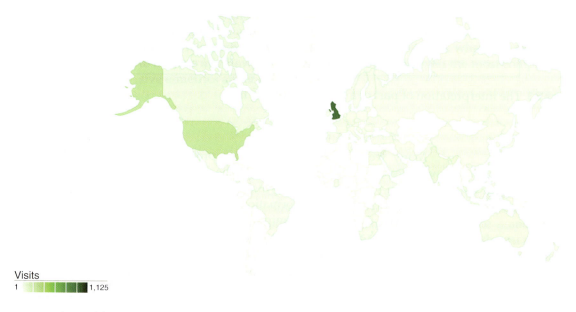

**Figure 2.5** A world map indicating where visits to alancharlesworth.eu originate.

A further advantage of out-sourcing the analytics is that the work can be done on a regular basis, with a periodic report delivered which hi-lights significant events or returns. Without this it is easy for the manager – who probably has a multitude of other things to do – to forget regular examination of the statistics.

## Practical Insight

**With time and money – there is no limit to analytics**

As with other aspects of the Internet, technology drives on relentlessly – and this includes the e–metrics environment. One application, dubbed part of 'experience management', is software that tracks – and saves – every action each visitor makes on a website, then allows the e–marketer to replay a page-by-page, browser-level recording of an actual customer's on–site experience. So if customers are leaving a site midway through a form (for example) analytical staff can look at the *actual* screen seen by the user in order to access what has gone wrong.

For those who want to take the other extreme and be 'hands–on' in tracking metrics, software is now available that allows you to monitor site traffic in real time-as it happens. Particularly useful for social media sites, this means you can pick up on emerging trends and so take action to stay ahead of the crowd. Of course, it also means someone watching the analytics for every minute of every day – and so you would have to be sure the organization was going to benefit from the commitment of such resources.

Essentially the decision is governed by:

1   What are the objectives of the site?
2   How can those objectives be best assessed, given:
    • The data available
    • How it is collected and presented
    • The expertise available to complete the analysis.

However, all of the above is a pointless exercise if the ability – and will – to act on any information gleaned is not high on the organization's agenda.

*You Decide*   Advise Phil and his team at the Cleethorpes Visitors Association (case study 4) on which web analytics should be collected to help meet their online marketing objectives.
   Alternatively, conduct the same exercise for your organization or that of your employer.

## 2.6   THE INTERNET AS A TOOL FOR MARKET RESEARCH

Although this section on market research is included in this (early) chapter, marketers will be aware that research is actually an ongoing process – more commonly referred to as market *intelligence*. However, given that research into the market should take place early in any strategic

59

| Rank | Top 10 2007 | % | % change | Rank | Top 10 2006 | % |
|------|-------------|-----|----------|------|-------------|-----|
| 1 - | France | 32% | −13% | 1 | France | 37% |
| 2 - | Spain | 17% | 7% | 2 | Spain | 16% |
| 3 ⇑ | Italy | 7% | 19% | 3 | Bulgaria | 14% |
| 4 ⇑ | Portugal | 6% | 41% | 4 | Italy | 5% |
| 5 ⇑ | Cyprus | 6% | 104% | 5 | Turkey | 5% |
| 6 ⇑ | Greece | 5% | 35% | 6 | Portugal | 4% |
| 7 ⇓ | Bulgaria | 5% | −65% | 7 | Greece | 4% |
| 8 ⇓ | Turkey | 3% | −34% | 8 | Cyprus | 3% |
| 9 | New Zealand | 3% | 5% | 9 | New Zealand | 3% |
| 10 ⇑ | Ireland | 2% | 33% | 10 | Australia | 2% |

Source: Hitwise United Kingdom (www.hitwise.co.uk)

**Figure 2.6** Keyword searches on "property abroad".

## Practical Insight

### Use qualitative as well as quantitative research

Perhaps because they are so easily available, over–reliance on e-metrics can be a mistake – according to Forrester (www.forrester.com) senior analyst Sucharita Mulpuru in a speech at the Shop.org Annual Summit in September 2007. She said that online retailers are *watching* customers (the web analytics) instead of *listening* to them by conducting surveys, focus groups or polls.

## Primary research

The first point of call for any Internet–based primary research must be the metrics of your own online activities. Having covered these in detail in the previous section there is little more to add other than to point out that although analytics are generally performance–related, the data that is gathered can be used in planning for the future as well as correcting the past. Other methods of collecting primary data using the Internet are – effectively – online applications of traditional offline techniques.

Note that the following is concerned with using the Internet in conducting research on behalf of the marketer – hosting questionnaires for other organizations and/or collecting data that can then be sold to third parties is a business model in its own right – see Rappa's online trading business models in section 1.7.

The most common form of research offline is the survey – where selected respondents are asked to answer questions or complete questionnaires. Naturally there is an inherent flaw in conducting surveys online in that the only respondents are those who have access to the web – which is fine for online–related questions, but not so for other research. Whilst email can be used simply as a method of communication for questionnaires – as the post is offline – the interactive nature of the Internet can increase response rates.

On-page surveys do not have to be full-blown questionnaires, however. A small box in a prominent position on a busy web page, for example, could provide a wealth of data about customer behaviour. A simple question like 'how did you get to this site?' with a 'check-box' response for either: 'search engine', 'link from other site', 'saw web address in ad', 'knew web address' and 'in my favourites/bookmarks' as the options. It's very simple, but it does give human – rather than e-metrics-sourced technical – data. Even more simplistic is a simply yes/no response to a direct question that is related to a product or service offered on the site – 'have you ever purchased a holiday online?' for example – or as in Figure 2.7, a direct question at the foot of a FAQ page.

**Was this information helpful?**

◎ Yes    ◎ No

**Figure 2.7** A simply yes/no response form.

Long questionnaires are too complex to include on a web page, but they can be accessed from a link – perhaps a banner or a pop–up promoting the survey. To use websites other than your own it is necessary to engage agents who develop then host or distribute questionnaires. One such company is American Consumer Opinion (www.acop.com) who conduct online research through users who have registered to take part in surveys – offering financial rewards as an inducement to participate. Surveys are bespoke depending on the needs of American Consumer Opinion's clients.

It is also worth noting that the results of research – if not confidential – can be released into the public domain – making surveys achieve double objectives of both data gathering and PR – and subsequent search engine optimization as a spin–off.

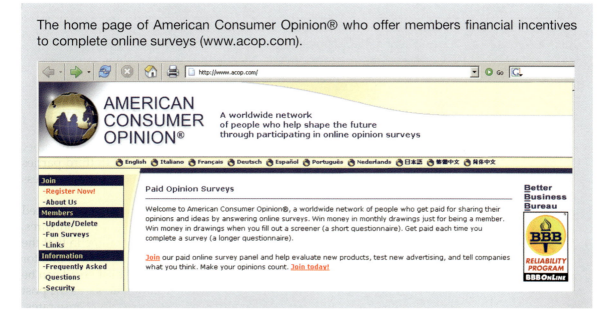

The home page of American Consumer Opinion® who offer members financial incentives to complete online surveys (www.acop.com).

As well as using the Internet to host and distribute questionnaires, it is also possible to host online focus groups. Although this technique has flaws – most significantly that members cannot be observed for reactions or body language – the cost of assembling a group of individuals in a chat room scenario is significantly cheaper than bringing them together physically. It is also the case that participants can be drawn from a much wider geographic area – even different continents – for just as low a cost, so expanding the scope for research.

Building on the notion that secondary research can be gathered through observation of consumer activity (for example, the use of keywords covered in the previous section on secondary research), is the concept of *ethnography* – an overt or covert participation in the everyday lives of people over an extended period of time (Hammersley & Atkinson, 1995). Dubbed as *netnography* (Internet–ethnography) in an early study by Kozinets (1997) the online version of this social science is practiced by joining online social media sites and entering into community discussion. Whether or not the researcher should disclose their [true] identity and purpose is an ethical question debated by netnographers, but whichever path is chosen valuable data on consumer behaviour and attitudes can be gleaned. As with any marketing–oriented involvement on social media sites, however, care must be taken to not be perceived as advertising products or brands – even when a bias has been declared. This may lead to the exercise being (a) rejected by community members, (b) flawed though 'unnatural' responses or, (c) effectively becoming a online focus group.

Note that how online marketers can use social media sites as part of their marketing efforts is covered in chapter 9 – which includes observing user behaviour in what might be described as *basic* netnography – and so could be considered as an element of intelligence gathering.

*Go Online*   A significant aspect of simply observing (i.e. without commenting) what customers write on social media sites is that the content is in the first person – and so is very revealing in its content. Someone complaining about being ignored by staff in a store, for example, should alert the company that their staff recruitment and training programmes aren't working as they should be. For an excellent article on how to analyse this kind of intelligence, follow the link on the chapter's web page.

## DECISION TIME

Although marketers might refer to research and intelligence with regard to data collected, for many – especially small businesses – the information is no more than that knowledge gained as part of their every day commercial operations. Tracking a competitor's activities has always been something that is expected – almost naturally. In pre–Internet days this meant that you signed up for competitors' mailshots (to your home – not business – address, of course) in order to track their promotions and rang up for fictitious 'quotes'. Now, instead of having to physically visit the stores of competitors (I have spent many hours noting prices in competitors' shops) the prices are on their website – or you might be able to use a comparison shopping engine (see section 4.6) to do the job for you. You can even set up numerous 'hotmail–type' email accounts and register for competitors' email campaigns.

## Practical Insight

### What – and tell my competitors?

In the mid to late 1990s I spent time both 'preaching' the advantages of the Internet as a business tool as well as representing a company that designed websites. After 'it's a fad and won't catch on', the biggest excuse I came across from small business owners for not having a website was that they thought it would make life too easy for competitors to find out details of their products and organization.

For the uninitiated, please note: I am not talking about any kind of 'industrial spying' here – that is illegal. Simply gathering information that is in the public domain is very much an expected aspect of doing business. Now, simply by spending a few hours a week surfing the web (it can even be at home, after 'office' hours – an important issue for small business owners and managers who spend all day actually running their business) you can:

- Keep up to date on what is happening in your industry and/or market
- Track competitors' activities by visiting their websites
- Read what customers have to say about you or your competitors on 'review sites'
- Find new markets – by, for example, visiting the websites of organizations that might use your products or already use those of your competitors
- Develop new product offerings – the owner of a small hotel, for example, could visit the websites of national or global chains to 'adopt' their ideas for their own accommodation.

More specific data–gathering efforts – primary or secondary – will depend on the objectives of that research, what information is required from the data and how it will be used. Essentially, the same criteria for offline market research should be applied to online research initiatives – and data should certainly not be gathered simply because technology makes it easy to do so (see website analytics in the previous section). Any subsequent research will then be expected to give a return on investments made.

## MINI CASE

**Do it yourself – with a little help.**

As a marketer you might know the questions you want to ask – but are not aware of how to use Internet technology in order to ask them. Although some companies will handle the whole package for you, others offer the opportunity to develop it yourself. SurveyMonkey facilitate the creation of your own surveys that can be (a) hosted on your website or blog, or (b) distributed by email.

**The home page of SurveyMonkey (www.surveymonkey.com)**

*You Decide*  Advise members of the consortium that owns The Gilded Truffle Hotel (case study 3) on what kind of data could be gathered using online market research, how it might be collected and what use could be made of it.

Alternatively, conduct the same exercise for your organization or that of your employer.

## 2.7 PROMOTING THE WEBSITE OFFLINE

Although not strictly part of Internet marketing – it is actually the *offline* promotion of an *online* entity – it is worth considering how a website can be promoted in the offline environment.

In the case of the pure online business, they need to advertise offline in order to drive the necessary volumes of traffic to their sites. An example would be the shopping comparison sites, particularly in the insurance and travel industries where hardly a TV ad break goes by without there being an ad for such sites. Essentially, in these cases, the website is the product that is being advertised.

For the offline entity, as with all marketing activities, the answer to this question is that it depends on the objectives of those activities. Closely allied to the issue of objectives is the contemplation of which domain name is to be used. If the company has only one product or is known by an established brand name then the chances are that only one domain name is used. However, there will be instances where the organization has more than one website (several products, each with their own site) – or perhaps a mini-site has been set up (on its own domain name) to support a particular promotion. Obviously, such promotions will include offline advertising, and any ad will include the pertinent website address.

As well as in ads, there are a number of other places where a domain name could be featured – effectively it is everywhere that potential customers might see it. This would include all or any of the following.

- On all stationery, including letter-headed paper, invoices, receipts and business cards.
- All promotional literature. This includes not only direct marketing letters, flyers and so on, but product catalogues, trade show hand-outs and any other kind of printed materials.
- Promotional give-a-ways. This is an infinite list of virtually any item that can be given away, from pens and note blocks to sports bags and mugs.
- Where appropriate, on the products themselves. This has obvious limited applications – few businesses can put their domain name on the side of an aeroplane as do Virgin and easyJet, for example. Putting your domain name on a piece of furniture would be unlikely to impress customers (though it could be included on a label on the underside). However, 'flymo.com' on the side of a lawnmower instead of just 'flymo', for example, is not unreasonable.
- Product packaging, including labels and boxes, cartons etc.
- Point of sale materials used in both retail and wholesale outlets.
- Company vehicles. Trucks and vans obviously, but cars can also be suitable if they are used by staff while performing their duties – estate agents, for example.
- Employee's clothing. Whilst business suits do not lend themselves to the practice, polo shirts, overalls and work coats can actually be enhanced by a discrete – but readable – domain name. Note that baseball caps and tee shirts could be included here, but although employees *might* wear them, they are better included under promotional give-a-ways.
- On anything related to any sponsorship the organization might be involved in. This would include event banners, press releases, literature or other promotional material.
- On any materials or tools used in the course of the day-to-day operations of a business – scaffolding on a construction site, for example.
- At the bottom of all general communications emails (that is non-direct marketing emails).

It is worth noting that when a domain name appears in print, no matter what it is on, the issue of aesthetic is a serious consideration. This issue is addressed in the earlier section – 'creating the right domain name'.

## DECISION TIME

This is, essentially, about the justification of cost for any offline marketing activity that might drive customers online. In many cases the cost will be absorbed within existing costs. For example, a business card with 'www. companyname.com' on the bottom will cost no more than a similar card without it. Similarly, a URL at the bottom of a van or truck's livery will add little to the cost of that livery.

Consideration should also be given to the presentation. Not only are the aesthetics important, but also how the domain name or URL is announced. It is reasonable to suggest that in the majority of contemporary markets the buyers – be they customers or consumers – would expect both vendors or manufacturers to have a website, in which case a simple 'alancharlesworth.eu' at the bottom of a page, packaging or similar will suffice. Note that users recognise a web address when they see one – hence the www is not really necessary. By the same token a message such as 'visit us online at … ' is pretty much redundant.

*You Decide*

Advise the Lindsey Naegle (case study 12) on where her website should be promoted offline – and what she would hope to gain from this kind of promotion.

Alternatively, conduct the same exercise for your organization or that of your employer.

### CHAPTER EXERCISE

Giving justifications for all your decisions, advise Two Cities Manufacturing Ltd (case study 11) on all aspects of Internet marketing covered in this chapter.

Alternatively, conduct the same exercise on your own organization or that of your employer.

## REFERENCES

Creese, G. & Kahlow, A.E. (2003). E-channel awareness: Usage, Satisfaction and Buying Intentions. Aberdeen Group, Aberdeen.

FMI Group (2001). Website Visitor Analysis – Statistics or Intelligence? FMI Group, Basingstoke.

Gay, R., Charlesworth, A. & Esen, R. (2007). *Online Marketing – A Customer-Led Approach*. Oxford University Press.

Hammersley, M. & Atkinson, P. (1997). *Ethnography: Principles in Practice*, 2nd edn. Routledge.

Hughes, T. (2007). Regaining a seat at the table: marketing management and the e-service opportunity. *Journal of Services Marketing*. Vol. 21, No. 4, pp. 270–289.

Kozinets, R. (1997). I Want To Believe : A Netnography of The X-Philes' Subculture of Consumption. *Advances in Consumer Research.* Vol. 24, pp. 470–475.

Long, B.S. (2002). How to avoid common web mistakes. *Public Relations Tactics.* Vol. 9, No. 11.

Pitta, D.A. & Fowler, D. (2005). Online consumer communities and their value to new product developers. *Journal of Product and Brand Management.* Vol. 14, No. 5.

Schlosser, A.E., White, T.B. & Lloyd, S.M. (2006). Converting website visitors into buyers: how website investment increases consumer trusting beliefs and online purchase intention. *Journal of Marketing.* Vol. 70, No. 2, pp. 133–148.

Weischedel, B., Matear, S. & Deans, K. (2005). A qualitative approach to investigating online strategic decision making. *Qualitative Market Research: An International Journal.* Vol. 8, No. 1, pp. 61–76.

Welling, R. & White, L. (2006). Website performance measurement: promise and reality. *Managing Service Quality.* Vol. 16, No. 6, pp. 654–670.

# Website development

> *The three golden rules of good design are:*
> *Eliminate the superfluous,*
> *Emphasize the comfortable, and*
> *Acknowledge the elegance of the uncomplicated*
>
> Giorgio Armani

## CHAPTER AT A GLANCE

## 3.1   INTRODUCTION

> " all online marketing – be it strategic or operational – revolves around the web presence "

Whilst there are other essential elements to Internet marketing, it is an inescapable fact that all online marketing – be it strategic or operational – revolves around the web presence. The importance of the website is acknowledged by the fact that three chapters of this book are devoted to the subject. Readers should note, however, that whilst other aspects of e-marketing depend on the website, it too relies on elements of marketing that go beyond what the customer sees on their computer screen.

Concentrating on presentation, usability and navigation, this chapter considers best practice in the development of the organization's web presence so that customer needs are met and organizational objectives achieved. Note that this chapter – in keeping with the philosophy of the book – considers the marketing elements of web design and not the technical (IT) issues. This 'non–technical' approach is not meant to ignore or devalue the input from programmers – this is particularly the case for *back–end* design (the visible page is the site's *front–end*). Google, for example, has a very simplistic page design and presentation that efficiently and effectively help the users achieve their aim (generate a search). It is behind the scenes in the back–end design – the search algorithm – where Google programmers earn their pay.

### Practical Insight

**The technical basics**

From a technical perspective, there are many ways of developing a website. The most basic is using hypertext mark-up language (HTML). This is a programming 'code' that makes the content of a document appear on a computer screen. For example, to make a word appear in bold you place <b> (start bold) in front of it, and <b> (end bold) after it. Other types of coding are more complex. In this book such forms are referred to as 'Flash'-type. Although this is a significant generalization, it serves the purpose of this book.

To check the code of a web page, right click on your mouse and then in Internet Explorer (IE) click on 'view source'-or on Firefox/Netscape 'view page source' and you will see the source code used.

The main issues of a web presence – like marketing itself – do not exist in isolation, with each aspect having influence or effect on the others. Online credibility, for example, might be influenced by the presentation of the site and the quality of its content – all of which depends on the way the site is managed. However, to aid the learning process, I have presented all of the key aspects in separate sections.

If the objective of this chapter is to address the issue of developing an effective web presence, we must first consider what constitutes a *good* website. A review of the academic research reveals a preponderance of similar criteria for assessing the quality website design. For example, note the commonality of the terms used by the following when presenting their key aspects of quality website design: Ease of use, aesthetic design, processing speed, security (Yoo & Donthu, 2001); business function, corporate credibility, content readability, attractiveness, structure, navigation (Kim et al, 2003); accessibility, communication, credibility, understanding, appearance, availability (Cox & Dale, 2001); usability, usefulness, adequacy of information, accessibility, interaction (Yang et al, 2004); usability, information quality, service interaction (Barnes & Vidgen, 2002); core service, supporting services, user interface (Van Riel et al, 2001); quality of information, service, security, playfulness, design (Liu & Arnett, 2000).

---

*Go Online*    **When you're inside the bottle, you can't read the label**

Although this philosophy can be applied to all marketing, it is particularly relevant to website development. Essentially, it means that if you are too close to the design of a website (inside the bottle) you do not see the site (the label) in the same way that the site's visitors might. For more on my views follow the link from the chapter's web page.

---

Note that these all have an element of intangibility about them, and that the qualities could well be perceptions of users – perceptions that might be different from those of the site's developers. It is also the case that the underpinning of these criteria is mainly strategic, that is, they do not tell the developer how to *practically* apply these things to a website (e.g. what is 'ease of use' and how do you achieve it?)

A further criticism of this research is that little mention is made of any weighting for the criteria. If, for example, in Kim et al's criteria listed above, the home page of the website was not attractive to the target audience, or the navigation was poor, the users would leave the site before the other four criteria could even be addressed. Similarly, if students feel that the answer to an assignment question can be found within the text of a website they will ignore criteria of readability, attractiveness, structure and battle their way through poor navigation in order to track down that assessment solution.

Readers should also note that this is the first of three chapters that cover website development. In this chapter we look at the basics that are applicable to all sites. In the two subsequent chapters elements of website design that are specific to B2C and B2B are addressed.

## 3.2   THE BASICS

An often–used comment on website development is that designers design for themselves instead of designing for the user, which invariably means using technology for technology's sake – something Loizides (2003) describes as 'one of the worst offences [online] marketers can make'. Although for the best examples of successful websites this is not true – sadly it is still the case for many sites. Dadzie et al (2005) advocate that website features can be categorized into website design features and customer service functions. Although this might be considered a sensible a way of separating *design* and *marketing* elements of the site, it may also suggest to some that design and customer service are divorced – which is not the case. A common example of technology for its own sake is the use of 'splash' home pages. Online marketing practitioner and trainer Dr R. F. Wilson (2003) defines 'splash' pages as *'home pages with dancing logos powered by Macromedia Flash technology designed to annoy and turn away visitors before they reach the real home page'*. His opinion is shared by many – myself included – but not necessarily by all designers. For designers, web pages such as those on my website (www.alancharlesworth.eu) carry no kudos in design circles – indeed, they might brand mine as being 'bad' because it is so basic. My argument is that the site is designed for its target readership – and if you were to visit that site it would be for easy–to–find information, not entertainment. Sadly, that 'splash' pages do nothing to meet the needs of the visitors is too often not a concern of those who design them.

a customer. If you doubt this, consider: would you go into a shop to buy shoes if nothing on the outside of the shop suggests that it sells footwear? Or would you enter a restaurant if the entrance was dirty? Here are a few tips.

The front page should:

- Download quickly
- Be short and to the point
- Offer a value proposition – a reason for visitors to stay
- Be professional
- *Inspire* visitors to go deeper into the site
- *Direct* visitors deeper into the site
- Appeal to the target audience
- Include contact details

The front page should not have:

- Flash/splash type technology [e.g. it has a 'skip intro']
- Self-serving statements
- A company description
- Advertising banners
- Any 'award' logos
- The designer/developers name or logo
- A 'home' button
- External links

In chapter 7 I have included a quote from advertiser Alvin Hampel who makes the point that if an ad is clever and entertaining but sells no products it has failed as an advert – the same can be said of websites. Writing in a white paper on website design, practitioner Rick Tobin (2008) sums up this subject well. He suggests that the [web] page is (or should be) designed for a key audience – the content written for them in a voice they want to listen to; the navigation intuitive to them specifically; and the benefit messaging built around their needs. He goes on to say that more often than not this is an accepted best practice in other media but is frequently ignored in website design because:

- web designers build for ego and flash, not users.
- web designers test based on a coolness factor and not on how a user actually interacts.
- design theories are based on a push media perspective, where a glossy graphic grabs attention and brand association – very few design theories focus on a pull medium, where the user is in the driver's set and has explicit intentions.

*Go Online* The use of Flash type technologies in website design is a hotly debated subject. See the chapter's web page for a link to the web page that fuelled much of the debate – 'Flash: 99% Bad' by Jacob Nielsen.

In this section we will consider the basic elements of presenting information on a website. These are presented as guides and not rules. Obviously the objectives of the site might dictate how the guides are interpreted – but they are ignored at the publisher's peril. It is also worth noting that this book is about marketing on the Internet – and so this chapter refers only to sites that perform a commercial or public service and from which a return on investment is required. If you want to create an 'all–about–my–favourite– rock–band' website then ignoring the guides will not impinge on any objectives – commercial or otherwise. In fact, the chances are that only your family and friends will ever visit it, and so the design is of little consequence.

In addressing the basics of website development we are going to start by looking at two fundamental issues: presentation and usability. As with many aspects of Internet marketing, opinion is divided on what is meant by various terms and concepts, and this section is no exception. In this case I will be combining website *navigation* with *usability* – others might consider them separate subjects.

## MINI CASE

### Ads on your home page

This is the home page of one of my domain names. The company with which it is registered offers 'free' hosting of a web page – which is what I accepted. However, the page appears with a number of links down the right hand side (the 'related links') that are beyond my control. Given the nature of the page's content, it is not a significant problem for me. However, if this was my businesses' home page, what might potential customers think of those 'ads'?

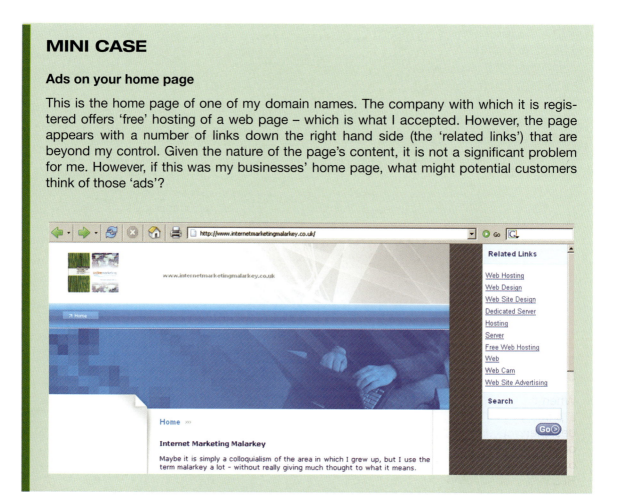

# Presentation

As with so many things in life, 'keep it simple' is an excellent maxim to follow when developing a web presence. Indeed, even in what many would conceive as a technically–liberated age, many shy away from new online applications. The American Customer Satisfaction Index (2007) – who present reports on a myriad of industries – commented on the fall in satisfaction of pure online e–business companies as potentially being because recent innovations such as maps and social networking sites are of interest only to the most 'tech–savvy' users and not the general web users. Usability expert Steve Krugg attempts to get the message across in the very title of his book on the subject: Don't Make Me Think (2000). His point being that using the site should be instinctive – leaving users to concentrate on the objectives of their visit.

## MINI CASE

### Simplicity is the key

Those who advocate against simplicity on grounds of it being 'boring' might want to consider Morgan Stanley's 'State of the Internet' report (2006). According to it, the three most visited websites were (1) Microsoft, (2) Yahoo!, and (3) Google. In describing these sites the key word would be 'plain'. More specifically, they meet the needs of the user – simply.

Presented in no particular order, the following are some of the key issues in presenting a website to its visitors.

- Download time. In the early days of the web, research suggested that around eight seconds was as long as most people were willing to wait for a page to download. The widespread availability of broadband has reduced this waiting time – web users are an impatient lot. Technology–heavy sites download slowly, simple ones quickly. Cutting edge technology has a place – but is it on your website?

## RESEARCH SNAPSHOT

### Download it or lose 'em

When connection was through low–capacity dial-ups, the download speed of pages was a primary concern when designing sites. With the advent of broadband, however, many designers have forgotten about the issue – and yet 18 per cent of Internet users are still on dial-up connections (PEW/Internet and American Life, 2007). Furthermore, designers of technology rich splash-style front pages should revisit the issue for another reason. Research, conducted in 2006, by US Internet performance tracking company Gomez

> *Go Online*     For more on how text looks on the web, follow the link to my web page on online text presentation.

- Avoid non-standard characters that not all browsers can read – the subscript™ for example, does not appear as such on some browsers.
- Home page link. So that a visitor is never completely lost on your site, or because they may have arrived deep in the site from a search engine, there should be a link to the home page on every other page on the site – although it is surprising how many home pages include a link to themselves.
- Ensure the design features of the site are appropriate to its objectives. You would expect the presentation of a website for a funeral director to be different to that of an amusement park. An extreme example perhaps, but what sort of website might your target audience expect to find?

## Practical Insight

### Knowledge of all fonts?

The most easily read font on a website is one from the Arial/Helvetica family. Times New Roman, the most commonly used font in printed media, should be avoided.

The reason is in the presentation of the fonts. Arial and its cohorts are *sans serif* fonts – they have no *tails* at the end of each line in the letter. Times New Roman is a serif font – it has the additional tails. In print, characters are 'solid' and so the tails make the words easier for the human eye to identify – and so read. Online, however, all characters are presented in pixels – effectively thousands of dots on the screen that when put together represent letters, numbers and so on. Because of this pixilation it is better if each character is distinct from the next – and the tails in serif fonts tend to 'blend' each character into its neighbours, so making it more difficult to read on a computer screen.

Incidentally, it is the same issue that makes words in italics difficult to read online – and so they should be avoided.

Follow the links on the chapter's web page to see my examples of how different fonts look online.

- It may be true that a picture paints a thousand words – but online there are caveats. Be aware of using large images on a website (and never on the front page) as they can take a long time to download. If your product sells on what it looks like, then pictures are essential – but make sure consideration is given to the file size of any image (for download times). Also, the quality of any pictures is important, they should be professionally produced. Having pictures on a website simply because 'they look nice' is not good practice. The custom of having a picture take prominence on a web page is a legacy from the print media and advertising. Often referred to as 'the hero shot', having a big picture of a film star next to a story about them might work in magazines and images of gorgeous women on perfume ads might work offline – but online such illustrations simply take up valuable on–screen space.

- Grammar and spelling. Sadly this final point should go without saying, but unfortunately it is a common problem on pages ranging from blogs to corporate sites. Ensure any textual content is grammatically correct and has no spelling errors. How credible is a business if it cannot even take the effort to have its website content checked for errors?

## RESEARCH SNAPSHOT

### Leaving is easy

If a website is difficult to use, people leave. If the homepage fails to clearly state what a company offers and what users can do on the site, people leave. If users get lost on a website, they leave. If a website's information is hard to read or doesn't answer users' key questions, they leave.

*Source: Usability guru, Jacob Nielsen (2003)*

## Usability

Website usability is all about how easy it is for a visitor to achieve their objectives for visiting the site. If it is to find the address of a local store – is there a prominent link on the front page that says 'store locations'? If it is to purchase a silk tie as a present – is there clear categorization: e.g. menswear > ties > silk. Any block on the visitor's smooth flow through the site is a reason for them to leave – and a click on the back button represents a lost sale. Naturally, the opposite is also true – as Kamarulzamam (2007) commented 'it is evident [in this study] that in order to convert Internet browsers into e-shoppers, the ease of use and usefulness of e-shopping must be enhanced'. Similarly, research from Hung-Pin (2004) showed that *perceived* ease of use and usefulness help drive shopping attitudes. In Gay et al (2007) I make the point that in website design, familiarity breeds *acceptance* and so endorse the commonly used – and so easily acceptable – 'header-columns-footer' model. Because the design is so frequently used – not least by some of the most visited sites on the web – when people arrive on a page with this design characteristic they are immediately at ease with the presentation.

> " usability is all about how easy it is for a visitor to achieve their objectives for visiting the site "

## MINI CASE

**Don't confuse your site's visitors**

My own website uses a standard 'header – 3 columns – footer' set-up. At the time of writing, other examples include: the BBC (www.bbc.co.uk), MSN (www.msn.com), yahoo! (www.yahoo.com) and Wikipedia (www.wikipedia.org) – so I think I am in good company.

**The page construction of the home page of alancharlesworth.eu**

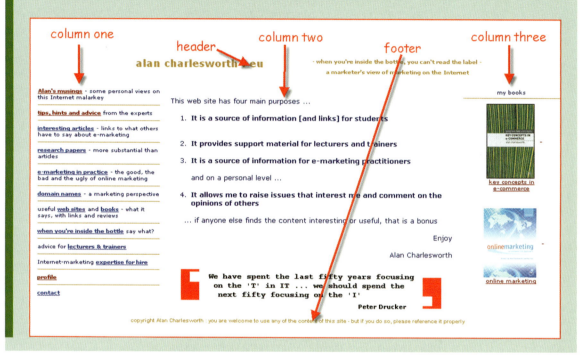

Navigation refers to how visitors find their way – *navigate* – around your website. If you only have a couple of pages this shouldn't be an issue, but if the site has more than three pages this is vital. It is also the case that in an era where search rules the web, many visitors will arrive not on your front page – but deep in the site. Navigation systems should take this into account so that potential customers do not simply bounce straight off your site because (a) they are not aware of other content, or (b) can't find their way to it.

## Practical Insight

**There are right visitors, and there are wrong visitors**

Over the years numerous commentators, authors and practitioners have made the point that there are several distinct categories for people who arrive at a commercial website – and they should be considered in the design of the site. Nearly all agree that the list is something like this:

1  They're there by mistake – they followed a link, miss-typed a URL, miss-interpreted the domain name – or one of a dozen other reasons. No part of your web development efforts should be aimed at them.
2  They don't really know what they are looking for, but they think you might have it – think of the window shopper who wanders in off the street. A front page which says whose site it is and what they offer – plus a clear navigation bar should tell this visitor whether they belong there or not.
3  They have some inkling of what they want and believe that you sell it – perhaps because they have been on the site before. As with previous group, clear navigation should help them out – though as they know what they are after, more comprehensive listings might be necessary – or an in-site search facility.
4  They know what they want and they know that you sell it. For these visitors 'one-click' type navigation is necessary so that they can get to their purchase as quickly as possible.

Of course, grey areas will exist in this list – and developers should never forget that a visitor who is #4 for one product might be a #2 or #3 for others.

Although you may know your way around your site, you should not assume others find it as easy. Pages, sections, categories, products – whatever your site is made up of – should be signposted clearly. There should be an unambiguous contents list. If every page has a 'return to home/index page link then the visitor is only ever one click away from base – where they can start again. If your website is massive – provide an in–site search facility. Seen by many as essential to navigation around major sites, internal search facilities can be problematic – suffering from what I call 'red sweater syndrome'. The problem lies in who is responsible for the development of any search facility – and it is too often left to IT staff. By the very nature of computer programming – it is binary – coding is developed in a yes/no way. The algorithm is asked for a 'red sweater', if there is no 'red sweater' the search return is 'none found'. And this is where marketing must work with IT in developing the facility. Here's the reason.

Different people recognise the same products by different names and descriptions – a red sweater and maroon pullover, for example – and so marketing input is required to ensure provision is made for matching searchers with products that meet their needs: e.g. a search for 'red sweater' will trigger the response that 'maroon pullover' is actually the same thing. To avoid the 'no return' page – which is bound to send the potential customer elsewhere – marketers should help make sure that:

• If there are no matching products, a *marketing* message is offered (e.g. 'you might want to try …' or 'no shirts in this colour are available, but you might want to consider this range [link] that has other colours that might work with your outfit').

- As indicated with the red sweater, where synonyms are used, the search terms that visitors might use should be predicted. This also includes popular terminology (e.g. a car enthusiast might search on 'alloys', not 'alloy wheels').
- Common misspellings (in the products and descriptions) can be predicted – similarly, different international terms should be catered for.
- Too many results are as bad as none. The visitor has used the search to save them time in navigating the whole site, it's no good presenting them with a list that is longer than the site's navigation bar. Multiple results should be categorized, or if necessary an 'advanced search' option should be offered to help users narrow down their alternatives.

Technical staff can build all of these elements into the search engine's parameters – but they should not be expected to determine those parameters themselves. In the last section I emphasized the importance of input from sale staff in the website development. This is a good example of where their experience is essential – it is they who know what customers ask for.

## RESEARCH SNAPSHOT

### Nice flight, shame about the website

Research by user experience specialists Webcredible (2008) which evaluated 20 of the top UK travel agent and airline carrier websites against 20 best practice usability guidelines suggests that it is not only late flights and lost baggage that are problems for the industry. The best score (out of 100) was gained by airline consortium–owned opodo (opodo.co.uk) – but that merited only a mark of 67. Room for improvement all round, I think.

Although good navigation is important for *branding* and *service* websites (see section 1.7), for revenue-generating sites *important* becomes *absolutely essential*. As the site's objective is more tangible – make a sale, for example – the web designer can look to influence the way a visitor navigates their way around the site. One way of doing this is to use an online adaptation of the sales funnel. (Note that the sales funnel is a development from the buying cycle and AIDA concepts – both of which are covered in more detail in section 1.6.) In the traditional version, potential customers might be exposed to an advert (the top, or widest, part of the funnel). People interested in the product might respond to the ad by ringing up to request a brochure (they enter the funnel). After reading the brochure, the prospective customer then contacts the firm to arrange a demonstration of the product, and so on until a purchase is made (they fall out of the funnel at its narrowest point). At each step the customer can either (a) go deeper into the funnel, or (b) step out by rejecting the offering. Sales (and marketing) teams can then study users' progression through the funnel – and address issues that cause them to step out at the various stages. It is also the case that customers can be 'rejected' at any stage if sales staff identify them as 'not-serious' purchasers.

Online, web designers might consider the website to be the 'funnel'. Potential customers might arrive at the front page (mouth of the funnel) from a search engine. What they see on the page will determine whether or not they click deeper into the site (funnel). At each stage the prospect might withdraw (click away). The final stage – the narrow end of the funnel – is where the customer clicks on 'buy now'.

---

*Go Online*

### Give site visitors a personality

One way of developing a successful e–commerce website is to match its presentation and content with the intended visitors. A popular method of doing this is to create visitor 'personas' – follow the links on the chapter's web page for more on this concept.

---

The funnel model is applied in a concept called 'persuasive – or per-suas*ion* – architecture', where the navigational design of the site leads a prospect to the objective of the site by having them follow a series of com-mands. For example, a product description page might sell its attributes and end with the comment 'to find out what colours are available, click here'; 'to select a size, click here' – and so on. However, the model also depends on the hyperlinks to each be a 'call to action' that motivates the user to move to the next stage. A persuasive call to action can be the dif-ference between a visitor continuing down the funnel or leaving the site. For example, consider how the inclusion of a benefit and an imperative or active verb help make the second of these hyperlinks more persuasive.

1  Bob discovered a work opportunity that changed his life. **Read More**
2  Bob discovered a work opportunity that changed his life. **See how Bob doubled his earnings in less than a year**

As with its offline version, the online sales funnel can be used as an ana-lytical tool. If, for example, most prospects leave the site from the 'price' page then it suggests that either (a) there is a problem with the content of that page, or (b) there is a problem with the product's price. To find out which of the two is the main problem, testing is the answer.

---

## Practical Insight

### Access for the Disabled

Although the arguments offered by the Royal National Institute for the Blind (RNIB) – ranging from moral (it's fair), through commercial (it's good business sense), to legal (it's the law) – are valid, they are not reflected in the attitude of many website publishers towards the issue of making sites accessible to disabled users, with far too many not meeting the criteria.

Designers can seek advice from a number of sources, not least the Worldwide Web Consortium (www.w3.org).

However, online retailers are still failing accessibility tests. Wide ranging research by usability and accessibility specialists, Webcredible (published in December 2007), showed that although some of the UK's leading retailers are making strides when it comes to making their websites more accessible, but there's still a long way to go. Follow the link on the chapter's web page to download the report.

As a footnote, although under the terms of the Disability Discrimination Act of 1995, all UK websites should be accessible to *all* users, prosecution under – or even policing of – the Act seem to be minimal.

## Testing

Although testing should be considered as a basic element to website development it is too often the case that it is seen as an add–on, a luxury, or worst still – not a necessity. Before any site is made live to the public it should go through two stages of testing – *technical* and *human*. It should also be noted that this testing is related to the end user and how they are able to access and use the site. Aesthetically beautiful websites that win design awards or feature high in search engine results pages are not necessarily user friendly. As with all marketing, the only important opinions are those of the end users – the customers.

Technical issues that can be tested and addressed during development include:

- Performance on the various browsers which customers might use, including not only the most popular (Internet Explorer and Netscape/ Firefox) but also AppleMac, Web-TV and any other system made available through Internet service providers.
- Download speeds on a variety of broadband and dial–up facilities – with high and low specification PCs and laptops also being brought into the equation.
- How pages present on various sizes of computer screen – including portable devices (e.g. Blackberry) if the target audience is known to use them.

It is also worth noting that testing should not end when the site goes live. Whilst ongoing improvements can be made to all of the elements listed above, other aspects of the site can be constantly tested for better results. For example, the text used in calls to action as part of the sales funnel can be tested for increasing clickthrough rates. For major online retailers like Amazon, such testing is constant with virtually every aspect of the web presence including (but not limited to) background colour, headlines, copy, graphical images, banner ads, PPC ads, button colours – indeed, anything where there is the potential to improve the response and be able to measure the improvements – being subject to testing in order to achieve maximum sales.

## RESEARCH SNAPSHOT

**For useful feedback, ask the shopper – not the website designer**

The 2007 'Retail Customer Experience Study' from Future Now (www.futurenowinc.com) was interesting not only for its results – but the methodology of the research.

The study consisted of having 'mystery shoppers' visit a retailer's website and answer a series of Yes/No questions about the availability of 69 different factors that reflect a focus on customer experience. The features addressed included:

- Did product copy descriptions answer the shopper's implicit questions
- Whether the retailer offers customer reviews
- Were shoppers' gift buying needs catered for
- Ease and simplicity of checkout
- Retailer's ability to address the shopper's concerns (e.g. return policies, guarantees)
- Ease and clarity of retailer return policies
- Offering estimated delivery times and showing in-stock availability for items

Of further interest – and relevance – are the issues that weren't included in the survey, so making findings objective rather than subject. Ignored issues included:

- The ease in locating the products
- The efficacy of the brand in conveying confidence
- The impact of overall design on credibility and sales

*Source: Future Now Inc (2007)*

Human – or *usability* – testing is task oriented and should not be performed by anyone who has been involved in the project as they will have an insight into what is expected and how they should act. Neither should questionnaires or focus groups be used as people rarely say how they *actually* act online – few people like to admit they struggled with a task that they think others will perceive as being easy. Although advanced testing using such techniques as eye–tracking (where the user's eye line is tracked as it moves around a web page) are available, much can be learned by taking a member of the Internet–using general public, and simply putting them in front of the site's home page and asking them to perform a series of commands. If the website has a specific target market, then people who fit the right demographic profile should be used for testing. The respondents should be observed (and un–prompted – keep the design team out of the room) as they, for example, find the organization's postal address, a complaints phone number, the cost of shipping a product to America, a whitepaper download, how many colours a shirt is available in or make a purchase. Essentially, ask them to perform tasks that ordinary users will expect to complete (easily) in order to meet their objectives for visiting the site. Simple observation will tell the developers whether or not the site is usable or not.

## Practical Insight

**'White van' vs 'eye candy' websites**

Also known in the US as *panel van* websites, these are commercial sites of limited content and functionality, but which meet the objectives of the business they represent. The term comes from the ubiquitous vans that are a staple of businesses around the world that need to transport goods from A to B with the least fuss and best return on investment. Like their namesake websites, white vans are not a glamorous aspect of business, but they get the job done – hence the analogy. The opposite of such a site would be an *eye candy* website that looks good but does not meet any business objectives.

Note that these descriptions draw on content from my book *Key Concepts in e-Commerce*.

## DECISION TIME

This section follows on directly from the previous chapters where the website's objectives and who takes responsibility for its development are addressed. In my experience, however, it is not always the case that these two fundamental issues have been addressed before work starts – or is even completed – on the site.

From the strategic objectives will come the answers to such issues as:

- What technology is most appropriate for the target market?
- How will the target users access the site – and what types of hard and software might they use?
- What style of presentation best suites the organization, brand and customers?
- How will the site be used – quick information gathering or deeper research?
- Are there existing offline brand aesthetics that should be mirrored online – corporate colours, logo fonts etc.?
- Should the site meet with accepted online conventions – or will the target market be expecting something more unusual?
- Will pictures add to the users' experience of the site – or detract from it?
- What is the best method of navigation that best facilitates the user meeting their on–site needs – and the objectives of the site?
- Is an in–site search facility needed, or will good navigation suffice?
- What testing is necessary to ensure both user experience and site objectives are optimized?

The answers to these issues will give the designers a direction to take in the way the site is developed to best suit target users.

*Go Online*   Whilst there is no finite 'right' way for website design, numerous 'design guides' exist – follow the links on the chapter's web page to see some of the best.

*You Decide*    Advise Quincy Adams Wagstaff and his staff at Huxley University (case study 10) on what aspects of the basic website design are specifically relevant to the university's web presence.

Alternatively, conduct the same exercise for your organization or that of your employer.

## 3.3   ONLINE CREDIBILITY

In the *real* world, customers can use all of their senses in making a judgement on a brand or organization. They can *look* at the building they are in – how it is decorated; how well maintained; how clean. They can *listen* to what staff say – and note their tone of voice for sincerity or humour. They can *touch* products; feel the characteristics; assess the quality. They can *smell* the product – or if it is relevant, the place in which it is processed or sold. They can *taste* the product – or ingredients. They can also use their *sixth* sense – the one that gives them a *insight* of the organization – its ethos and culture, for example. Online they are limited to the square foot or so of computer screen on which the words and images that make up your web presence appears. Chen & Barnes (2007) make the point that web–based transactions are more impersonal and anonymous and so building online trust is an essential component for vendors to succeed in an e-commerce environment.

A term I have used for some time in an effort to emphasize to organizations that cost cutting on website development will come back to haunt them in the future is: *online-you are your website*. Essentially this notion reflects the fact that in the intangible world that is the Internet the only thing that on which the (potential) customer can judge your organization is what they see on their computer screen. Of course, bad website equals bad organization is a perception – but then so too is much of marketing. If *online, you are your website* ever carried any validity, it is with regard to online credibility. Long before the commercial Internet, Mowen (1987) made the point that the consumer evaluates a retailer and its products/services before deciding on whether or not to develop a relationship with them. This is not only equally true in the online marketplace, but it can be applied to B2B trading as well as retailing.

> **❝** online, you are your website **❞**

## MINI CASE

### Fast talking advice

When asked about the secret to success, Groucho Marx once replied: '*To get on in life the thing you really need is a reputation for honesty and fair dealing – and if you can fake that you're laughing*'.

Whilst you should always look to present your organization in as good a light as possible, beware of overstepping the mark. Such is the nature of the web that you will be found out.

So how do we build trust and credibility into a website? Teo and Yu (2005) suggest that a consumer's willingness to buy online is positively influenced by (a) the dependability of the store, (b) reduction of uncertainty, and (c) their online experience. Fogg (1999) suggests credibility is a combination of trustworthiness – unbiased, truthful, good, honest – and expertise – experienced, intelligent, powerful, knowledgeable. The last of Teo and Yu's points is emphasised by Poirier (2003) who says that website visitors form impressions about your company based on the totality of the experience they have whilst on your site. He goes on to make recommendations as to what makes up that *experience* – including ease of navigation, clarity of writing, quality of customer service and professional visual presentation of material.

A number of practitioner websites offer more tangible solutions, though many are based around Stanford University's Persuasive Technology Lab's research into web credibility – whose guidelines include:

- Making it easy to verify the accuracy of the information on your site.
- Showing that there's a real organisation behind your site.
- Highlighting the expertise in the organization.
- Showing that honest and trustworthy people stand behind your site.
- Making it easy to contact the organization.

However, the limitations of the computer screen can also be an advantage – particularly to the smaller business. Online, all organizations are measured in the pixels of a computer screen – and so a well crafted site can be a great equalizer in a competitive marketplace. Providing they can meet the needs of the their customers, the small business that is tucked away on a trading estate in an unfashionable northern town can be an *credible* online competitor of that mega–corp based in London's Docklands.

## Practical Insight

### Look outward, not inward

When Jonathan Kranz-Collier, the author of 'Writing Copy for Dummies' was asked (in an interview with marketingprofs.com, 2007): 'What is the most common mistake that you've seen companies make in crafting its collateral?' He replied: 'Narcissism. We think we can distinguish our business from the competition by talking about ourselves: our company, our mission, our philosophy, our products. Yet the more we talk about ourselves, ironically, the more we sound like everyone else … and we lose potential customers as a result.

## DECISION TIME

For the pure online organization the website is everything – and so it should receive all the attention that the sole source of income demands. However, for any 21st century marketer it is likely that the website will play an important role in any marketing strategy – and so how that website represents the organization is an essential consideration. The site must present a credible organization so that trust with customers can be developed – as Gefen & Straub (2004) point out, the higher the degree of consumer's trust, the higher the degree of purchase intentions of consumers.

Just as every business – and marketing mix – is different, so too is every website. However, there are a number of issues that should be addressed in order to suggest credibility to the customer. These would include such things as:

- Incorporate contact details, including full mailing address
- Provide details of staff to make the organization real
- Have an FAQ section that answers all potential customer questions
- Include details of complaints procedures
- Explain in full the organization's email and data protection policies
- Use customer endorsements

## RESEARCH SNAPSHOT

Researchers at Massachusetts Institute of Technology's Sloan School of Management found that slightly more than half of the consumers were willing to pay more for a product if it came from a reputable vendor.

*Source: Brynjolfsson, E. & Smith, M. (2001)*

However, these are generic topics, and each publisher should look for specific issues that are relevant to that site's visitors. For example, JupiterResearch (2006) found that 29 per cent of buyers were positively influenced by shipping cut-off information (the last date for orders for guaranteed delivery by a certain day) – suggesting credibility through reliability. Also – as is a constant theme throughout this book – multiple aspects of Internet marketing impact on each other. Researchers from iProspect (2006) for example, found that 36 per cent of search engine users considered that seeing a company listed among the top results on a search engine results page raised the credibility of that company within its field. Note, however, that whilst we have considered trust as a distinct aspect of website design, effectively all the other elements of this chapter are components of online credibility.

*You Decide*   Advise Robert Terwilliger (case study 9) on specific issues of credibility with regard to the website for the Modeller's Stand that would be important to potential customers, and suggest how that might be addressed.

Alternatively, conduct the same exercise for your organization or that of your employer.

## 3.4   CONTENT DEVELOPMENT

As we established in section 1.6, it is in the consumers' search for information that the web has the greatest impact on marketing. This should not come as a great surprise, customers' thirst for information to aid their purchase decision has long since been recognised as a key element in the buying process – Glazer (1991) makes the point that a major component of exchange is the exchange of information.

### RESEARCH SNAPSHOT

**Most searches are for information**

Using a software application that automatically classified over a million and a half queries submitted by several hundred thousand users, Jansen et al (2008) found that around 80 per cent of searches are informational in nature. The remaining 20 per cent of searches are evenly split between those that are navigational or transactional.

> textual content is
> often the last thing
> considered in website
> development

If it is a search for information that is the primary motive for visiting a website, then that information must be not only of a high quality – but presented in a way that it is acceptable to the visitor. It is necessary, therefore, that further examination of this aspect of website development is included here. Although content developers have long argued the value of their contribution to the success of a website, their arguments have been equally long ignored by too many developers. Indeed, it is the experience of many – including myself – that the textual content is often the last thing considered in website development. It is not unusual for a site to be months in development and the content written in the last few days before it goes live – with it often being simply lifted from existing offline publications. Not only that, but the task is delegated to anyone who might be available at the time. So it is that arguably the most important element of the website – that will be available to customers 365 days a year, seven days a week, 24 hours a day – is written by the office junior or placement student. Author and practitioner, David Meerman Scott (2007) acknowledges that website design is important, but suggests that it dominates the focus of too many organizations' online thinking, to the detriment of good content development – in his opinion, because it is *easier* to do so. Supporters of quality content development point to traditional media, where professional input has always been a prerequisite of any content that is put into the public domain and attributed to an organization – and yet that ethos is largely ignored where websites are concerned.

## Practical Insight

**Content is king!**

On a commercial website, visitors arrive looking for information that will meet the needs that have driven them to the website in the first place. That information is the *content* of the website. While much of the sought-after information will be in textual format, do not forget that appropriate images, graphics, audio and video content can add to the readers' stimulus.

Good content will overcome basic design – but excessive design will not disguise poor content.

And who decides whether the content is good or not? It is the website visitor – if it is relevant to their needs then the content is good. As with all marketing, however, the trick is to know what the potential customers' needs are.

For both successful practitioners and academics, however, the value of content is being recognised. Chen & Barnes (2007) comment that shoppers make purchase decisions based on the information provided by online retailers and according to a survey by CompleteInc (2006) 20 per cent of consumers changed their original purchase decision based on information gleaned online. Online product merchandising specialists WebCollage's (www.webcollage.com) 2007 survey of online consumer product research habits suggests that 91 per cent of shoppers consider that it is important that they are able to find complete product information online, whilst 82 per cent of respondents said they were more likely to return to sites that provided them with complete product information. Both Koufaris & Hampton-Sosa (2004) and Cao et al (2005) continue the theme of the relationship between information availability and purchase decision in their research which found that useful and easily understood information on a website lifts the degree of online trust and positively influences purchase intention. Furthermore, the perception that it is only high–value items that are researched online is proving to be misconceived. Results of a study – the Digital Shelf (2007) – conducted jointly between comScore, Procter & Gamble, the Search Engine Marketing Professional Organization (SEMPO) and Yahoo! into the role of online search in the purchase of consumer packaged goods (CPG) revealed that it is not just cars and travel that draw users online. The research showed that people use the web to compare alternative products in all four categories investigated – food products, personal care products, baby products and household products. That 73 per cent of respondents said that the motivation for visiting a CPG site was for 'information and help' only goes to reinforce the notion that the availability and presentation of information is paramount in website content – even if the product costs less than a couple of pounds.

## Practical Insight

**Content or copy?**

It is important to appreciate that while the two may blend into each other, there is a fundamental difference between content and copy. Essentially, content has the objective of being informative. Copy, on the other hand, is persuasive in its nature – hence the common term, *sales* copy. It is copy that will encourage a visitor to become a customer. The textual content presented in an advert will have been developed by a copywriter. Online this aspect of the web content is often referred to as the *call-to-action* – 'click here for more information' is a basic example. The online blurring of where one stops and the other starts is commonly found in product descriptions. If a product is described only by its attributes or capabilities ('it is 50 cm long and will last two hours on one charge') then that is content. However if it is described by how it best meets a customer's needs ('smaller than its competitors at a mere 50 cm and practical in hundreds of outdoor applications because of its astonishing two hour charge') it is copy. That many website developers are confused by the terms only emphasizes their lack of awareness in the importance of both.

Having determined the importance of a website's content, let's now consider the development of that content by looking at the two distinct elements: (1) textual, and (2) images and other features.

## The development of textual content

A common mistake in many aspects of marketing is that organizations are organization–centric rather than customer–centric. This manifests itself in website content development in that too many organizations determine the content be asking 'what do we want to say' rather than 'what does the market want to read'?

*Go Online*    **Words, what words?**

If you had any doubt as to the importance of text on a web page, try removing it with the Netdisaster 'text-sucker' tool. Follow the link from the chapter's web page to try it for yourself.

In content development there are four key issues that need to be addressed. In chronological order, they are: (1) The solution to what need is being sought when the target market chooses to visit your website, (2) What information does the target market expect to be told to help meet that need, (3) How does the target market expect that information to be presented, and (4) How is this information best developed? Let's consider them in more detail.

1   The solution to what need is being sought when the target market chooses to visit your website? This is natural progression from the objectives for the website. As discussed in section 1.7, key objectives for

a web presence are essential prior to any development taking place – and this is clear example of how a website cannot possibly be successfully developed without those objectives being clear.

2   What information does the target market expect to be told to meet that need? Obviously, specific information will vary from product to product and site to site. However, the developer must be clear what constitutes information. Gary Klein (2004) says that *'the defining feature of information is that it reduces uncertainty'* – and in a marketing environment this is definitely true. Klein goes on to give the example that saying 'customer satisfaction is my number-one priority' is public relations (PR), not information. Carrying Klein's point into my theme of saying what the market want to read, rather than what we want to say, an example would be an organization saying 'we offer world-class customer service at our call centres' – that is PR. Information would be something like; 'your phone call will be answered by a human being within six rings. We never use automated answering services.' That is *information* that might prompt a customer to your company rather than a competitor.

## RESEARCH SNAPSHOT

### Online scholarly activity

Representing the kind of research that offline entities must soon consider to be the norm when developing website content, Pew Internet & American Life Project (2007) found that nearly 80 per cent of African American teenagers (who go online) researched universities online compared with 51 per cent of white online teens and 55 per cent of online teens overall. I cannot help but wonder how many UK universities know the demographic breakdown for their web–using potential students?

3   How does the target market expect that information to be presented? An overriding consideration in this regard is that the information is easily understood by the target audience. Considering consumers who were at the information seeking stage of the buying cycle, research from Enquiro (2007) found that they were reliant on the presentation of information being in a straightforward traditional way – which suggests clear dark characters on a light background (see the presentation element of section 2 of this chapter). However, this does not address the *style* in which it is presented. First of all, it needs to be appropriate. If you sell goods to pensioners, for example, your target audience will expect a certain tone in the text, perhaps formal and reserved, certainly respectful – though not straying into being condescending. A further consideration is the character of the site. Martineau (1958) proposed that a retail store has its own personality – this is also true of a website, or more accurately it reflects the personality (or culture) of the brand, product or organization. Although its aesthetic presentation will also have an influence, it is the presentation of the textual content that will determine that personality.

Similarly, the *language* used in the text needs to be appropriate – and I do not simply mean English, Spanish, Chinese and so on (see the next section for more on this particular subject). What I am referring to is that in the same way that 'yo dude, wassup?' won't work on a website selling long–stay holidays to retired people, neither will 'good morning ladies and gentlemen' suit a site selling skate board accessories to teenagers. Another consideration is the use of jargon associated with the product. For many B2C markets the jargon and the *style* may be closely related – not least in the teenage market or anything that is sport, hobby or interest related.

## Practical Insight

### Page headlines must provide a welcome

Common on websites is that the first page includes the salutation 'welcome' – as is the case when you enter a physical store. The problem is that when a potential customer arrives on your homepage they are not actually in the store. They are standing on the outside and looking in – and the headings on your page, like the signage and window displays in a bricks and mortar shop, will determine whether or not they enter your sales area. So don't waste important space with a 'welcome' – give them the information they need to make that next step.

Essentially, you use jargon if the target reader will understand it – indeed, in some circumstances to explain terminology might be perceived as insulting to the experienced reader. However, a caveat is that in some markets the *buyer* may not be the *consumer*. Parents, for example, looking to buy a present for their child may not understand the terminology used – and so not make a purchase. In a B2B environment, jargon becomes even more important as it can be part of the description of the product or its application – we look at this in more detail in chapter 5.3 where we consider the impact of the decision-making unit.

## MINI CASE

### The gobbledygook manifesto

Author of 'the New Rules of Marketing & PR' and all–round expert on web content, David Meerman Scott was so fed up with self–serving nonsensical comments in PR releases and on websites that he set up the gobbledygook manifesto to help rid the world of 'corporate' phrases like: scalable, groundbreaking, cutting–edge, situational fluency and paradigm shift (what do these terms mean when an organization uses them to describe itself?). In his book, Scott highlights that in their marketing, Disney talks about 'quality entertainment content', and points out that is 'movies and TV shows' to you and me. I liked this phrase from a software company's site: 'We're dedicated to developing applications that empower users to be more productive' – it sounds like they might make bigger shovels. Follow the link on the chapter's web page for a link to the gobbledygook manifesto.

Another key issue that is pertinent here – and another that is too often forgotten by website developers is this: where is the customer on their buying cycle? As we covered in section 1.6, the buying cycle is a model that describes the buyer's behaviour from problem recognition to purchase. The problem for content developers is that if you design the site to meet the needs of someone who is at the 'information search' stage then that content will do little to satisfy someone who is reached their 'purchase decision' – and, of course, vice versa. Unless you are certain that site visitors are always at a certain stage, the content must try to meet both groups' needs – and so consequently is a compromise to all stages in the buying cycle.

## RESEARCH SNAPSHOT

### Travel segmentation

Data from Experian (www.Experian.co.uk) – in their 'Mosaic Segmentation System' – suggests that over a quarter of visitors to travel websites are aged 55 and over. Given that many holiday destinations are aimed at specific age groups, this means that certain web pages on travel sites can be developed to appeal to this demographic group in both content and presentation.

A final consideration that is an accumulation of all of the factors covered in this section is how the presentation of information impacts on the relationship that will (hopefully) develop between customer and organization. In an attempt to assess the relationships between users and websites, Maulana & Eckhardt (2007) asked respondents to imagine websites they visited regularly as people – with three primary relationship types: just friends, good acquaintances and soul mates. With the exception of pure–play online businesses, few sites operate in isolation in developing a relationship with users. For example, my affinity to Nottingham Forest is with the football club, not any website that features the club. In behavioural terms, this is an issue of what need I am meeting when I visit a site – let's say to find out the latest news about player's injuries – and how well the site meets that need. However, how that information is presented might help develop a relationship. When discussing online behaviour in the first chapter I commented on how the development of a relationship with a website can vary depending on what need the website meets. To continue the example of my relationship with websites that contain news about my favourite football team, it could be that a number of sites meet that need – but I might develop a relationship with a particular site depending on the style of the writer(s) of that site. For example, the 'official' site is more formal – presenting the news as fact, whilst other sites use a more informal manner – with the addition of personal opinion. Essentially, it is that personal opinion – the *personality* of the site – which will help develop my relationship – but put off others. In marketing we call this segmentation.

## MINI CASE

### The virtual voice of the terraces

An example of how a writer's personality can attract repeat visitors to a website that – essentially – carries the same content as a number of other sites is the nffcblog.com – an unofficial site covering the activities of Nottingham Forest football club. On the page pictured below – lauding a long–awaited success – the club's site matches this one for its celebratory mood, but the nottinghamforest.co.uk page was more formal in its presentation. Can you imagine an officially sanctioned report where the writer announces that he is 'off to the pub'? The writer catches the mood of the fans – for they too were all going to the pub to celebrate, as was I.

## How is this information best developed?

In this section it is impossible to divorce the issue of *how* (is the content best developed) with *who* is responsible for its development. Therefore, although we address the issue of website management in detail in section 6 of this chapter – and we also considered the website development team in section 2.4 – before we continue to consider the *actual* content, let's consider who writes it. As mentioned earlier, it often falls to junior members of staff to produce the textual content – and with the greatest respect to office juniors around the world (who may one day become *great* content writers) they are the wrong people to whom you should give this crucial task. In the same way that without the necessary education and training, not every one can write a book, or a newspaper article, or advertising copy – why should they be able to write website copy? At the least a professional should be paid to *edit* the text. At the *very* least have someone who knows what they are doing check the spelling and grammar. I find personal assistants and secretaries good for this task – indeed, if you *must* insist on 'DIY' content writing such employees (who are used to writing things *properly*) will do a better job than most. Of course this is a option of last resort – as expert in the practice, Bob Bly (2003) says, you should write you own copy *only* if you are (1) an excellent copywriter, (2) you enjoy writing copy, and (3) you have the time to write copy.

## MINI CASE

### Passion can sell

It is rare, but sometimes amateur–content can score over that which is professionally written. The primary reason for this is that the writer's enthusiasm for their subject comes through in the text. Naturally, proof reading to correct any major errors in spelling or grammar should be conducted – but poor syntax can sometimes add to the charm of the content.

An example of successful amateur writer is on the website of Cervelo Cycles (www.cervelo.com). Much of the content is written by the company's co–founder, Gerard Vroomen. This is not the text of a qualified journalist or copyrighter, but it reflects the zeal that the writer has for his product and for competition cycling. It also happens to be in the language his customers understand.

### The home page of cervelo.com

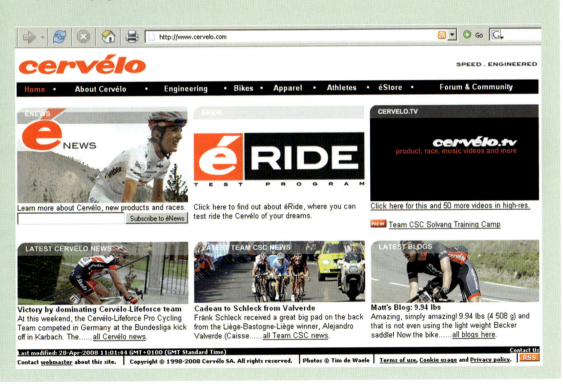

> " to get the style of the content right, the copywriter must get a feel for the product, service, organization or brand that he or she is writing about "

In order to get the style of the content right, the copywriter must get a feel for the product, service, organization or brand that he or she is writing about. Copywriting expert John Carlton (www.john-carlton.com) calls this process 'sales detective work'. *Clues* would come from such things as previous ads, brochures, reports, press releases, technical manuals and product specifications. As well as also interviewing staff from senior management through to 'shop floor' workers, online social media sites can provide an insight of how the organization, brand or product is perceived by the general public – i.e. its customers. Perhaps most importantly – if it is possible – speaking directly to existing customers will help in presenting the content in their 'language'. A phrase often used in sales training which applies equally to copy writing is 'selling is the transference of enthusiasm' – website content should reflect this.

A common mistake made in website development – because it requires no further effort or cost – is to simply reproduce content that was written for other media. Jacob Nielsen (1997) makes the point that a movie is not made by filming a play – although the story and characters are the same, but the two media require different presentation skills. Content written for offline publication has been developed to be read in a different context than it is on a website. On the web, any tangible aspects of the publication – you physically hold a book or newspaper, for example – do not exist. Where printed content is linear (the last word on page two leads to the first word on page three, for example) web content not only exists on a *bottomless* page, but it has links to multiple other pages – allowing users to read them in any order. Similarly, this page (that you are reading now) exists as part of a book – would this page be useful without the rest of the book? Web pages, on the other hand, must be able to exist in their own right, meaning that the content must provide the context and purpose of every page so that a user arriving deep in a site from a search engine, for example, will comprehend what the page is about.

### Don't sell a product – solve a problem

Although this phrase could be a motto for not just website content, but all marketing messages, online it serves another purpose in that it is applicable to good on–site navigation. Links to content deeper in the web should be explicit on how the visitor will benefit from clicking on the link – and eventually buying the product. For example, a company that specialises in lawn products might have the following as the links on its home page navigation bar:

I need a greener lawn
I need to get rid of moss
I need to get rid of weeds
  Or maybe:

My kids are ruining my lawn

My dog is ruining my lawn

Notice how in all of these examples are written in the first person (I, my) which (a) makes the issue personal and (b) gets away from 'we' and 'us' – the language of an organization that is talking about itself.

A further consideration in the 'don't take it from other literature' argument is the way in which we read the textual content of web pages. Simply put, we find it harder to read text on a computer screen than we do printed on paper, so we rarely read whole pages of textual content. Instead, we scan the text, picking out keywords, sentences, and paragraphs of interest and skipping over other text that has no appeal to us. Obviously, therefore, the web writer must pamper to this practice by writing content that uses descriptive headers (and sub-headers), short paragraphs, bullet points and content that gets to the point quickly. Finally on the subject of writing specifically for the online context, web pages have hyperlinks that can be used to direct readers to further associated or supportive information – and they certainly won't be present in any offline publication.

The question of whether the textual content of websites should be short (to retain attention) or long (to cover the subject in detail) is one that has experts in the field arguing. The answer, of course, comes in what the customer expects – but that is too simplistic. Consider the customer's position on the buying cycle issue discussed in the previous section, for example. In real life the competent sales person knows within a minute or so if the customer is new to the product or is a repeat buyer – and so can adjust the length (as well as content) of their sales 'patter' accordingly. Online, we cannot make that decision about the customer and so have to gamble on long or short – or present a compromise that may or may not suit all customers. That content developers are left between a rock and a hard place with regard to the short vs long debate is confirmed by research into health information websites by Huntington et al (2007). They found that although users found shorter content easy to read, they thought the information presented was too short to meet their needs. As with a number of aspects of web development covered in this chapter, publishers must accept that they can please some of the people all of the time and all of the people some of time, but not all of the people all of the time. This same adage can be carried into the consideration of the *actual* content.

In his book, *The Long Tail*, Chris Anderson (2006) suggests examples of criteria people might use for their evaluation of content – whether it is high or low quality.

| HIGH QUALITY | LOW QUALITY |
|---|---|
| Addresses my interests | Not for me |
| Well made | Badly made |
| Fresh | Stale |
| Substantive | Superficial |
| Compelling | Boring |

As Anderson rightly points out, beauty is in the eye of the beholder – the assessment being not one of the tangible quality of the content (i.e. well researched and written, grammatically correct, to the point etc.) but how *appropriate* it is to them (for some years, I have actively used the term 'beauty is in the eye of the customer'). My wife, for example, has quite recently taken up horse riding. A website on the subject would definitely be 'not for me' and 'boring'. My wife would obviously think the opposite for these two criteria, but might also – being a newcomer to the subject – be happy enough with 'stale' and 'superficial' content. Similarly, if the content were addressing her interest, would poor spelling and grammar ('badly made') be an issue? My sister, however – who has been riding horses for as long as I can remember – would have yet another opinion of the same website content.

## Practical Insight

**Testimonials work – if you treat them right**

Sean D'Souza, ace content writer and founder of PsychoTactics (www.psychotactics.com) endorses testimonials but warns against 'the–company–was–wonderful–I–would–recommend–them–to–anyone' type tributes. He advises you use the following structure:

1. Paint a detailed picture of the customer giving the testimonial.
2. Explain the situation before the customer made the purchase. Make sure to put in the reluctance factor.
3. Explain the result of having made the decision and how the customer has benefited.

Practiced correctly this method helps the potential customer visualize how they might benefit from the product or service on offer.

The *actual* content of the website will depend on the objectives of the site – but there are some elements that are essential to most (if not all) sites if they are to be successful. Although no list can be absolute – and inevitably, grey areas will exist – figure 3.1 is a rough guide to what users might find (a) essential, or (b) useful or interesting. It is the latter which differentiates the online presence of the organization. Note that in a competitive environment all competitors' websites are likely to contain the 'essential' elements. It is the 'useful or interesting' content that adds value and so differentiates the organization in the marketplace.

| Essential | Value added |
|---|---|
| The organization's name. What the organization does – its business or if non-commercial, its objectives Where the organization is located (address). Full contact details. Note that all of these should be on the site's front page. On an extensive site that is likely to have visitors arrive deep in the site from search engines, the first two should be on *every* page. If the website facilitates online transactions or collects visitor data then legal notices are also a must (see section 7 of this chapter). | How the organization / brand / product / service will meet the needs of the reader. Extensive product/service descriptions including static or – where appropriate – moving images. Articles about topical issues in your market or industry sector – these can be written in-house or commissioned. An insight to the organization – over and above the standard 'about us'. Pen – pics of staff, perhaps. Reviews of products – car accessory retailers commenting on the performance characteristics of cleaners and polishes, for example. Endorsements or testimonials from satisfied customers A frequently asked questions (FAQ) section – this has the added advantage of reducing repetitive requests from the public. A directory of useful books and websites – a brief review of each adds a personal touch. A glossary of terms used in your industry – particularly if your business attracts customers who are new to the marketplace. |

An addendum to the above could be a 'do not include' list, which would include:

- Self – serving statements – 'we are … ', 'we do …' 'our …'. Customers want to know how the company can help meet their needs, not how wonderful the organization thinks it is.
- Errors in grammar and spelling.

**Figure 3.1** Website content.

## Practical Insight

### Stand out – or run with the crowd?

In markets where many companies offer what is essentially the same product you need to differentiate yourself – including online. So are you one of the crowd? Try these.

1 Take your website content – in particular the 'about us' section. Now substitute the name of your biggest competitor. If the content still makes sense, you are in with the crowd.
2 Take the content of your competitor's site and substitute your organization's name. If the resulting text is not accurate when your name is substituted then your competitors have made an effort to differentiate their online offering.

## The development of images and other features

After text, the next most common type of content is pictures. As mentioned in section 3.2, pictures are often included on a web page for purely aesthetic purposes – they look nice. However, the organization's website is its online real estate (with the front page being prime property) and so taking up space with a picture that does nothing to meet the online needs of the target market is a waste of that valuable resource – with the aforementioned 'hero shot' being the worst offender.

Note that no matter which of the above you use, all videos should be:

- As short as is feasible to get the message across – any more than a few minutes and you should condense the message.
- Of *professional* quality – poor video quality will be perceived as representing an organization that has little emphasis on quality.
- Of benefit to the user – grandiose rhetoric from the CEO or MD extolling the virtues of the organization or any aspect of it are for the presenter, not the customer.
- Key words tagged according to their content – more and more search engines are presenting videos in response to searches.

Spoken content is a further option that has become more viable due to the popularity of the MP3 player – a means of recording verbal content from a website and replaying it at a time that is more convenient to the listener. Dubbed the podcast as the iPod brand dominates the MP3 arena, such digital recordings can also be used in more creative ways than simply being a spoken version of a written article. A spoken explanation of assembly instructions for flat pack furniture, for example. Or what about a spoken recipe? In this case, the listener/cook can easily pause or replay sections where necessary.

## Practical Insight

### Idle symbols?

I have long cautioned against the use of icons in place of text. This is not simply a personal opinion. Back in 1985, after finding that pretty but unlabelled icons confused customers, the Apple Computer Human Interface Group is said to have adopted the motto; *a word is worth a thousand pictures*. After that, a descriptive word or phrase was added beneath all Macintosh icons.

For bricks and mortar traders, interactive maps – such as those from Google – can make finding the store easier than just directions or a *static* map. Similarly, a hotel can use such maps to emphasise how good a location they are in. The caveat remains, however, interactive maps should be used to satisfy the needs of the customer, not 'jazz–up' a website whose textual content is poor.

Other interactive website content includes:

- Widgets – pieces of scripting code that facilitate the delivery of live content from a third party site without the website owner constantly having to update their site, applications include such things as calendars, clocks, weather forecast and calculators.
- Online forums on which customers can ask questions about products and services. Although viewed with suspicion by some users – they are perceived as not being independent of the organization hosting the forum – some companies (Cisco is a prime example) have successfully used

forums as a kind of after–sales service that is provided by the consumers themselves, so reducing costs in that department.

## DECISION TIME

As website development practitioner and writer Gerry McGovern (2007) says, *'there are three things a great website must be: useful, useful and useful'*. Note that McGovern doesn't use terms such as 'entertaining' or 'a show-case for the designer's skills' or 'at the cutting edge of Internet technology'. If these things help meet the needs of the target market, fine. But for the majority of visitors that need is information – presented in a way they find easy to access and understand.

### Practical Insight

**Oi – you're not allowed in here**

Something users find frustrating is when they arrive on a site only to be shown a message telling them they must upgrade a version of software to allow them to access a site. Most times, this means the visitor immediately leaves the site as the (a) don't know how to download software (my wife), (b) don't have the necessary administrator access to their computer (me, when I'm at work), or (c) they just can't be bothered (me when I'm at home).

No matter what the reason, the objectives of the site are not being met. Developers should always consider carefully the results of them using 'leading edge' technology in site design. In most instances they are best advised to design for one software release behind the newest – or at least give a reasonable time period for the new version to be adopted. My offline analogy is that a clothes shop would soon go bankrupt if security staff barred entry to anyone wearing 'last years' fashions.

The content of a website is wholly dependent on the objectives the organization has for that site. Essentially – the four key decisions to be made are:

1. The solution to what need is being sought when the target market chooses to visit your website? Why are people coming to your site? Remember, the web is a pull medium, they have chosen to go to your site – what is it that they are going there for?
2. What information does the target market expect to be told to help meet that need? Visitors are on your site to solve a problem – what is it that they think will help them?
3. How does the target market expect that information to be presented? What language – over and above that of nationality – will the visitor want the information in? Put simply, how will they best understand and accept what you have to say?
4. How is this information best developed? Should the content be purely text – or can pictures help meet the customers' needs? Or are video clips or podcasts a better solution? And finally – who is responsible for its development?

Kim, J., Suh, E. & Hwang, H. (2003). A model for evaluating the effectiveness of CRM using the balanced scorecard. *Journal of Interactive Marketing.* Vol. 17, No. 2, pp. 5–19.

Klein, G. (2004). The Power of Intuition. Currency.

Koufaris, M. & Hampton-Sosa, W. (2004). The development of initial trust in an online company by new customers. *Information & Management.* Vol. 41, pp. 377–397.

Kranz-Collier, J (2007). *Make every word count.* Available online: www.marketingprofs.com/7/make-every-word-count-qa-jonathan-kranz-collier.asp

Krugg, S. (2000). Don't Make Me Think. New riders.

Lindgaard, G., Fernandes, G., Dudek, C. & Browñ, J. (March-April 2006). Attention web designers: You have 50 milliseconds to make a good first impression! *Journal of Behaviour & Information Technology.* Vol. 25, No. 2, pp. 115–126.

Liu, C. & Arnett, K. (2000). Exploring the factors associated with website success in the context of electronic commerce. *Information & Management.* Vol. 38, No. 1, pp. 23–33.

Loizides, L. (2003). *Lesson in the Art of Flash* INT Media Group. Available online at www.clickz.com/mkt/capital/print.php/2240791

Martineau, P. (1958). The personality of the retail store. *Harvard Business Review.* Vol. 36, pp. 47–55.

Maulana, A.E. & Eckhardt, G.M. (2007). Just friends, good axquaintances or soul mates? An exploration of website connectedness. *Qualitative Market research: An International Journal.* Vol. 10, No. 3, pp. 227–242.

McGovern, G. (2007). New Thinking Newsletter, July 2007.

McGovern, G. (2002). *Demystifying Content Management* Available on: www.clickz.com

Morgan Stanley (2006). *The State of the Internet, Part 3.* Available on www.morganstanley.com/institutional/techresearch/pdfs/webtwopto2006.pdf

Mowen, J.C. (1987). *Consumer Behaviour.* MacMillan Publishing, New York.

Nielsen, J. (2003). *Usability 101: Introduction to Usability.* Available online at www.useit.com/alertbox/20030825.HTML

Okazaki., S. (2006). Searching the web for global brands: how American brands standardise their websites in Europe. *European Journal of marketing.* Vol. 39, No. 1/2, pp. 87–109.

PEW/Internet and American Life (2007). *Information searches that solve problems.* Available online at http://www.pewinternet.org/pdfs/Pew_UI_LibrariesReport.pdf

Pew Internet & American Life Project (2007). *Teens and Social Media* Available on www.pewinternet.org

Poirier, P. (2003). *Can Your Site Stop Your Telephone From Ringing?* Available online at MarketingProfs.com.

Scott, D.M. (2007). The New Rules of Marketing & PR. Wiley.

Teo, T.S.H. & Yu, Y. (2005). Online buyer behaviour: a transaction cost economics perspective. *Omega (Oxford)*. Vol. 33, No. 5, pp. 451–465.

Tobin, R (2008). *Barriers on a website*. EnquiroResearch. Available on www. Enquiroresearch.com

Van Riel, A.C.R., Liljander, V. & Jurriens, P. (2001). Exploring consumer evaluations of e-services: a portal site. *International Journal of Service Management*. Vol. 12, No. 4, pp. 359–377.

Webcredible (2008). *Flights Online–Ensuring Your Site Takes Off*. Available online at www.webcredible.co.uk

Wilson, R. F. (2003). *12 website design decisions your business or organisation will need to make correctly*. Web Marketing Today, July 9, 2003. Available online at Wilsonweb.com.

Yang, Z., Cai, S., Zhou, Z. & Zhou, N. (2004). Development and validation of an instrument to measure user perceived service quality of information presenting web portals. *Information & Management*. Vol. 42, No. 4, pp. 575–589.

Yasin, M.M. & Yavas, U. (2007). An analysis of e-business practices in the Arab culture. *Cross Cultural Management: An International Journal*. Vol. 14, No. 1, pp. 68–73.

Yoo, B. & Donthu, N. (2001). Developing a scale to measure the perceived service quality of Internet shopping sites (sitequal). *Quarterly Journal of Electronic Commerce*. Vol. 2, No. 1, pp. 31–47.

# The B2C online presence

> *I am the world's worst salesman – therefore,*
> *I must make it easy for people to buy*
>
> Frank W Woolworth

## CHAPTER AT A GLANCE

4.1 Introduction
4.2 Niche markets
4.3 The retail website
4.4 Checkout process
4.5 Fulfilment
4.6 Comparison Shopping Engines
4.7 Bricks and clicks – integrated retailing

## 4.1 INTRODUCTION

This chapter concentrates on selling goods to the end consumer via a website – essentially, online retailing – or e–tailing, as it is also known. It is, however, impossible to divorce the subject of this chapter from that of others throughout the book. Most obvious is the previous chapter that looks at website development, with a second being the final chapter that considers integrated Internet marketing.

---

### RESEARCH SNAPSHOT

**If you go online, you shop online**

More than 85 per cent of the world's *online* population has used the web to make a purchase. Focusing only on users of the Internet, South Koreans lead the way with 99 per cent having shopped online. The UK comes in at joint second – with Germany – on 97 per cent. The USA and Europe are neck and neck at 94 and 93 per cent respectively.

*Source: The Nielsen Company, 2007/Marketing Charts, January 2008.*

---

Online retailers can be divided into three main categories:

1. Pure–play – where the organization trades online only. In this case, the online sale is the be all and end all of the site's objectives. The site's design and content must reflect this.
2. Bricks and clicks – where the firm sells goods both offline (bricks) and online (clicks). Although online sales are important in this instant – the website must also act as a sales lead generator for the bricks element of the business.
3. Niche operators who may or may not have a physical retail presence, but are smaller businesses than those featured in 1 and 2 above and concentrate on small – *niche* – markets (we look at this group specifically in the next section).

A fourth group is offline retailers who have a web presence, but do not *sell* online. In essence, such traders are using their web presence for brand development, lead generation or customer service (see section 1.7), and so the web content is developed accordingly – in this chapter we are concentrating on those sites that facilitate online B2C transactions.

Note, however, that 'retail' covers far more than the shop (off– or online) that sells a tangible product to the end user. The element of financial institutions that offers online banking facilities, for example, is *retail* banking. Similarly, some of the most popular online purchases are travel–related – a travel agent is a retail outlet and the sale of car and household insurance to end users is a retail transaction. Both of the latter routinely offer customers discounts if policies are purchased online.

## Practical Insight

### Customer, consumer – or both?

Fundamental to marketing – and equally essential online – is the customer/consumer issue. Basically, the customer pays for the product and the consumer … well, consumes it. This can, of course, be the same person who buys a chocolate bar and then eats it. However, they might have bought the chocolate as a gift for their daughter – in which case the child is the consumer. In marketing this is important as the marketing message might be targeted at the consumer or the customer – babies' nappies is an obvious example.

Online the customer/consumer targeting issue is important in that it determines the nature of the content of the website – and its presentation.

Throughout this chapter we will build on the basics of web design covered in chapter 3 and address elements of online marketing that are either specific, or peculiar, to online retailing. Before doing so, however, it is worth putting online retail into context with its offline older relation.

Although online sales have increased exponentially since the birth of the web, they still only represent a small percentage of all retail sales – so whilst online B2C sales will represent a significant sum of business for a relatively few retailers, it will always be a minority of overall retail sales. Indeed, this could well be used to support the argument that the Internet's main benefit in B2C trading is as a marketing platform used to influence offline consumer purchases rather than an additional channel of distribution.

## MINI CASE

### Delivering the goods – but not profit (yet?)

With online sales predicted to represent 10 per cent of the grocery market by 2112 (IGD, 2007) and currently enjoying annual sales of £325m, the future for online grocery store Ocado looks good. But although it delivers around 12,000 orders a day to customers' homes from its state of the art distribution centre in Hatfield on the outskirts of London the company is still operating at a pre–tax loss of around £43m (as of the financial year to December, 2006). Although it is expected to turn a profit in 2007, there is another caveat for would–be online grocery moguls – the venture has swallowed some £277m of investment in its seven years of existence.

## 4.2  NICHE MARKETS

Before we look in detail at the key elements of online retailing it is worthwhile considering the role that the Internet has played on the development of *niche* markets in the B2C environment. It has always been the case that a segment of small retailers have operated in specialist – niche – markets that are too small (or specialised) for mainstream retailers to contemplate. Although they might attract customers who are willing to travel long distances, such buyers are few, with the majority of customers coming from the locale of the shop. By definition, this means that turnover is low – but still sufficient for small businesses to make a reasonable living. This return on limited turnover stems from two basic business principles; (1) low costs – such shops are rarely in premium–rent malls or high streets, and (2) high selling prices – anyone who is willing to search hard for a particular product will not expect to purchase at discount prices.

The niche outlet is normally proprietor–run, and the owner is likely to be an expert in the product being sold – often because the product area relates to their profession or long–standing hobby. Fishing tackle, equestrian supplies, model–making kits, tapestry materials and musical instruments would be typical examples of such – though also common are outlets dedicated to specialist elements of popular markets. An example of this might be the bathroom fittings supplier who stocks more unusual products than can be found in national–chain DIY superstores.

For existing *bricks and mortar* niche operators the web provided an obvious additional outlet for their products, but in the early days of the commercial web most saw it as an 'add–on' to the offline store rather than being an essential element of an integrated retailing strategy. It did not take too long, however, for the more forward–thinking traders to realise that niche products featured highly in search queries on related subjects and so online sales could easily eclipse those made in the physical shop. The next logical stage was for people who were experts in a topic to open online–only (pure–play) outlets. For many of these individuals selling goods related to their interest was a long–held dream, but the cost – and financial risks – of opening a physical store meant it had remained a dream. However, websites can be set up for very little, minimal stock holding is required for the e–shop and – equally importantly – you do not need to be on the retail premises for all the hours the shop is open. This last point is the reason for it to be common for many small, niche e–shops to be run part time, with the owner being either (1) in full–time employment (so guaranteeing income), or (2) a parent who fits in the online business with child care responsibilities. So common is this model in the USA that the terms 'mom and pop operation' and 'stay–at–home moms' are both closely linked with part-time online trading.

A further issue that played a vital role in the spread of the online niche retailer was the advances in software that made the provision of online–sales facilities both easy and relatively inexpensive. However, such is the way that e–commerce has developed, you do not even have to develop your own website. A number of Internet brand names offer shop facilities within their own web presence – charging either a fixed or commission–based fee. Such sites – Yahoo! and eBay are obvious examples – not only offer

> " The niche outlet is normally proprietor–run, and the owner is likely to be an expert in the product being sold "

the niche seller a platform for online sales and guaranteed virtual–footfall, but also lend their brand value, promotional activities and – importantly – search engine rankings to the small business. A further attraction is that that the host brand will facilitate online payment (on eBay, it is through PayPal), meaning that sellers need not set up their own credit card account. Although the original concept was for the general public to sell off – by auction – unwanted items in a kind of online boot–sale, eBay is now more commonly used by SME retailers as a method of reaching a market that prior to the Internet was simply not possible. Furthermore, many shun the auction model, simply listing goods at a fixed price. This makes much of the eBay site a facilitator of B2C retail transactions rather than the C2C auction site that it was originally. Building your eBay store requires little in the way of technical knowledge – simply choose a name, pick a template and write a description for your shop and you are away. A customised logo and a colour scheme will help personalize your online presence. Up to 300 categories can be created for your store, so there is little you cannot consider for this virtual shopping mall. Obviously, fees must be paid – eBay charges store owners a monthly subscription fee, a listing fee and a final value fee for items that sell. In addition, postage and packaging costs must also be considered when deciding on a profitable selling price – but given that these will be the only marketing costs to be added to the products' cost price, healthy profits can still be made. Adopting the traditional retailing practice of 'loss leaders', common practice is to list 'bargain' products in auctions to attract online browsers, and then direct them to your online store where all of your products are listed.

Note that although sites such as eBay and Yahoo! provide templates and easy–to–use page development tools for the online niche retailer, users should still exercise those elements of good practice covered in this and other chapters – writing the textual content in such a way as to best promote products being an obvious example.

## MINI CASE

### The long tail of online business

Closely associated with the Internet – not least because it was promoted virally online – Chris Anderson's Long Tail (*the Long Tail*, 2006) model is based around the concept of niche marketing. Anderson – using the music industry as an example – suggests that whilst the main retailers (off– and online) concentrate on selling only the top 20 selling CDs at low prices, there is a long tail of less–popular CDs which cannot match sales figures of the top sellers, but can still sell in numbers that are sufficient to generate profits for niche sellers. The Internet connection is that the web not only helps niche sellers reach potential customers, but social media-type recommendations ('if you enjoy this, you might like this …') can make buyers aware of artists they have not previously considered – or even heard of.

Although focused on the long tail model, Anderson's book provides an excellent background to the development of B2C e–commerce. For my review on the book, follow the link on this chapter's web page.

## DECISION TIME

The use of third party websites to host online shops can work for some organizations, with the advantages – particularly for small or micro businesses – being significant. Many of the issues raised in chapter 2 (website hosting, for example) are negated by partnering your business to a branded website in much the same way as *concessions* have worked in traditional retailing for scores of years.

However, such a route to market can have disadvantages, particularly if the organization has ambitions to expand beyond being a small player in a particular market. This is because the business is inextricably linked with the host organization and so all those benefits gained from the partnership can be an impediment in developing an online brand of its own – not least because the third party retailer can be perceived by customers as being just that – a business too small to trade in its own right.

The use of such sites is not limited to SMEs, however. Though not as popular in the UK, in America a number of high street brands use eBay (or similar) auctions to sell–off goods that might be end–of–range, unpopular sizes or colours or simply over–stocks.

> *You Decide*
>
> Advise Robert Terwilliger on the advantages and drawbacks of using a third party website to sell the Modeller's Stand (case study 9).
>
> Alternatively, conduct the same exercise on your organization or that of your employer.

## 4.3  THE RETAIL WEBSITE

In this section we will take a look at elements of website design that apply specifically to websites on which consumers can make purchases. However, to concentrate only on the online purchase element is to under-value the site as a retail outlet. As mentioned in the introduction to this chapter, there are three types of retail website: pure–play, niche and bricks and clicks. Although all three offer online purchase facilities, the latter must also consider the customer who might be on the site as *part* of their buying process, with a decision to buy being made either off– or online and the actual purchase made in the other medium. Similarly, few custom-ers will make a purchase on their first visit to a site. This being the case, the website must cater not only to the potential online purchaser, but those who have not yet made up their mind. Recognizing that all visitors to the B2C website can be valuable, Moe and Fader (2001) identified four types of online shopping visits that the customer might make:

1. Directed-purchase visits. The consumer is ready to make a purchase.
2. Search and deliberation visits. The consumer is researching not only the product, its price and availability, but also the terms, conditions and cred-ibility of the site – although they do intend to make a purchase eventually.

3. Knowledge-building visits. The consumer is engaged in exploratory browsing that *may* lead to a purchase at some time in the future.
4. Hedonic-browsing visits. The consumer is doing electronic window shopping — that is, shopping for pleasure or recreation.

Offline, it is easy for the experienced sales person to identify these groups. Online, the website must cater for them all – for even the latter is a recipient for a branding message that may eventually influence a purchase.

---

*Go Online*  **e–tail – or e–commerce?**

It is becoming common practice for websites that allow consumers to make online purchases to be called 'e–commerce sites' – although, by definition, they are *retail* sites. For more on my views on the various terms used in describing elements of online trading, follow the links from the chapter's web page.

---

We have seen this notion of different *types* of website visitor in previous sections – notably 1.6 and 3.4 – where we considered the issue of buyer behaviour and where potential customers are in the buying cycle. A concept popular in offline retailing is that of the early-stage buyers and late-stage buyers. In this model, the sales person takes a different approach to customers depending where they are in their buying-decision making process. Early-stage buyers are looking for information that will help them make a purchase decision, while late-stagers have done their research and are ready to buy. Getting it wrong in-store costs you sales – the same is true online. As with Moe and Fader's four types of visitor, in the offline environment identifying the different kinds of shopper is relatively easy for the experienced salesperson. Online, however, it is not possible to immediately identify which category each visitor is in, so the site must pamper to both. This is particularly true if the goods that have a long buying cycle – with the website having to cater for visitors who are at all the stages in the cycle. This could be discrete or obvious. For example, links on the front or product page might that say something like; 'weighing up the options?' and 'ready to buy?' Subsequent pages for each link would have appropriate content – details of finance schemes or deliver schedules in the latter, for example.

Although e–commerce evangelists commonly give the glib reply of 'anything and everything' to the question of what can be sold (and purchased) online, this is not the case. For some products the web provides information on which to base a buying decision – and no more. This is particularly true of big and/or heavy items, where delivery costs may make the online selling price un–competitive. The reasoning behind this is rooted in psychology – as is much of buyer behaviour – but in an attempt to make tangible why some products are more suitable to online sales than others, Michael de Kare Silver (1998) suggested a framework he dubbed his electronic shopping (ES) test. De Kare Silver's ES test consists of three elements, each of which must be addressed to determine the product's suitability for online sales.

1. Product characteristics – what is the product's primal appeal to the senses? Products that appeal to sight and sound senses are good contenders for ES – books and music, for example. Conversely, products that appeal to touch, taste and smell are less likely to suit ES – De Kare Silver suggested clothing, food and perfume as examples.
2. Familiarity and confidence – to what degree does the customer recognize and trust the product. The more familiar the product, brand and organization is to the customer, the more confidence they have in making an online purchase.
3. Consumer attributes – what are their underlying motivations and attitudes towards online shopping? Is it convenience or price that influences their buyer behaviour, for example?

Note that De Kare Silver's first point is often quoted by those who say books and CDs are the only things that sell online. However, in a Shop.org sponsored survey in 2008, 'apparel' was the top–selling online goods category. Similarly, research conducted by the University of Southern California's Annenberg School for Communication's Center for the Digital Future (2008) found that clothes come second only to books in the ten most popular online purchases. Travel arrangements, gifts, CDs, videos, electronic goods, software/games, products for hobbies and computers/peripherals make up the other eight categories. Although this would appear to be a rather limited list of products, several – notably gifts and hobbies – cover a wide array of goods, including (for example) virtually any sports–related product. Although not categorical, these results suggest that the ES Test has in some ways stood the test of time. However, it is elements two and three that have become more influential as the Internet has established itself as an integral part of society The second element is particularly pertinent to this section as 'familiarity and confidence' is becoming more and more applicable to the actual website – whether the website represents a brand or not. The familiarity aspect can be applied to website design in that the major websites follow certain *norms* in presentation, the location of navigation bars, for example. Sites that break from the standard presentation style can confuse or even alienate visitors. Similarly, a site with good usability will generate confidence, as will elements of the site included to enhance its credibility.

An obvious advantage that virtual retailers have over their offline counterparts is that online, there is no display–product cost. Part of the success of Amazon, for example, is that the online store needs only list a description and image of a book's cover to display it for sale. Therefore millions of books can be listed with no stock–unit cost – no physical store could ever afford to stock and display the extensive range offered by the online sellers. Note that there will be a cost of page development and website hosting, but this would be nothing like the cost of buying even one of each book offered for sale – it is

> **"** An obvious advantage that virtual retailers have over their offline counterparts is that online, there is no display–product cost **"**

also the case that Amazon stock only the fastest selling books, others are ordered from publishers as online orders are placed.

This issue of stock cost extends beyond simply displaying a book on a shelf – there is also the matter of merchandising to increase sales volume. For example, a bricks and mortar bookstore must decide on whether a book is displayed by author, genre or subject. To display a book in more than one category means increasing stock holding by that multiple – for the chain retailer this number is then multiplied by the number of stores. Online, however, books can be 'listed' in multiple categories at no extra cost. The same concept can be applied to other product categories – mens' polo shirts, for example, could be listed (displayed) in 'casual wear', 'summer shirts' 'sports wear' and 'gift suggestions' as well as by manufacturer or brand. This ability to multi–list goods means that stock can be arranged by consumer–need, so providing an efficient navigational structure for the website from a consumer perspective (Taylor & England, 2006).

## Practical Insight

### Online, merchandising skills are still essential

Effective stock categorization, listing and display emphasizes the point I made in section 2.4 when considering the website development team. It is only an experienced retailer or salesperson that can make merchandising decisions – delegating the task to anyone else will inevitably cost sales.

An additional benefit to abundant merchandise information is that the customer should have an increased perception of the probability that their needs will be met (Szymanski & Hise, 2000). This is the same concept that sees offline retailers fill large stores with goods – many of which they know customers have little interest in but add to the perception that the store will have what they want. At the core of this practice is the so–called 80/20 rule – that is that 80 per cent of all sales will come from 20 per cent of products.

## DECISION TIME

In essence, the issues raised in this section mirror many of those included in the previous chapter on website development. However, it is worthwhile emphasizing some elements in the online shopping scenario. Key issues will vary depending on the product being sold, but the following should be common to most sites.

- Navigation. Obviously important to any website, good navigation is absolutely essential for the retail website where customers will soon click away to a competitor if they cannot easily find what they are looking for.

- Product pages. Commenting on their extensive research into e-tail store image attributes, Yun & Good (2007) made the point that textual and visual description is crucial. This point is well made, and the visual element of the B2C website is an opportunity for designers to show the full range of their skills and programmers the added value that technology *can* bring. Textual descriptions should follow all the criteria covered in section 3.4 – and as ever, it is the needs of the customer that should be paramount. For example, giving an extensive technical description of the inner workings of a laptop is not what the average customer is looking for – they simply want to know what that technology does for them, e.g. it will play CDs and DVDs.

  In some instances a simple one–dimensional image of a product is sufficient to display its qualities – a book cover is a book cover, no matter what angle you view it from, for example. However, common software now makes possible applications that allow the customer to move around the image as if it were in three dimensions. Cars, for example, can be moved so that the customer can view it from 360 degrees or a hotel bedroom can be rotated so all of its attributes can be viewed. The widespread use of broadband also makes video clips of products feasible for many markets. This could be instructional (using a mobile phone), a demonstration (how to use a power tool safely) or aesthetic (a video tour of a cruise ship).

- Cross and up–selling. Also known as associated selling, this technique is well established in offline retail – and technology can be used to transfer it online. The model for cross selling is for the sales person to offer related or associated products to increase sales. Done properly, the practice is perceived by the buyer as being part of good service – drill bits with a drill, or matching tie with a shirt, for example. Up selling is where the salesperson offers an upgraded or higher specification product to increase sales value. As with cross selling this can be seen as being part of good service. For example, a customer might select a laptop off the shelf, but when the salesperson asks pertinent questions they discover that the buyer needs a higher specification machine to handle the uses for which they are buying the computer, and so advises one with a higher specification. Online, carefully prepared software programs can take the place of the attentive salesperson, with an automated notice of the need for an accessory or advice on an associated product appearing when a purchase is made. Whilst technology can be applied to automate these facilities, human input from an experienced sales person (to identify the associated products) is essential.

## MINI CASE

### Do you want fries with that?

After introducing its Internet ordering facility in March 2007, a year later saw PizzaHut (www.pizzahut.com) roll out 'virtual waiter' technology that suggests additional associated menu items based on data gathered from millions of online orders. In addition, returning visitors to the online restaurant can also can develop their own 'Pizza Playlist' so that future orders can be a one-click operation.

> **a retail website must not lose focus of its purpose – to sell things**

- Frequently asked questions. These pages can be extremely useful to not only customers, but also the selling organization (it reduces the necessity to employ staff to respond to telephone or email enquiries). As with all aspects of the website content, the FAQ section should be developed by sales and marketing staff who will be aware of (a) the kind of questions that might arise, (b) what the answers are, and (c) how the answers should be presented. This page could be divided into sections, e.g. questions on: products, shipping, payment methods etc. It can also be dynamic, moving the most asked questions to the top of the list in response to customers' enquiries.
- Calls to action. Part of the site's sales copy (see section 3.4) and the site's sales funnel (see section 3.2), a retail website must not lose focus of its purpose – to sell things. To this end, the visitor must be constantly prompted to make a purchase. The most common call to action is an

## DECISION TIME

Worth noting at this point is that in *marketing* terms – in much the same way that a 'customer' might not hand over any cash for a service – an online 'check–out' need not include a financial payment. For example, if the web page has an objective of signing up users for a free newsletter, the form they have to complete for the service is, effectively, the check–out. Similarly, the form that I complete in order to register my interest in a new service offered by my local council should be designed with the same criteria as a checkout on an online retail site.

Although a reasonably effective website can be developed with limited technical expertise, a checkout facility is a specialist area that would need either expert in–house skills or – as is common – it is out–sourced. The latter is popular as not only are specialist skills required, so too is a secure server. Most small companies will pay for secure hosting – business website hosting companies all offer a full checkout facility on their servers. A further option is to use a third party for both checkout and payment handling. As mentioned in section 2 of this chapter, using the shopping sites of the likes of eBay or Yahoo! is a sensible option for small online retailers.

## Practical Insight

### S is for secure

To identify when you are on a secure site, take a look at the URL in the browser window. A secure site will start with 'https://'. If the site is using the secure check facility of a hosting company the URL will switch from that of the website (e.g. www.retailwebsite.com) to that of the secure server (e.g. www.secureservercompany.com). Although you have moved to the secure server when you clicked on 'buy now', it is the norm that the page will carry the same livery as the company site – all part of the secure hosting service.

Another option for traders – though in a limited number of industries – is to use agents to accept customer payments. One example of this is hotels. It is the travel and tourism industry that has seen most sites that – as a business model – operate as intermediaries for numerous hotels, airlines and car hire companies. These companies then seek high listings on both organic and paid listings for keywords related to locations in which they have clients. For individual hotels, partnering with one or more online booking agencies alleviates the problem of maintaining an online booking form. Obviously, a fee will be involved, but such sites will normally feature highly on search engine listings, and so generate business that the hotel might otherwise miss. So widespread are the online booking agents that many hotel chains use them in addition to their own online booking systems.

Finally, an issue that is missed by many website developers – making sure that customers know how to use the checkout facility. Allred et al

(2006) make the point that online vendors should routinely provide hand-holding assistance to the new shopper. This can be detailed instructions including screen shots of completed elements or a 'dummy' checkout that allows new users to experiment with the checkout procedure without having to commit to an actual payment. Having said this, if customers want something badly enough, they will get it. For example, when The Popcorn Factory (www.thepopcornfactory.com) came top of the Nielsen Online/ Marketing Charts' top converting websites from the Christmas holiday season 2007, a number of practitioners asked 'how come?' They pointed out a far from perfect conversion optimization and checkout process on the site. Online conversion specialist Bryan Eisenberg offered a more basic reason why customers were willing to work their way through the imperfect system, commenting: 'people's motivations trump any great or poor design, if shoppers have made up their mind to buy a product from a particular retailer, then they'll work through almost any poor shopping process – especially if they're comfortable with the brand'.

*You Decide*    Advise Robert Terwilliger on checkout issues that are specific to the Modeller's Stand website (case study 9). How might this differ from a website that offers more than one product for sale.
   Alternatively, conduct the same exercise for your organization or that of your employer.

## 4.5  FULFILMENT

> " fulfilment is often the neglected element of online B2C trading "

As with its offline equivalent – commonly referred to as 'logistics' – fulfilment is often the neglected element of online B2C trading. Nevertheless, despite its less than glamorous image, making sure the customer receives the product they have ordered is just as important as any other aspect of Internet marketing. In this section we will consider the four key building blocks of online fulfilment: stock control, shipping costs, outbound logistics and returns. Although each is an element of the business (i.e. a cost) and so in itself an integral aspect of any strategic decision, in this section we will consider the important operational aspects and how they are presented to the customer on the website.

### Stock control

One of the great advantages of selling online is that customers do not expect to carry the goods out of the shop with them, so you do not have to physically hold them in stock. Therefore, if a supplier has short lead times – next day delivery is common – the e–tailer can source the ordered product from a supplier (or the manufacturer) and still offer delivery to their customer within a reasonable period.

## MINI CASE

### The virtual business

Much touted as the 'future of commerce' in the early days of the web, the concept of the virtual business has never reached its predicted popularity – with few genuine examples existing. A scenario of the model is this:

I set up a website selling promotional mugs to businesses. The site shows the different types of mug and a selection of images to choose from. Software allows the buyer to put their own company logo and message onto each mug. That done, they complete my check-out procedure and pay for the goods by credit card. When I receive the order I pass it straight over to my supplier who not only makes up the mugs, but despatches them to my customer. I then settle the invoice from the mug company – which will be less than the customer paid me. Therefore, without sales staff, offices, warehousing or manufacturing facilities – or ever touching a mug – my virtual business has made a profit. The concept becomes even more virtual if the product is fixed – i.e. not customisable. I could use software, for example, to forward a retail book order direct to the publisher who posts it direct to the customer. Profits may be low, but as overheads are virtually zero, positive income can be generated.

For the company that actually carries stock, the same issues of stock control that impact offline apply online. However, with regard to out-of-stock (OoS) products there are a number of issues unique to the online sales environment. These include:

- In an offline store the sales person can direct customers to substitute products or the customer – having made the effort to visit the store – will look for alternatives. Online, however, consumers can easily switch to another website in a click or two (Dadzie & Winston, 2007).
- Online, it is easy to withdraw a product from sale or post a temporary 'out of stock notice' – preferably with an indication of when it will be available again.
- If the OoS is temporary (e.g. a day or two) the customer need never know if shipping/delivery time is outside that period.

## Shipping costs

In a B2C environment it is common practice for the customer to pay for both actual shipping (transport) costs and 'handling' or 'packaging' (in the UK, the term 'post and packaging' is an accepted term to describe the cost). These two costs should be considered in isolation:

- Packaging. This element also has two aspects, the cost of labour and that of materials. Firstly, all products must be placed in a suitable package that is appropriate, e.g. packing for fragile items. Any packaging – even the ubiquitous 'jiffy bag' – costs money. Similarly, the operation of physically placing the goods into packaging can be labour intensive – and so, expensive.

Obviously, for a high–volume retailer automation is an option, but that would involve significant capital expenditure (for any machinery) that is beyond the resources of a smaller business. Any costs incurred must be recovered in either (1) the shipping cost charged to each customer, or (2) the product's selling price.

## MINI CASE

### Quick fingers and small boxes

Several years ago – before music downloads became popular – I became involved in the marketing of an online-only business selling CDs. This was a 'cottage industry' in the truest sense of the term – with the entire operation being run from a picturesque village in the North Yorkshire Dales. As our marketing and SEO improved, so did the sales. But therein lay the biggest problem we had. Having solved the issue of reasonably priced, high quality boxes in a variety of sizes (two-CD cases are bigger than those for single units), we were then faced with the time it was taking to select a CD from the boxes in which they arrived (we purchased CDs only in response to orders and had them delivered in bulk), place it in the appropriate box and print and affix the address label. With practice our best worker got this down to a couple of minutes, but the average was more like three. I never bettered five minutes per order. Simple arithmetic tells the story. We increased sales to around 500 orders per day. So 500 times three minutes equals 1500 minutes. Yes, we needed 25 person-hours per day to dispatch the customers' CDs. Effectively, three full time members of staff. Despite healthy sales, the owner sold the business shortly afterwards – the cost of fulfillment meant that making a profit in a competitive market was simply not possible.

- Transport. The cost of transport can be fixed quite easily by weighing every item in advance and so be able to calculate how much to charge the customer (note, don't forget to weigh the products with any packaging – boxes can be quite heavy). If you sell only a few products, weighing each will take only a few minutes – even with a wide range of products on offer it is not too onerous a job, and it will be a one–off task. By adding a fixed sum to cover packaging, shipping charges can then be listed in either a chart (weight x location) or use software to tabulate the same numbers based on customers selecting (1) product, (2) where they are, and (3) type of shipping option (first class etc). Although this sum can be shown as a total at the end of the checkout process, best practice would be to include it as a running total in the shopping basket. This is particularly the case if you offer free shipping when an order reaches a set total – seeing that they are close to the 'free' figure will often prompt shoppers to buy extra items. A survey by JupiterResearch in 2006 revealed that 18 per cent of shoppers admitted to buying unplanned items to get free shipping.

A further consideration of packaging is whether or not the shop offers special wrapping services – a product that has been purchased as a gift, for example. Although this service does add value to the overall product offering – and it can be offered at an additional fee – it does add to costs in terms of both time and packaging (the gift wrapping).

## Outbound logistics

After the ordered product has been sourced and packaged, delivery to the customer must be arranged. The costs are not a significant issue for the seller because they will have been paid by the customer – specifically, or intrinsic to the buying price. Neither is dispatch a problem, most carriers will collect. The most significant problems arise at the other end of the delivery chain – where, and how, the customer actually takes possession of the goods.

For some items there is no problem. A boxed CD, for example, will go through the average house's letter–box. However, if the goods are bigger, or a signature is required for the delivery, there must be someone at home to take that delivery. Despite the fact that online shoppers have many questions to ask about delivery costs, shipping returns and privacy issues (Forrester, 2005) extensive research by industry analysts IMRG (2005) found that the online retailing industry could be losing a significant number of orders because potential customers are dissatisfied with delivery services. Their research revealed – amongst other things – that 80 per cent of the UK retail sites assessed did not allow customers to specify delivery instructions. Furthermore, Page-Thomas et al (2006) found that although customers consider delivery a vital component of customer service, online retailers are not matching expectations concerning the information they provide about the delivery of ordered goods. The same survey revealed delivery pricing guides, delivery guarantees and delivery schedules as the most important information that potential buyers seek.

> although customers consider delivery service a vital component of customer service, online retailers are not matching expectations

Over the years a number of initiatives have been tried to address the issue of unattended and deferred home deliveries. These include basic arrangements such as having the delivery driver phone the recipient an hour or so before their expected time of arrival or more accurately predicted deliveries times using GPS tracking. Other more complex schemes have been the subject of numerous start–up business models – all recognizing that any system that might be widely accepted will generate healthy profits. The following have been, or are being, tried, but to date nothing has caught the public's imagination:

- Redelivery services – the customer directs goods to a depot, from where they collect it
- Pickup points at convenience stores and filling station forecourts
- Removable boxes secured to an electronically-controlled anchor point outside the recipient's house
- Collection points at self-storage depots
- Box banks outside supermarkets, including a card-swipe facility on the boxes

A final issue with regards to delivery is that of sending to an address that is not the one associated with the name on the credit card used for the transaction. Many firms, fearing fraud, will refuse to do this. However, for many people being at home all day to receive goods is problematic – if not impossible. For the gift–seller (a florist, for example) such a policy would be a recipe for bankruptcy. There are ways around this, but it generally involves having the bank make further checks on the validity of the credit card – which involves a higher cost for the seller. For the smaller company, it makes sense to sell through a third party where PayPal–type facilities tackle such issues for the retailer.

## Practical Insight

### There's more money in picks and shovels than gold

Although hard facts do not exist to support the notion, a number of industry insiders point to the profits made by the major delivery companies and suggest that of all the industries that have profited from the rise of the Internet, it is those courier and parcel services that deliver the online–ordered products who have benefited most. This is based on a similar hypothesis from the great American gold rushes in the 19th century. The adage was that the businesses selling mining tools made far more money than the gold prospectors who bought them.

## Returns

Also known as reverse logistics, the organization must give consideration to customers who want to return the goods to the vendor. The quantity of potential returns will depend on both the product and the organization's

needs, many other products – from cars to kettles – simply list the relative attributes of the products. As with so many aspects of the Internet, it is the travel industry that has been a primary exponent of the concept – with sites like Expedia (www.expedia.com) and Travelocity (www.travelocity.com) being able to search their databases to present flight and hotel options for wherever the traveller wishes to go.

However, the convenience of free on–demand product comparison comes at price – that being the lack of total impartiality of the options offered to users. Despite the fact that most CSEs explain their links with sponsors, it is normally only in the small print – and how they generate income and how commercial relationships affect their content is not so clear (Defaqto, 2007). Similarly, when considering – for example – car insurance, whilst a number of brands might offer their own insurance policies, there are a limited amount of policy underwriters. For example, Britain's largest motor insurer, the Royal Bank of Scotland (RBS) underwrites policies for Direct Line, Churchill, Privilege, Tesco, Mint and Virgin. In a similar vein of questioning the independence of some CSEs, the problem might be one of conflict rather than allegiance. It is common practice, for example, to omit results from key suppliers in a market because they choose not to pay the fees charged by the comparison site.

As is the case in so much of online marketing CSEs have added to their content to take them beyond offering comparisons of similar products. Not only are shipping and any other additional costs for each listed seller included in the comparison, but many now offer customer reviews (see section 9.2) – essentially they are trying to present themselves as a kind of online shopping community site (see section 9.3).

## DECISION TIME

As with all aspects of Internet marketing, using CSEs is not for every retailer, with advantages and disadvantages to the service offered. These include the following:

- The comparison results are price–based. If you offer a premium price for a premium service, then you will fare badly in the CSE results. Remember, CSE users are in the segment of the market that is shopping on price. If this is not your demographic then stay away from comparison sites.
- Not all of your products have to be listed, selected products can be used to raise the seller's profile – the equivalent of the long established offline loss–leader principle.
- The major CSEs rank highly with search engines. If you are struggling with both SEO and search engine advertising, perhaps the CSE can put your product on the search engine results pages.
- There is a cost to the retailers of selling through a price comparison website. Whilst this can be built in to selling prices and marketing budgets, paying a commission to sell your product cheaper than your competitors might be a risky long-term strategy.

- The CSE might not have many visitors, or its visitors might not be shopping for your products – though in a pay-per-click arrangement, no traffic equals no cost (other than that involved in setting up the listing).

Although the CSEs all provide a guide on submitting to their engines, before adding products to their listings you should be prepared to provide details of all of the following attributes for each:

- The product's full name
- A description of the product
- The product's manufacturer and assigned part number
- The category on the CSE in which you wish it to be listed
- How you want the product to be classified
- Your selling price – and the retail price if you are discounting it
- The URL of the product's page (on your site)
- The URL of any image to be presented on the CSE

To increase clickthrough volume, it is also advisable to include:

- Stock availability
- The weight and size of the product (for shipping purposes)
- Shipping costs

*You Decide*    Advise the owners how suitable the use of CSEs might be for the Gilded Truffle Hotel (case study 3). Explain both the positive and negative aspects of the practice for the hotel.
Alternatively, conduct the same exercise for your organization or that of your employer.

## 4.7   BRICKS AND CLICKS – INTEGRATED RETAILING

In this section the concentration is on the way in which retailers can integrate off – and online sales. The issue's wider context – how all organizations can use the Internet in their marketing, both strategically and operationally – is addressed in the final chapter. It is inevitable, however, that there is some crossover in the content of the two sections, therefore readers are advised to read both this section and chapter 10 in order to get a full appreciation of the subject.

Before considering the role of the Internet in any retail strategy, let's consider its impact so far. Throughout this book I have attempted to present facts and figures that are both relevant and accurate. However, for this particular subject the data is complex or biased, resulting in it being confusing – or all of these. The complexity comes from different bodies' interpretation of what 'retail' is within their research. For example, some include services

> " ... there may well be around a third of the population who will never shop online "

such as online booking of holidays or flights whilst others include only tangible products. This has an obvious impact in that just one family trip booked online would be the equivalent of dozens, if not hundreds, of books or CDs. Other statistics, such as those from the UK Office for National Statistics (ONS), include 'online' with other 'non–store' retail figures. The problem itself is made more difficult by the researchers not always publishing their own definition of what they have counted as retail. Bias comes in the form of research published by organizations that are in some way involved in – or would gain from – online retailing, and so may have a natural inclination to be positive about any numbers involved. Examples of research into online retail include:

- US government figures that suggest online represents only three per cent of total retail sales
- The British Retail Consortium (BRC) saying that online sales for 2007 were 6% of all retail sales
- A 2008 report released by Shop.org suggesting that e–commerce would account for 7% of all retail sales in that year
- The Interactive Media in Retail Group (IMRG) – the industry body for the e–retail industry – put the proposed 2008 figure at 17 per cent

Furthermore, surveys like that by Forrester Research (2008) show that online retailing, whilst still growing, is doing so much slower. It is also worth mentioning that even in countries where the Internet plays a significant role, usage is not 100 per cent – indeed, in the USA that figure has stalled at around 70 per cent of the population, so there may well be around a third of the population who will never shop online. Although it is likely that this 30 per cent represent the poorer segment of society and so their retail spending will be low for many classifications of product – their existence alone will prevent online sales achieving a majority of overall retail sales.

In the mid 1990s, the low cost of entry into (theoretically) global markets saw a wave of new online retailers. At that time most of the major offline – 'bricks and mortar' – retailers shied away from the web, many thinking it was simply a fad and others concerned that they could not operate both physically and electronically without one cannibalizing the other (Gay et al 2007). Those that did go online did so with a half-hearted effort that was neither e-tail nor e-marketing strategy. Although nearly 60 per cent of respondents to a 2008 US Direct Marketing Association (DMA) survey said they have both brick-and-mortar and online shops, it is still the case that a significant number of retailers either do not sell online at all, or offer only a limited range. This is not to say that offline retailers do not use the web – they do, but as part of their strategic marketing effort – branding and after sales service being the most common online objectives. Whatever their online objectives, the offline retailers have now entered the online environment with a vengeance – and so present competition to those entrepreneurial dot com retailers who were first to sell to consumers online. What began as a pioneering form of retailing practiced only by the new e-tailers is now part of a multichannel strategy for established retailers (Grewal et al, 2004). Despite this, there is still a tendency to treat online as the poor relation. At the Shop.org Annual Summit in September 2007, Forrester (forrester.com) senior analyst Sucharita Mulpuru delivered a speech that included a warning that retailers still have not truly embraced multiple channels. In particular, offline is not being used to drive online sales, with retailers continuing to silo web sales, with the result that online divisions continue to incur promotional costs to drive traffic to the site. It is also the case that traditional retailers neglect the standard of their web presence at their peril. Research, conducted in 2006, by US Internet performance tracking company Gomez (www.gomez.com), revealed that 65 per cent of online shoppers would stop or reconsider shopping at an organization's physical outlets if they had a poor online experience.

## Research Snapshot

### What is integrated retailing?

According to one of the leading publications on the subject – Internet retailing – 'the cross–channel ideal envisages the customer being able to walk through the store door after a few hours of surfing the web to purchase or pick up the perfect product, with the expectation that the local store should be aware of their order and able to fully support them'.

*Source: Internet retailing (2008) Out of Touch Retailers Throw Away High Street Sales, Issue 5, September 2008*

Although the issue was introduced in section 1.6, where we looked at online buying behaviour and it is addressed again in chapter 10 (the Internet as part of an integrated marketing strategy) it is worth hi–lighting the options open to the contemporary shopper. Only 15 years ago, for many products, the consumer was limited to visiting a single retail outlet, considering the options available there, and making a purchase. Now, however, not only can shoppers use the web to research products, they have a choice of purchasing off–or online as well as having the product delivered or collecting it from a local store (Canavan et al, 2007). Indeed, the practice of buying online and picking up in store is developing fast. Speaking at the Search Marketing Expo West convention in 2008, Krillion-E-Tailing Group CEO, Joel Toledano, reported that 40 per cent of WalMart's online sales and 55 per cent of Circuit City's e-commerce transactions in 2007 resulted in goods being collected from a bricks and mortar store. Furthermore, comments made by Comet's content manager, Robbie Tutt – in an interview with e–consultancy (in August 2008) – suggest the practice is also common in the UK, with around half of the electrical retailer's online customers electing to take the 'collect in store' option. The Krillion survey also found that when customers were questioned on their primary motivation for utilizing in-store pick up, the top three responses were:

- Save shipping expense – 50 per cent
- Convenience – 22 per cent
- Immediate need – 18 per cent

# MINI CASE

## Catalogue retailer transfers experience online

Some of the best proponents of online sales have been those companies that started out as catalogue, or direct mail, retailers. The reason for this (I believe) is that e–tailing is – effectively – catalogue selling, but the catalogue is viewed on a computer screen instead of paper. All the experience of distance selling and fulfilment gained over decades has been applied to the online environment – with sales and marketing asking the question of IT 'how can technology help us do this better', rather than the web presence being driven by IT displaying their design talents.

In the integrated retailing stakes, the UK's Argos is showing the way. Early proponents of making catalogue–viewed goods available in physical depots as well as mail order, they now offer a whole host of permutations in how the customer can view, choose, order, pay for and take possession of goods. This includes making a purchase online and having the goods delivered or picking them up from a store, or ordering the goods online so that they are reserved for you when you collect, and pay for, them. Argos also allow telephone ordering and text reservations. Or customers can simply go into an outlet and make a purchase.

**The home page of Argos.co.uk**

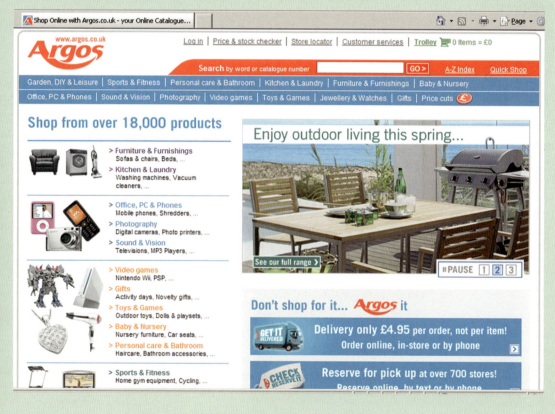

# DECISION TIME

The decision on integrated retailing needs to be considered from two points of view – the offline retailer going online and the online retailer developing a 'bricks and mortar' presence. Let's consider the latter first.

In many cases – particularly for the niche retailer – the online presence is actually a development of an offline business, with the online fulfillment being handled from the bricks and mortar store – something that can add to the credibility of the e-commerce website. For others, the online business is only profitable because there are not the costs (both fixed and variable) associated with running a physical outlet, with many 'eBay'-type retailers running their operation as a part time venture. Furthermore, the goods are normally dispatched outside of the immediate area, so having a single outlet would not increase sales to a wider demographic – and multiple stores is simply not a consideration. However, if the business is full time, and premises rented with stock held, it does make sense to open to the public.

## RESEARCH SNAPSHOT

**High street retailers are winning the online shopping competition**

The websites of the 100 largest high street retailers in the UK received 19.3 per cent more UK Internet visits during July 2008 than the 100 largest online-only retailers.

*Source: Hitwise.co.uk*

More significant is the first issue raised – that of bricks and mortar stores moving online. For some retailers the potential of channel conflict is a problem. This is particularly true of manufacturers who have their own outlets but sell through other stores as well. The introduction of online sales might cause shops stocking lines to withdraw from the distribution chain – particularly if the goods are cheaper or the choice wider online. For other stores the reason for *not* having online sales is more puzzling. Obviously there is the issue of the cost of setting up and maintaining the online presence – but this would be marginal compared with the up-keep of physical stores. It is also the case that with a minimum of restructuring of staff and premises, online fulfilment could be handled from existing stores – as do Tesco with their online grocery deliveries.

## MINI CASE

**Leveraging your offline assets**

An example of a traditional store adapting to being 'clicks and mortar' in order to respond to competition from new online-only stores – in particular, Amazon – is Barnes and Noble.

Trading online as BN.com, the US book giant integrates its channels of distribution by offering discount cards that can be used off-and online and making deliveries for online orders from bricks and mortar outlets – on the same day if one is local enough to your home or workplace. In-store, sales staff will process online orders for any books that are not in stock – with the customer having the required item delivered to their home. In the UK, a similar scenario exists, where Tesco distributes online orders from local stores – whereas its competitor in e–grocery sales, Ocado (www.ocado.co.uk), delivers from a single distribution hub located in London.

However, as with all marketing problems, the answer lies with the organization's customers. If they *expect* that a retailer has a web presence on which goods can be purchased or ordered, then that retailer should have an e-commerce website that supports their offline sales and marketing efforts. Schoenbachler & Gordon (2002) suggest that there are three issue to consider in identifying customer expectations with regard to their channel–choice; demographics, past experience and convenience. Whilst these will vary from firm to firm, the concept has its roots in *traditional* segmentation models. Briefly considering each of Schoenbachler and Gordon's points in turn:

- Demographics – this might apply to geographic issues (where are your customers, are there local shops?) but be more specific to Internet users' demographics. If your product is aimed at affluent 30 year olds who are cash–rich but time–poor then online has to be an option. A target segment of low–income families, on the other hand, is not likely to have access to the Internet, or even a credit card, and so would never use a website to purchase goods.
- Past experience – do your competitors have online sales? If this is the case then people in your market will expect an online option, to not have one is to send customers to your competition.
- Convenience – as with the cash–rich but time–poor segment, do your customers value the convenience of online purchases? Insurance and banking services would come under this heading. Also of significance is that not only do customers like to be able to pick up merchandise at a store after ordering online but they see it as a significant advantage (to the online shop) if they are able to return online–purchases to a physical outlet.

*You Decide*    Advise Frank and his staff at Hill Street Motorist Shops (case study 8) on extending their limited online offering and how it can be further integrated into their overall sales strategy.

A second option is to identify a well–known high street retailer that does not sell online and consider why it has taken that decision.

Alternatively, if your organization or that of your employer is a retailer, consider the implications of integrated off– and online retailing.

## CHAPTER EXERCISE

Giving justifications for all your decisions, advise Martha and her team at Phelps Online Department Store (case study 13) on all aspects of online retailing covered in this chapter. Alternatively, conduct the same exercise on your own organization or that of your employer.

## REFERENCES

Allred, C.R., Smith, S.M. & Swinyard, W.R. (2006). E-shopping lovers and fearful conservatives: a market segmentation analysis. Marriott School of Management, Brigham Young University, Provo, Utah, USA.

Canavan, O., Henchion, M. & O'Reilly, S. (2007). The use of the Internet as a marketing channel for Irish speciality food. *International Journal of Retail & Distribution Management.* Vol. 35, No. 2, pp. 178–195.

Center for the Digital Future (2008). *Surveying the Digital Future.* The University of Southern California's Annenberg School for Communication.

Dadzie, K.Q. & Winston, E. (2007). Consumer response to stock-out in the online supply chain. *International Journal of Physical Distribution management.* Vol. 37, No. 1, pp. 19–42.

Defaqto (2007). Motor Insurance in the UK 2007 – the rise of the aggregator. Defaqto Ltd.

De Kare Silver, M. (1998). *E-shock.* MacMillan Press.

Direct Marketing Association (2008) Channel Integration and Benchmarks in the Retail Industry

Forrester Research Inc (2005). Poor Contextual Help Erodes Shoppers' trust, (www.forrester.com). Forrester research, Cambridge, MA.

Forrester Research Inc (2008) U.S. *E-commerce Forecast: 2008 to 2012.* www.forrester.com

Gay, R., Charlesworth, A. & Esen, R. (2007). Online Marketing – A Customer-Led Approach. Oxford University Press.

Gomez (2006) *Online Shopping Experience Report.* Available on www.switch2gomez.com

Grewal, D., Iyer, G.R. & Levy, M. (2004). Internet retailing: enablers, limiters, and market consequences. *Journal of Business Research.* Vol. 57 pp. 703–713.

IGD (2007). *UK Grocery Outlook.* Available on www.igd.com

IMRG (2005). E-retail Industry Home Delivery Trust Scheme Phase 2 Gets Go Ahead. Interactive Media in Research Group. (IMRG. organization).

Kamarulzamam, Y. (2007). Adoption of travel e-shopping in the UK. *International Journal of Retail and Distribution Management.* Vol. 35, No. 9, pp. 703–719.

Moe, W.W. & Fader, P.S. (2001). Which Visits Lead to Purchases? Dynamic Conversion Behavior at E-Commerce Sites. *Sloan Management Review.* Vol. 42, No. 2, pp. 8–9.

## 5.1  INTRODUCTION

Where the last chapter – on the B2C web presence – built on the previous chapter on website development, this chapter is developed from both. Obviously, the basic tenants of website design apply to B2B sites (chapter 3) just as much as a check–out facility on a B2B site should comply with the same guidelines as those covered in section 4.4 on B2C. This chapter, then, concentrates on those issues that relate specifically to the B2B online presence – that it is relatively short should not give readers the perception that the subject is any less important than those covered in the previous chapters, it is simply that many of the key issues have already been addressed.

Also worth noting is that in a B2B environment, online marketing should be seen as part of the wider entity that is e–business. This issue is addressed in detail in section 1.4 – the impact of the Internet on business – and referring to that section will be beneficial to your understanding of this chapter. Similarly, this book concentrates on the use of the Internet in marketing – and not the use of the Internet in business in its entirety. For example, it is now common practice to use the web as part of project and logistics management and although there will be elements of good practice in web design incorporated to sites in those fields (e.g. navigation and usability), they are not marketing specific, and so are not covered in this book.

A final point of note with regard to this chapter is that I have differentiated only B2C and B2B in separate chapters. Essentially, this chapter – despite its title – actually considers all non–B2C online marketing. Therefore, where reference is made to a B2B market or environment, this could just as easily apply to selling to a government department or university as it could another profit–driven business. In this context, perhaps the term B2O – business to *organization* – should be in common use?

Two issues are significant in B2B marketing, they are that (1) the method of both the decision–making process and the actual purchase differs from B2C, and (2) the range of products varies dramatically. The first of these is addressed in detail in both section 1.4 (actual purchase) and the next section of this chapter (buying practices). The diversity of products purchased by an organization means that the marketer must be prepared to adapt their online selling to suit different product lines. Garrido Samaniego et al (2006) make the point that in a similar manner to consumer markets, firms make use of the Internet in their purchasing as a source of information and, sometimes, as a transaction channel. This second point means that it is sometimes necessary to have a website that is – essentially – a retail site, with goods being selected, ordered paid for (using a credit card) and fulfilled in exactly the same way as on a B2C web presence, in chapter 1, I gave the example of relatively low–value stationery being an example of this. Indeed, research from Enquiro (2007a) suggests that it is only smaller value B2B purchases that are likely to be conducted online. In instances such as these, the website developer is advised to treat the site as a retail site – following all best practice used in that environment. It is perhaps this similarity between B2C and B2B sites with a 'shopping' facility that has resulted in such sites being dubbed 'e–commerce' sites.

For other products – in total value terms, the majority – the website is not the medium on which the actual purchase is made. As we will see in subsequent sections of this chapter, the organization's online presence can play a significant role in the commercial buying process but rarely is it the end of the process, more often being a medium for marketing communication. As Brews & Tucci (2004) comment, *'efficiency in the communications channel can reduce customers' search and bargaining costs'.*

## 5.2  B2B BUYING PRACTICES

Throughout this book it has been my intention to avoid covering *offline* marketing theory and models – there are plenty of books that do that – this book being about *Internet* marketing. However, there are a number of offline issues that must be addressed in order to practice online marketing and – as with buyer behaviour (section 1.6) – how organizations go about their business purchases is an essential consideration for the B2B Internet marketer. Key to this issue is *who* makes the buying decision, and in this regard Webster & Wind's 1972 paper on the subject is still relevant. They suggested that the buying decision can depend on input from *some* or *all* of: initiators, users, influencers, deciders, approvers, buyers and gate-keepers. Dubbed the decision making unit (DMU) these have remained the same in the online environment – with each of them being able to use the web to help them in their own aspect of the decision–making process. More lately, in a survey on B2B trading, search engine marketing firm, Enquiro, (2007 b) suggested that there are three elements to the contemporary, Internet–using B2B buying unit:

1.  The economic buyer who releases funds and holds power of veto
2.  The user buyer – who judges the impact of the purchase on the job
3.  The technical buyer who considers not only the technicalities of the product, but also aspects such as logistics and shipping costs

The same report also proposes that B2B purchases follow a chronological order of: awareness, research/consideration, negotiation and purchase – a sequence similar to the recognized B2C buying process. The difference being the inclusion of 'negotiation' – though it might be argued that the retail customer's ability to seek out lower prices online (for example, see comparison search engines, section 4.6) is a B2C equivalent of 'negotiation'.

As previously mentioned, it would be rare for a purchase order to be raised based purely on information gleaned from a website. More likely is that the Internet will be used to gather information that will then be used to narrow down a field of potential suppliers, who will then be contacted on a personal basis. This reflects the way that B2B purchasing has been conducted for hundreds of years – with the web replacing (or supplementing) catalogues, brochures, trade shows and to a lesser degree, advertising. This means that the B2B website has the key objective of lead generation – making the presentation of information an essential element of the B2B website. It is also the case that in a branding context, the site can also help develop the relationship that is essential in B2B commerce. Supporting the argument that in a B2B context there is little opportunity for direct sales, but opportunities

>  the Internet would only be exploited effectively as a marketing tool when practitioners moved beyond its ability to support transactions

for lead generation and relationship building exists, Gummerson (1994) – one of the originators of the concept of relationship marketing – predicted that the Internet would only be exploited effectively as a marketing tool when practitioners moved beyond its ability to support transactions and recognised that information delivered online provides a foundation for developing relationships with customers. Needless to say, the quality of the web presence can end a relationship before it has chance to begin – this is particularly relevant where an initial order (once negotiated) will result in repeat orders over a long period of time.

## DECISION TIME

The key decisions to be made with regard to B2B buying practices revolve around being aware of:

1. How your potential customers go about their buying decision, and
2. Who – within the buying organization – has the responsibility for seeking information on the product that will meet its needs.

Both of these issues can be addressed by reviewing the B2B buying process – or *cycle* – that might follow a sequence something like that shown in Figure 5.1.

It cannot be emphasized how much this process can vary depending on the almost infinite number of products that might be purchased in the B2B environment. In describing consumer transactions it is relatively easy for a marketing tutor to use examples such as cars, mobile phones or soft drinks when teaching marketing practice. In a B2B scenario, however, students tend to be unaware of just how many B2B products are manufactured – and so marketed. These products range from the one–inch long metal bracket that holds up the classroom whiteboard to the tons of concrete used in building a motorway flyover – and yes, people earn a living marketing both of these products!

Having assessed the potential buying process used by the target market – or industry – the e–marketer can then draw some conclusions as to (1) who is likely to make up the DMU, and (2) what information they might seek online – and how they will expect it to be presented.

*You Decide*    Advise Syd Carton and Charlie Darnay at Two Cities Manufacturing Ltd (case study 11) on what type of buying process might be common in their industry (or markets) and consider how that might impact on their web presence. Remember, you are looking at them as vendors, not buyers.

Alternatively, conduct the same exercise on your organization or that of your employer.

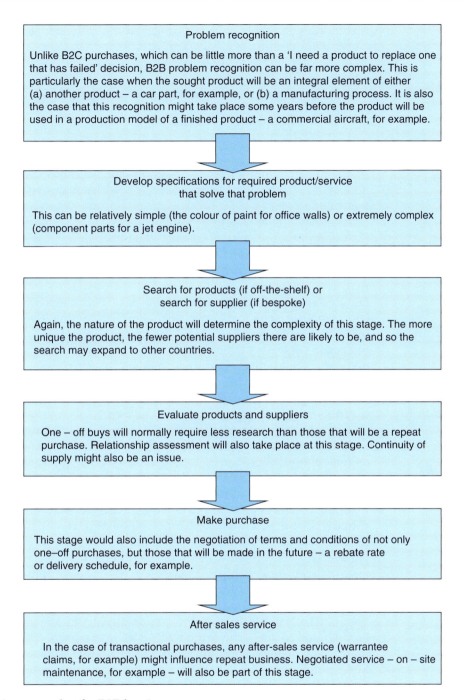

**Figure 5.1** An example of a B2B buying process.

## 5.3   THE B2B WEBSITE

In chapter three, the importance of website content development is stressed, and the point is emphasized in B2B marketing in that the site is likely to be visited by different people – all of whom have a different agenda in deciding whether or not they will buy from you. As we have seen in the previous section, the problem stems from the way businesses go about making their purchases.

In the previous section we considered a sample B2B buying cycle. In order to build a web presence that meets the needs of B2B buyers it is worthwhile giving that cycle further consideration by looking at each element in more detail.

1. Problem recognition – likely to be an in–house decision, though buyers do use the web to keep up to date with news in their sector. This means that online press releases for new developments or products should be distributed to those sites that might be visited by industry workers – with the organization's own website including content on new products, new applications or any other advances that are important in the industry or marketplace. Such content might prompt the B2B buyer to recognise that they have a problem.

2. Develop specifications for required product/service that solves that problem – another issue that is probably completed within the organization, though as in the previous stage, staff may use the web to stay in touch with developments in their industry that may influence any specification decisions. The company website should address any issues that might be specific – although it should be inherent in any product description.

3. Search for products (if off-the-shelf) or search for supplier (if bespoke). It is this stage where the website really earns its keep – when asked if they used the web in their purchase decision–making, 85 per cent of B2B buyers said yes. (Enquiro, 2007a, b). Not only are there search engine optimization issues to consider, but the information that the buyers seek must be made easily available on the site – and in a format that they would find most useful.

4. Evaluate products and suppliers – offline this would normally involve contacting the potential suppliers, online this is not necessary. The phrase 'online – you are your website' (introduced in chapter 3.3) is particularly relevant here. Based on their perception of the organization from its website, a company may or may not make initial contact via email or telephone – a call that could lead to a multi-thousand pound order or contract. Would you trust the manufacture of a vital, high–specification safety component for your product to a firm that couldn't be bothered to spell–check the text on its home page? Or returns '404' messages when you click on a product link on their site?

5. Make purchase – as stated earlier in the chapter, online purchase (i.e. with a credit card) is not the norm in a B2B transaction. However, the product might be suitable for online ordering – in which case a retail–style site might be appropriate. If the goods being sold lend themselves to regular repeat orders, then once the initial order has been negotiated (price, discounts, delivery etc) an online provision should be made to accommodate those orders. This could be as simple as a designated email address or a more complex password–protected order form. It may even be an opportunity for a personalized web page, as described in chapter 8.5.

6. After sales service – as with other web presences, this can be a specific objective of the site. In the B2B environment, this could go beyond a standard FAQ page to being part of any contractual agreement made with regard to the product – installation instructions or application updates, for example.

There are several caveats to add to this cycle that might impact on the Internet marketer, including:

- The online information gathering exercise might be given to a junior member of staff who is tasked with finding potential suppliers (via a search engine – another complication for key word selection – see section 6.3) who then simply prints out web pages that they think are relevant. Printed pages are then distributed amongst members of the DMU.
- A B2B buyer is often starting at square one with no knowledge of the market – therefore brand affinity does not play any part. On the other hand, if you have previously dipped a toe into that market you might be drawn to a brand you have come across before.
- Inspecting, sampling and negotiation are integral aspects of B2B buying – although it might not be possible for them to be completed wholly online, they should be introduced on the website.
- In B2B purchases risk avoidance is a significant issue. Buying a shirt in a colour that doesn't suit you (in a B2C transaction) might be annoying. Ordering bespoke products that are not suitable to your application in a B2B environment could spell bankruptcy for the company or the buyer losing his or her job. Website copy should reflect this concern.
- Similarly, there is a lack of emotion in a B2B purchase. When buying for ourselves the axiom 'buy with the heart, justify with the brain' is often true. This is not the case in commercial procurement where buying criteria must be adhered to.

## Practical Insight

### B2B has embraced the online presence

Although closer analysis can reveal some background to the bare statistics, the headline results of a survey from the Association of National Advertisers (2007) might surprise many. That is that B2B marketers have embraced 'new media' platforms more than their B2C compatriots. That most B2B marketers have smaller budgets and less opportunity for (offline) mass-media advertising may be one reason behind these results.

However, most significant is that [in the survey] a simple website is classed as 'new media'. So whilst many (if not most) B2B companies shun 'web 2.0' platforms such as bloggs, wikis and social networks, they do appreciate the value of a web presence.

Having said that, a 2008 survey from Junta42 Match, in conjunction with BtoB magazine, found that marketers are spending nearly 30 per cent of their budgets on custom–content projects such as email newsletters (69 per cent), white papers (50 per cent), and case studies (48 per cent) – all of which use the Internet as their medium of distribution.

# DECISION TIME

As with all marketing, the message and mode of transmission should correspond to customers' expectations, requirements and needs. Online – as we covered in chapter 3.4 – this is equally relevant. The additional problem, however, is that there can be a number of people involved in the buying decision – all of whom might be looking for something different on the vendor's website. For example, the *economic* buyer will be concentrating on price, discounts, rebates and so on. The *user* buyer will care less for cost and concentrate on whether or not the product will serve the purpose for what it is being purchased – with a natural inclination to desire the product that is actually *better* than they need. The *technical* buyer may look beyond the unit price and application and pay greater attention to lead times, delivery schedules and shipping costs. Any web content that does not address all of these issues and pampers to only one or two may find the 'neglected' group rejecting your offering and looking elsewhere.

How the relevant information is presented is another issue. Many products will be sold in niche markets where buyers will be experts in the industry. In this case, the content can be written in a language only they understand. Indeed, a lack of jargon, acronyms and abbreviations may well give the impression that you are not a serious player in that industry. When preparing the content it is essential to consult closely with the firm's sales staff who are familiar with the language used in the industry.

In any DMU, the person who accesses the website might need to relay the information to the other decision makers, and that may not be online – a board meeting, perhaps. Facilitating a printed format is an obvious requirement in the case – with PDF helping to ensure quality. However, as we covered in chapter 3.4, video and audio can enhance textual content and be effective in the conversion process. This is particularly true where video can be used to describe complex procedures, or an audio commentary from an expert in the product can bring to life the same content presented in one–dimensional fashion on a web page. Information presented in sound files that can be replayed on an mp3 player may be excellent for decision makers who are frequently away from the office (in the construction industry, perhaps). However, the same cannot be said of videos – which may also be unsuitable to play in meetings where several suppliers or products are being compared. As with all issues related to content, sales staff who have a history of dealing with industry buyers will be able to provide invaluable information in this regard.

*You Decide*

Advise Sam and Chris at BethSoft (case study 5) on how their website can address the needs of the target market for their product.

Alternatively, conduct the same exercise on your organization or that of your employer.

## 5.4  LEAD GENERATION

Such is the nature of B2B marketing and procurement that the key objective of the majority of B2B websites is that of lead generation. In essence, the website must present such a good impression of the organization and its products that potential buyers feel that both will meet their needs – and so are *obliged* to contact the firm.

Having said that, any sales person will tell you that moving the potential customer from *just looking* to being a genuine lead is far from easy. In real life, the sales person can watch, listen and react to the prospect. Online, the website does not have such aids, and so the 'call to action' must be delivered in the right way. A common mistake of many B2B sites is to push the lead-generation aspect too early – that is, force the searcher to contact the organization too early in their buying process. Information should be made available to help the decision makers to differentiate products and suppliers, so that when they do contact the vendor they are a more viable lead.

## DECISION TIME

**"** websites must *never* be created by folk with no sales and/or marketing experience **"**

In my experience, far too many organizations have their website designed so that the content does an excellent job in starting the customer down the sales funnel (see also sections 1.6 and 3.2), but then drops the ball when it comes to guiding them to the next step. This situation epitomizes the argument that websites must *never* be created by folk with no sales and/or marketing experience. The sales process is just that – a process, and experienced sales staff can do an excellent job in guiding potential customers through that process. To ignore their experience when developing a web presence is a significant mistake. Furthermore, a lack of cohesion between online and sales often results in leads being captured by the website, only to be dropped by the offline sales team. To address this inexcusable state of affairs three issues should be resolved. They are:

1. What are the most appropriate calls to action? In section 3.2 we looked at the concept of *persuasion* architecture, where the website content moves the visitor towards a desired action – in this case, to contact the organization. At the same time such navigation should also allow users to recognise if they are on the wrong site, that is, the seller cannot meet their needs – which is important as it cuts down the time wasted in responding to inquiries that will never generate sales. What *is* appropriate will depend on the product and the nature of the market in which it is being sold. For example, a product whose purchases are transactional (rather than relational) might suit a 'for 10 per cent discount on your next order … ' style of call to action. A lawyer offering to review an organization's health and safety policy, on the other hand, might be better advised to use a 'contact us before an injured employee does' type of call. Websites for products where viewing samples of work would be an integral part of the buying process could give the contact

to be effective, marketers must be aware of the e–marketplace's function so that they can make best use of them in the promotion and distribution of their products – hence their inclusion in this text.

A target for venture capitalists at the end of the last century, many start–up B2B e–marketplaces suffered in the dot–bomb collapse along with other online ventures. However, whilst many of these had suspect business plans and overspent on promotion and technology, research into the reasons for their demise (Day et al 2003) suggests that the key issue was that it was impossible to replace longstanding relationships in the B2B supply chain [with a website], therefore the e–marketplaces' greatest competition was existing ways of doing business. The intervening years, however, have seen a much more positive approach to the use of the Internet in the procurement and logistics fields – and so the use of e–marketplaces has become part of the way of doing business. Although some e–marketplaces are open to any and all members of an industry, many are restricted to membership of a restricted community – be they buyers or sellers (Cullen & Webster 2007).

## MINI CASE

In terms of the volume of B2B traffic, perhaps the ultimate e–marketplace is Alibaba.com, which successfully went public in November 2007. Based in China, Alibaba – according to its own website – provides *an efficient, trusted platform connecting small and medium-sized buyers and suppliers from China and around the world*, and its marketplaces *form a community of more than 30 million members from over 240 countries and regions*.

**The home page of alibaba.com**

# DECISION TIME

Often cited as an example of how many organizations' adoption of the Internet as a business tool has been fragmented, it is not unusual for a firm's buying department to actively use one or more e–marketplaces in their procurement activities – and yet the marketing department ignore them in their sales efforts.

How effectively the online marketer can use e–marketplaces obviously depends on the extent the industry in which they operate is served by them. If there is good coverage – and there may be a dominant player – then committing to selling via an e–marketplace can release physical resources (members of a sales team, for example) to concentrate on areas of the business where online marketing is not suitable or accepted. As with all online marketing efforts, however, using an e–marketplace is not a 'fit and forget' solution. The site should be constantly monitored for activity – particularly if there is a 'community' element to it. It is not unusual for the first firm to respond to a 'chat room' inquiry to be the one that gets an order. Similarly, frequent involvement in forums and the like will help build a profile of the organization and so help in any relationship marketing efforts.

Also worth noting is that e–marketplaces can be industry or market specific, and so the Internet marketer might need to join several. For example, a table manufacturer might be a member of a 'tables' portal that attracts anyone who wants to buy tables, but they could also join e–marketplaces for suppliers to the hotel and catering industry, education and local government.

Whilst joining some online marketplaces can be a simple as entering your email address into a box, in order to join an e–marketplace that is linked to e–procurement facilities, the online marketer will need to complete and 'application form'. Whilst some of the content will be standard issues related to the organization in order to establish credibility, other sections are an opportunity to market the company and its products. For these sections it is essential that thought and preparation is given to the entry.

Data relating to your company might include:

- The registered name of your company and its full address
- Your company number (as registered at Companies House) and its VAT number
- The name of any parent company if your company is part of a group
- The name of your managing, and any other, directors – and their responsibilities
- The annual turnover of your company as in the last set of published accounts
- The number of employees in your company

Although these will add credibility to the firm – and several might be classed as essential for many buyers – it is the following that require an element of 'sales copy':

- A description of the company – over and above the formal details listed above
- A description of the services and goods your company provides

- The URL of your website to enable buyers to see more about your company
- If you are a supplier of goods, an indication of stock holding and product availability
- An indication of the types of organisations you currently supply, including a list of existing customers
- Details of any industry accreditation, for example; ISO, Corgi, IIP etc.

Finally, there is the section that non–marketers always ignore. Most forms will have a section for 'other information' – this is your chance to make reading buyers contact you rather than any of your competitors. But remember, these will be professional buyers who will not be swayed by sales rhetoric.

*You Decide*

Spend some time online and see if you can find any B2B marketplaces that might be useful in the marketing of the Gilded Truffle Hotel (case study 3) Remember, you are selling, not buying – and yes, the hotel has a significant B2B market.

Alternatively, conduct the same exercise on your organization or that of your employer.

## 5.6 ONLINE AUCTIONS AND TENDERING

Staples of B2B trading for decades, both auctions and tendering have gained a new lease of life in the Internet age. As with so many other aspects of marketing, the concepts remain the same online as they are offline – but the technology has vastly enhanced the services available to both buyers and sellers. Although closely related as methods of doing business, the two models differ in their practice – as you will see as we look at each in more detail.

## Online auctions

Auctions are sub–divided into two types, the *forward* and the *reverse* – the forward (or *ordinary*) being the original. In normal transactional trading, the seller places goods for sale at a fixed cost and invites (potential) customers to buy the goods at that price. In a forward auction, the quality, quantity, specifications and so on of the goods are made known and identified as 'lots'. At a given time and date interested parties make bids against each other, with the one making the highest bid being the winner of the lot – and so become the buyer of the goods. Also popular in B2C and C2C trading, auctions are normally seen as a way of selling goods you already own but no longer have a use for – making them 'second hand', or 'used'. This is also the case in a B2B environment. Although it is a business model to buy new goods in bulk and then break them down into smaller units to be sold at auction, common auctions are for surplus or obsolete goods no longer needed by the organization – machinery that has been upgraded or furniture from refurbished offices, for example – the UK's Ministry of Defence even uses an online auction to sell surplus goods. Overstocks of goods that have not sold as well as was expected are another popular auction item, with goods being sold in bulk lots to smaller retailers or – as is now common practice amongst a number of brand names – sold on the likes of eBay. Similarly, the assets of bankrupt companies are a familiar component of B2B auctions. Although there is a perception that auctions are for relatively low–value items only, this is not always the case. In the oil industry, for example, it is common practice to use auctions to dispose of drilling rigs and refinery facilities – all selling for millions of dollars.

Traditional auctions require the buyers to be present in a specific location at a certain time to make bids – or at least have a representative to bid on their behalf. Although these do still exist and are popular in some industries (antiques, for example) the seller can reach a much wider audience – and so achieve a higher price – by using the web to advertise the lots and allow bids to be made over a longer period of time. This means that the industrial buyer can constantly monitor auction websites – most are industry or market specific – and bid on products or services that are of interest. The online facilities mean that they can watch bidding in real time and so be aware of whether of not they are likely to win the bidding within their budget – something that is not always possible when bidding takes place in a period of minutes some time after the goods were originally advertised.

With online reverse auctions – also known as *procurement* or *event* auctions – the role of the buyer and seller are reversed, with the buyer announcing what they wish to purchase and then inviting bids to satisfy those wants. Also, unlike the forward auction where the seller hopes to increase the selling price to its optimum, the reverse auction seeks to drive the selling price *down*. Although the buyer posts their requirements sometime before (in order for the bidders to prepare their quotes) the event normally takes place over a short period, typically an hour or so. As the bidding is performed in real-time via the Internet, the result is dynamic bidding – and so this helps achieve a downward price pressure not normally attainable with a traditional paper-based bidding processes. The model can help organizations make significant savings – Procter and Gamble, for example, is said to have made savings in its supply costs of around 20 per cent by conducting reverse auctions (Hooley et al, 2008). Whilst auctions are normally associated with tangible products, reverse auctions are also regularly used for services. A company might use one to secure cleaning services, for example.

# MINI CASE

### UK government shows the way in e–procurement.

One area of B2B trading that has been proactive in the adoption of reverse auctions is government purchasing. Indeed, e–auctions are an integral element of the UK Government's Procurement Strategy for central civil government. A natural extension to established tendering systems, bidders are evaluated for their ability to meet the requirement (of the product or service being bid on) before they are invited to take part in the auction. With these other issues being suitably resolved beforehand, the focus of the auction is on price. The OGC eAuction site (www.ogc.gov.uk) reported in May 2007 that their procurement auction facility had helped 14 councils and six NHS trusts save a combined £7 million on IT hardware purchases. Though primarily developed for buyers – the site lets public sector organisations place tenders together and buy in bulk, so helping drive prices down – marketers looking to sell goods in the public sector must be aware of how these auctions work in order to use them as part of their strategic marketing initiatives.

## Tendering

With its origins in fair and equitable trading – and the elimination of bribery and corruption – the concept of tendering has been common practice in the public sector for many years. The term itself is a form of legalize where an unconditional offer is made by one to another to enter into the contract of transaction of goods or services at certain specified cost. A rudimentary description of what can be a complex operation is this:

1. The buyer makes known their requirements. As with all aspects of B2B trading this can be as basic as the provision of pencils, to something as multifaceted as building a bridge or providing a computing infrastructure. Exact specifications are included so that interested parties can assess the potential costs in detail.
2. Potential bidders make known their interest and submit details of their organization, its resources and capabilities. This is then evaluated by the buyer to ensure that if the firm's bid is accepted they will be able to deliver on–time and to the standard of quality stipulated in the requirements document.
3. If they meet the required standards, the company is accepted to submit a tender.
4. All interested parties submit a bid by a pre–determined deadline. These bids are sealed – meaning that only the bidding organization knows their submission until all bids are opened after the deadline has passed.
5. The buyer reviews all of the bids. Although price will be the dominant characteristic of any decision, it is possible for a higher bid to incorporate better specifications – a shorter lead time or higher quality materials, for example.
6. All entrants are informed of the successful bid, with the winner being awarded a contract for the work.

Before the Internet such a process was unwieldy, complicated and time consuming, particularly for small to medium sized businesses – with big

## Practical Insight

### The EU leads the way with tendering systems

The home page of SIMAP, the online gateway to EU public procurement. Source: http://simap.europa.eu © European Communities, 2008.

Even before the Internet was a reality, the EU Treaty principles of non-discrimination, equal treatment and transparency were encouraged in the European community's procurement practices. The EU Public Procurement Directives require all contracting authorities (e.g. all national and local governments) to provide details of procurements in a prescribed format, which are then published in the Official Journal of the European Union (OJEU – formerly known as the OJEC). As this (paper) document is freely available, in theory all companies have an equal opportunity to express interest in being considered for tendering. In practice, however, many smaller businesses are not even aware of its existence, never mind how to access it – and that is before they attempt to develop an 'expression of interest'. However, the OJEU is now available online in the form of the Tenders Electronic Daily – TED (http://ted.europa.eu). Not only are all procurement requirements listed, the submission process is also online.

The home page of PEG (www.business-select.com).

Furthermore, in many regions local online help is at hand. For example, in the North East of England, the PEG (procurement – engagement – growth) facility – in its own words – helps companies *'gain access to many markets and have the chance to bid for numerous business opportunities, quotations and tenders above and below the E.C. tender threshold'.* Developed and run by Nimis Ltd (www.nimis.co.uk), the project also partners with business support organisation (councils, chambers, universities, facilitated networks etc.) to provide onward help and support to companies who wish to bid for EU tenders.

## MINI CASE

### Losers and winners in the search stakes

After reputedly upsetting Google by buying–in a whole load of links, shopping comparison site GoCompare (gocompare.com) found their ranking with the search giant 'punished' in the search results for the keywords "car insurance". The insurance–comparison website saw their rankings drop from top of the organic listings at the end of January to way down on page seven at the beginning of February 2008.

Online competitive intelligence company, Hitwise (www.hitwise.com) put this into context by estimating the cost to GoCompare of what is effectively search engine oblivion. In a matter of weeks the company went from attracting 17.49 per cent of *all* search traffic from the term "car insurance" to less than three per cent – a drop of some 87 per cent. Given that Hitwise estimate that one in six visits to GoCompare.com came from searches on the term, the effect on their income is easy to imagine.

GoCompare's self inflicted wound was a late Christmas present for its main competitors – Confused.com and Comparethemarket.com – whose traffic (for the term "car insurance") more than tripled as searches clicked on the 'new' number one SERP listing.

Essentially, if you want your website to be found by potential customers, then appearing high in the listings on SERPs for keywords pertinent to your organization, product or brand is a given. Not to be high on the organic listings means that increased resources must be committed to other ways of driving traffic to your site – from offline efforts (see chapter 2, section 6) to online advertising – including paid advertising on the SERPs, which we cover in the next chapter.

*You Decide*    Take a look at all of the case study organizations and consider the importance for each of having high listings on SERPs for relevant key words. List them in order of significance of SERP listings, with the organization for which high listings are essential at the top and the one for whom it isn't so important at the bottom.

Alternatively, consider the importance of high SERP listings for your organization or that of your employer.

## 6.3   KEYWORD SELECTION

As I explained in the introduction to this chapter, I have chosen to differentiate SEO and advertising on search engines. However, there is one area where they are inextricably linked – keywords.

This is because the structure of both organic and paid listings is governed by the keywords that are used by the searcher. Therefore, although this section is included in the chapter on search engine optimization, it is equally relevant in the sections on both search engine and network advertising in the next chapter as they are also developed around keyword

> **Simply put, keywords are the core of all search engine marketing**

matching. So why is deciding which keywords your website should be optimized for so important? Simply put, keywords are the core of all search engine marketing. If – as I described in the introduction to this chapter – the search engines are striving to match the searcher with websites that address their needs, it is the keywords that the searcher types into the search box that the search engine uses to make that match.

The issue for the online marketer is, therefore, to decide what terms the user will type into a search box when they want the product or information your website sells or provides. But, like many marketing problems, the question revolves around trying to get into the head of the potential customer to discern what they are thinking – not what you are thinking.

Some examples of mis–matches are rather obvious – holidaymakers search for "cheap flights" – but airline marketers sell flights that are *budget*, *bargain* or *best value*, for example. Similarly, someone seeking medical advice after a relative has had a *heart attack* would search on those words – yet website content written by a doctor would talk about an *acute myocardial infarction*. Inward–looking keyword decisions also place too much emphasis on product names, jargon and brands. Even if your latest model, the '123–500 series rodent eliminator' is the best in the business – and already well known in pest control industry circles – if I am new to the industry or I'm looking for the solution to a problem I'm going to type "rat killer" in my search box, not "123–500 series". This notion is reinforced by research from Jansen et al (2008) which found that 80 per cent of searches are informational, 10 per cent navigational and 10 per cent transactional – the definitions for each being:

- Informational – looking for a specific fact or topic
- Navigational – seeks to locate a specific website
- Transactional – searching for information related to buying a particular product or service

For content developers this means that they should be looking to provide keyword–rich information that helps the searcher meet their needs. That may lead to an (eventual) sale or traffic that will achieve website objectives (e.g. advertising income).

Furthermore, the English language doesn't help the e–marketer either, with some words being a heteronym – the same spelling, but different meanings. For example, 'bow' could be the front of a ship, a weapon used by Robin Hood, a hat decoration or something you do when you meet the queen. Similarly, to find films featuring the secret agent, typing "Bond" into a search engine will not give only returns devoted to 007. Somewhere in the SERP will be DVDs from the James Bond franchise, but the chances are the top return will be something to do with financial services. Plus there will also be entries for the UK organization for International development and the girl band with the same name as the sought-after spy with a licence to kill. There are also words that originate in other languages that are used differently in English – Jupiter, Zeus, Oden all refer to the same god, for example. Similarly, sometimes foreigners use 'localized' versions of place names instead of the name that natives use, for example Munich/Munchen and Majorca/Mallorca. In many of these cases the search engine will pick up on the duplicates – but it will be worth checking before you make keyword decisions.

## RESEARCH SNAPSHOT

**Search terms are getting longer**

According to Google's 'Analytics Evangelist' Avinash Kaushik, the final quarter of 2007 saw the average Google query rise from three words to four.

Keyword problems do not end there, however. The level of competition in the market will also be a consideration. If your product is represented by popular keywords then your website is competing with every other website that has been optimized for the same term. This is particularly true if you sell a product with a generic identification – such as 'mobile phone', 'laptop' or 'car insurance'. One way out of this is to optimize for more unusual terms that address niche markets – the so–called *long tail* of keywords. However, for some companies this is not feasible – consider how many combinations of types of car and customer locations in the UK a car insurer would have to optimize for to match all potential queries.

**The long tail of keywords**

This 'infographic' demonstrates how search terms get longer as they move down the long tail of keywords.

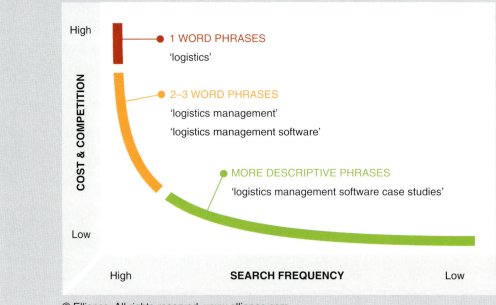

Still considering grammatical issues, search engines will *sometimes* correct misspellings and treat singular and plural as the same search – but this is not always the case (try searching on "hotel Athens" and "hotels Athens" and check both returns). A similar situation arises with *stemming*. For example, a search using the word 'swim' in a phrase may produce different results than the same term but with the word 'swimming'. In this example the chances are that the searcher was referring to 'movement in water', but the issue can be more complicated – the word 'swimmingly', for example, in a search term would have nothing to do with aquatic pursuits.

## Localization

A subject that has been around for a while, but is gaining greater recognition – and investment – by the search engines is that of searchers looking for something that is local to them. While the days of the printed Yellow Pages–type publications may not be under immediate threat, it is increasingly becoming the case that people use the Internet to find a local supplier, product, service or event. If this is so, the 'globalness' of the web loses its value. Having a SERP tell me that there are 2,330,000 vegetarian restaurants listed (as Google did on June 24, 2008) is pretty useless information if I want to eat out within a reasonable travelling distance from my home. My search is more likely to be "vegetarian restaurant Sunderland", "vegetarian restaurant Newcastle" or "vegetarian restaurant North East England" – and so the restaurants in those areas should optimize their sites accordingly. Needless to say, having a restaurant in Sunderland topping the SERP of a searcher in California is equally useless – and the search engines know it.

## MINI CASE

### I know you are there, but I can't find you

Carrying on from my point about vegetarian restaurants in 'localization', searches (on Google) for "vegetarian restaurant Sunderland", "vegetarian restaurant Newcastle" and "vegetarian restaurant North East England" all returned 'did not match any documents' messages, and yet I know that not only are there such eateries out there, but that they have websites. Furthermore, a number of meat–serving restaurants also feature extensive vegetarian menus – and they did not appear either.

Message to restaurants – optimize your websites for the different types of food that you serve. In reality, you need do little more than list some menus – just make sure your address is on each page to identify the geographic location of your outlet.

Localization impacts on keyword selection in a number of ways, not least that it can favour the smaller – local – business. The most obvious is in the address of the business, which – by definition – will include region, city or district that might be searched for by the customer. For the national (or even global) organization having a web page *optimized* for every outlet can be problematic – though not impossible for the can–do company. Another, less obvious, factor that can favour the local company is the use of *regional* phrases and terms. These are often difficult for the national company to adopt as they exist – and so are known – only in their own locale.

## Practical Insight

**We know where you live (well, almost)**

Ads are sometimes geotargeted – something achieved by looking at the user's IP address. If I am at work, for example, the IP address I am using will be that of the university that employs me. This means that ads that are more relevant to that geographical area are served first. Some practitioners suspect that search engines also use this technology in their organic listings.

## DECISION TIME

The best keywords must have both (1) strong relevance to your site – and so the product or service you are offering, and (2) high search volume – they should be the terms people *actually* look for. But how do you identify the right keywords? The following three options are available, in most cases all should be practiced.

1. Ask yourself. The chances are that you can think of a dozen or more keywords off the top of your head, but looking no further than these is a mistake. Your own ideas of what potential customers will use may differ wildly from what they will actually use.
2. Ask your customers. This can be offline or online, and can be part of a formal campaign or customers can be questioned in ad hoc fashion as and when they have contact with the organization. Simply asking a regular customer (of an offline business) what keywords they would use to find your website can be quite an eye–opener.
3. Use technology. An extension of asking your customers, the first step is to look at the metrics of your website to see what keywords people who actually visited your site used to find it. This concept can be taken a stage further by visiting one of the many websites that provide keyword research tools. Such tools collect data on search engine queries that have been conducted over a period of time. You can see what terms are searched on – normally by market or industry – as well as getting advice on related terms including synonyms and popular misspellings. Although the most comprehensive keyword research tools must be purchased, both Google's AdWords Keyword Tool and Yahoo's Keyword Selection Tool both provide keyword volume for free. Beware, however, if you are outside the USA. Many of the keyword research tools are US based and so may skew results for European searchers. Also, some of the most popular tools are based on Yahoo! searches – which may differ from the terms used on the more popular Google.

*Go Online*  There are a number of sites that publish the most popular search terms in given periods of time, follow the links from the chapter's web page for examples.

Another route to follow is to match your keywords with the *reason for purchase* of anything that you sell. Perhaps most obvious is where the purchase is a gift – so the search term a distant uncle might use is "Christmas present two year old girl". Similarly, those looking for inspiration might use "engagement gift ideas" or "surprise present for my wife". Along similar lines – and common practice in traditional advertising – is to provide a solution to a problem. In this scenario the searcher does not type in the name of a product (the solution), but the problem. For example, if the local wildlife is thwarting attempts to improve your lawn, you might use "birds eating grass seed" as the search term.

*You Decide*  Advise Robert Terwilliger on what keywords might match–up with what potential customers for the Modeller's Stand might type into a search engine. Bear in mind that most customers will not know of the existence of the product (case study 9).

Alternatively, conduct the same exercise on your organization or that of your employer.

## 6.4 ON-SITE OPTIMIZATION

Search engine optimization is based around two distinct categories, those that are concerned with the website itself, and those that are outside the parameters of the site. Evans (2007) refers to these as:

1. Query-factors – which consider the website content in relation to the keywords used in the search query, and
2. Query-independent factors – which rely on information from external web pages that link to the page being considered as a return for any search

In this and the following sections of this chapter we will look at these two elements in turn, starting with the on-site aspects.

### Keyword placement

The SE algorithm will consider the placement of the keywords within the web page, let's now have a look at some of those factors – or at least, what they are perceived to be. To fully appreciate these issues it is a good idea to put yourself in the place of the search engine. Its aim is to provide the searcher with results that will best satisfy their objectives of making that search. With this in mind, it is necessary to optimize your web pages to help the search engine achieve that objective.

The keywords can be placed in two aspects of the website, (1) that which is visible to the human visitor – its *content*, and (2) that which is part of the source code of the page and so is visible only to the search engines. Let's consider them both in turn.

## The web page content

Also known as the body text – because it fits into the source code in the *body* command – this is the textual content of the website that the visitor will read. Some put forward the argument that this is the most important aspect of SEO, and there is some validity – and sense – in their line of reasoning, which is this. If the search engine is looking to meet the needs of the searcher then the keywords that they use should be an inherent, organic aspect of the site's textual content. For example, consider this chapter as if it were a web page. Obviously it is about search engine optimization – that is its title. Now consider the keywords you might type into a search box if you were seeking answers to the sort of questions and issues I address in this chapter. I will [almost] guarantee that those keywords appear within my text. Three obvious search terms would be: "search engine optimization", "SEO" and "keywords". Now have a quick look to see how many times those three phrases appear on the pages of this chapter. How could I possibly write about the subject area without using those words? And that is the search engines' view as well – with the contrary also being true, a page that does not include those terms can't really be about SEO. Having said that, no matter what the benefits of keyword inclusion, you do not want a web page with content that reads something like:

> *'Search engine optimization, keywords, SEO are important to keyword, SEO and search engine optimization for web page's SEO, keywords and search engine optimization.'*

That too contains the keywords, but it makes no sense to the human reader – and the SE spider also realizes that it is search engine *spam* (nonsensical content designed to appeal to the SE). How often the keywords should appear within the text is debatable, though there is evidence that the SEs take *frequency* into account. For this reason there is some sense in keeping textual content short – keywords appearing twice in 50 words is a better ratio than four times in 400 words. There would also appear to be an advantage if the keywords are the first words on the page, or at least in the first sentence or paragraph. Once again, however, I refer you to *organic* content – a web page (or book) about apples would be strange if the word *apple* wasn't in the first sentence or two.

## Global SEO

For the organization that trades world–wide, SEO should take into account searches made in all of their geographic markets. This infographic illustrates some tips and best practices associated with successful international optimization.

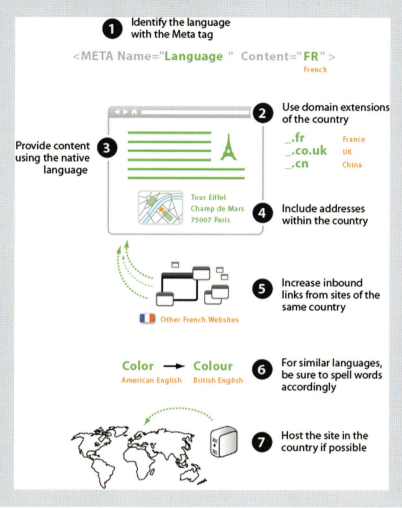

## The source code

The argument in favour of including keywords in a web page's source code is that it helps the SE spider identify the page's subject. In reality, with the exception of the page title – on which most agree – search engine optimizers disagree on the validity of this practice. However, given that each entry takes only a few minutes, the investment is not extreme – and as all of the entries should correspond with the actual content of each page it does encourage good content development.

The first batch of source code entries are the meta tags. These describe the contents of a web page, and can include 'status' information, the author's name or the name of the web design company for example. In the early days of SEO, because the meta tags were there to describe the page, the SEs focused on them. However, they are easy to abuse and for this reason the search engines reduced their reliance on them. The exception is the title tag – as it actually appears in the browser (at the very top of the browser window) it is a valid descriptor and so is foolishly abused. Other meta tags include the *description* and *keyword* tags. The latter is – it seems – universally ignored by the search engines. The former is also useless in SEO terms, but it is worth consideration as it can appear as the descriptive text for the web page on the SERP. Other places within the source code that may – or may not – be useful for SEO include:

- The *alt attribute* for an image. These are textual descriptions that appear as an alternative (hence *alt*) for an image. Although the practice is dying out as broadband availability increases, some people surf with the image function turned off (pages download faster), so the textual description says what 'missing' image is. More importantly, however, alt text tells the visually impaired what the image is – a legal requirement in the UK and much of the EU. Once again, the process is an exercise in *natural* SEO. If the image is a picture of a church in Humberston, the alt text should be 'Humberston church'. Not only does the visually impaired user know what it is, but the SE does also – so anyone searching on "Humberston church" will be presented with the page that features that picture. This is particularly true if the user has searched on the 'images' facility of the search engine. Sadly, many web designers treat both the disabled and SEs with some distain and simply tag the image as the file name – e.g. 123.gif – or nothing at all.
- The H1 tag. This is the source-code instruction that is used on page or paragraph headers (hence 'H') which makes the text bigger and bold. Again, the *natural* aspect of SEO comes in to play. If a website on Manchester United has a section on former players, there is likely to be a page for David Beckham. That page will – naturally – be headed with the player's name. Consequently the words 'David Beckham' would be in an H1 tag at the top of the page. It is obvious, therefore, that a search engine looking to match a search on "David Beckham" would offer up that page as containing content that is about the footballer. Note that other H tags present the text smaller than H1 – though H2, H3, H4 and so on are not thought to carry the strength of H1 in optimization terms. The same principle applies to the 'bold' command – the notion being that if a word is bolded within a paragraph then it is important to the reader and the subject – so the SE gives it more credence than other words on the page.
- Hyperlink text. These will be relevant to the SEO of the page to which they deliver the user. Rather than making a link on, for example, 'click',

or 'follow this link' – which mean nothing to a search engine – keywords should be used as the link text. Continuing the example of a Manchester United website, the former players page would have a link on it to the David Beckham page – if that link is on the words David Beckham, then that is telling the SE that the target page is, indeed, about that player.

- Part of the technical/design aspect of the website, but not in the source code, is another opportunity for keyword inclusion. This is the inclusion of keywords in the domain name and directory and file names used on the website.

  For example, consider the aforementioned David Beckham page. A logical URL for it would be:

  www.manutdwebsite.com/former-players/david-beckham.htm

  This makes it clear to both humans and search engines what the content of that page is. Although some doubt is laid on the SEO value of these, giving web page files names that match their content seems to be the type of logical practice that SEs favour. My own website – alancharlesworth.eu – is not likely to be about David Beckham, for example. By the same token, however, having too many slashes (/) in the URL might serve only to dilute the value of the page.

Worth noting at this point is that websites originally featured text and images only. Now they include such things as videos, PDFs, music, films and maps – which should all be optimized for the search. This is achieved by incorporating keywords in the titles and names of the various files. Other aspects of on–site SEO that fall outside of keyword placement include the following:

- Out–going links to external sites. In the next section we will consider the value SEs place on incoming links, however, outgoing links also add to the validity of your site in SEO terms. This does not mean that a page of links to every site you can think of will be looked on with any favour. As with all the other aspects covered so far, there is an element of how appropriate the link is – with SEs considering the quality and relevance of pages you link to. A link from my website to a site on dolls houses, for example, will gain no credit from a search engine. However – as is frequently the case on my site – if I have a paragraph of text describing an element of SEO, and it includes a link to an article on a search engine related website that is rated highly by the SE, then that approval will rub–off on my site.

- Advanced design technology. As with virtually every element of SEO, there is a divided opinion on how – or even *if* – the search engines spider websites developed in Flash or Ajax-type technologies. Without we go too far down the road of how these technologies work, it is fair to say that any site navigation that is embedded in the likes of Flash is more difficult for the spiders to read than is basic HTML or cascading style sheets (CSS). Another application that SE spiders don't like is that technology which is used to produce pages 'on the fly'. These are pages that are generated only when a user requests them – the results of an on-site search, for example. This means that the pages do not exist *permanently* – so the SE cannot refer searchers to them. Put simply, you cannot index something

- The web is fragmented. Advertising on traditional media is dominated by a limited number of players – on TV, for example, it is the commercial networks – and in print there is a narrow range of newspapers and magazines. Online, however, there are millions of websites, most of which have independent publishers. It is the development of the ad networks – predominantly Google's AdSense – that has opened up online advertising (ad networks are covered in section 7.6).

## RESEARCH SNAPSHOT

### Too busy doing other things

Small businesses appreciate the importance of advertising, but their focus is on running the business, therefore they do not *buy* advertising – it is *sold* to them.

*Source: Marchex (2008)*

The Internet does bring three significant benefits to the advertiser that are limited in other media, however. They are targeting, analytics and interactivity – let's consider them in more detail.

 Not only are web pages subject specific, but they must be *requested* by the visitor

1. Targeting. Not only are web pages subject specific, but as they must be *requested* by the visitor, there is an element of self–segmentation by all web users. For example, take a web page that has content about maintaining a good looking and healthy lawn. It is a reasonable assumption that if someone arrives on that page they have done so because they have an interest in gardening and grass, and so have clicked on a link (from a SERP, perhaps – which means they have searched on a term related to lawns) or they have typed the URL directly into their browser. This means that if I am marketing a related product – grass seed, lawn mowers, fertilizer or garden tools – that web page is an excellent place to host my ad. By definition, because the visitor is on that page, they are almost certainly in my target market and a potential customer for my product.

2. Analytics. As department store mogul John Wanamaker famously said *'I know half of my advertising is wasted, I just don't know which half.'* The reason for this is that with traditional media there is little or no evidence that any advert has worked. Some metrics are available, but they are limited in assessing actual results. For example, a TV ad might be shown during a programme that was viewed by 10 million people – but how many actually saw the ad? And of those who did, how many took any notice of it – and in that group, how many had an interest in the product? This is particularly true of branding ads where no direct sales can be attributed to the ad campaign. Online, the very technology that

runs the Internet can be used to assess the effectiveness – or otherwise – of any advertising.

Whilst the issue of whether or not a visitor actually saw, or took any notice of a banner ad on a page is still in question, if the customer clicked in the banner that it is a positive indication that the ad has succeeded in its immediate task. A further advantage of online advertising ROI assessment (often called return on advertising spend – ROAS) is the primary way of costing online ads. That is that you only pay if the ad has appeared on a web page, or if the visitor has clicked on it – meaning that Wanamaker's 'missing half' doesn't exist.

3. Interactivity. A final attribute of the online ad that is missing in all other media is its potential for interactivity. Arguably, an offline ad that prompts the customer to 'ring this number' is interactive in that it prompts a response and so is the instigator of an interaction. Online, however, the ad is truly interactive because the user can click on the ad for direct action related to it – ultimately (or perhaps idyllically) the customer could see an ad for a product and in a click or two, and within a few minutes, have purchased it without leaving their seat. It is also the interactive capability of the Internet that has seen a rise in online promotions, including contests and coupons. Although, strictly speaking, these are not ads per se – many of them are presented in such a way that it is hard for users to recognise a significant difference (e.g. if an ad on a web page includes a coupon, is that an ad or a promotion – or both?). Research by Borrell Associates (2008) suggested that such promotions may eclipse traditional banners and paid-search advertising by 2012 – with their measurability being a significant attraction to the e–marketer.

## Practical Insight

Online segmentation of ad delivery is broken into three distinct types of targeting – though the last can be used in unison with either of the first two:

1. Contextual – the ads served are relevant (in context) to the content of the web page.
2. Behavioural – ads are delivered in response to your prior actions on the web. Amazon's 'people who bought this book also bought this one' feature is an example.
3. Geographical – the use of IP recognition to identify where in the world the surfer is, with location–relevant ads then being served.

## 7.2  OBJECTIVES AND MANAGEMENT

The objectives of any ad campaign – and there should always be specific aims – will largely determine the nature and type of ad used, how it is managed and what analytics should be used in tracking its results. Like its ads' performance. As with websites (section 2.5) and email marketing (chapter 8.2) the actual analysis depends on the campaigns objectives. It is no use, for example, having a thousand users clickthrough on a sales–oriented ad if no one buys anything. However, there is a caveat to add with regard to measuring the overall success or failure of an ad campaign. It is entirely possible for all aspects of the ad to work perfectly – only for the experience of the customer after they have clicked on the ad destroy that good work. The 'significant experience' in question here is that of the *landing page* to which they are taken. So important are landing pages that I devote a full section to them at the end of this chapter. With regard to analytics, however, the advertiser should consider the whole process through which the respondent to the ad should pass in order to identify areas of failure – using a conversion funnel (see section 1.6) is recommended. If a potential customer clicks on an ad, continues through a landing page to a product page but leaves without making a purchase then it is unlikely that the fault lies with the ad, rather something else further down the funnel.

*You Decide*

Advise Martha Phelps on how she would be best advised to conduct – and measure – an online advertising campaign for her online department store (case study 13).

Alternatively, conduct the same exercise for your organization or that of your employer.

## 7.3   WHERE TO ADVERTISE ONLINE?

A marketer's response to this question would be 'those sites that members of the target market are likely to visit'. This is not the subject to be addressed in this section however, moreover the question is what *types* of websites can be considered to carry our ads.

Obviously, online ad placement is limited to those pages whose publishers accept ads as part of their income generation model. Until the advent of the search engine operated networks (see section 6 of this chapter) the majority of ads were limited to a relatively few categories of sites. In 2003, for example, 51 per cent of online ads were hosted on the major portals such as Yahoo! and MSN (Nielsen/NetRatings, 2003). Whilst this is still the case for banner ads, the ad networks have made it easy for even the smallest website publisher to include text ads on their pages, so opening up the scope for advertisers. The web has also changed over the last five years, with social media sites – which were few in number in 2003 – now hosting ads.

With comments on their suitability, the following are all potential hosts for online advertisers' offerings.

- Social media sites. These can be heavily targeted, but there are question marks over 'banner fatigue' – that is users ignoring ads on the pages. It is also the case that many social network members use them to 'escape' the barrage of ads that confront them in all other media. Simply reproducing that ad–saturated environment on social sites may well turn users away from them.

## Practical Insight

**Social media has few friends in advertising**

Although social media sites such as Facebook and MySpace report significant income from selling ad space on their sites, those paying for the ads are questioning the value of the ads – with clickthrough and conversion rates being generally poor. However, research into social network advertising by online brand specialists Prospective (2008) revealed that that 87 per cent of respondents felt that very few (58 per cent) or none (29 per cent) of the ads and offers on social media sites matched their specific interests and preferences – so maybe the advertisers need to consider their targeting strategies.

Poor contextual targeting can also generate problems for advertisers beyond low click-through rates. August 2007 saw a number of high profile brands – including Vodafone, Virgin Media, First Direct, the AA and the Central Office of Information (which coordinates UK government advertising) – withdraw from advertising on Facebook. The problem centred on the nature of the content that makes up the social media site – that is, unregulated user-generated content, some of which can be racially or politically sensitive. In the event, ads for these organizations appeared alongside a profile for the British National Party.

The social media sites, however, may look to the very nature of their sites to increase user acceptance of – and so interaction with – their on–page ads. Users selecting the products, brands or organizations that can advertise on 'their' pages, for example – in much the same way as they select their community 'friends'.

- Search engine results pages. Contextually accurate in that the ad's keywords match those of the searcher, but some industries are extremely competitive.
- Portals. High traffic, but there is often limited targeting potential for the top visited front page. Subsequent subject–specific sections can be better segmented, but attract fewer visitors.
- Community websites. Extremely good for targeting as, by definition, the page content is decided by the community members.
- Chat rooms, forums and message boards. Traffic might be low, but targeting can be accurate as the ads can be contextual to the subject being discussed.
- Blogs. Only a few blogs get meaningful traffic – and readers are often more interested in the blog content than any ads. Targeting can be accurate, however, and advertisers may benefit from the 'halo effect' of having ads on the page of an expert in the subject area (e.g. a search marketing company ad being displayed on the blog of a recognised 'guru' in SEO).
- Podcasts/video–clip pages. It is often the case that when a user clicks on a link to access an audio or video broadcast, it is hosted within its own 'page' – with any space (e.g. that surrounding the video window) being ideal for carrying display ads. This is particularly the case if the video takes a while to download – leaving the user as a captive audience for any ads that are running. Ads can also be embedded in the podcast or video.

- Print pages. Often neglected, some pages lend themselves to being printed – which means the ad gets printed along with the rest of the content. For example, a money–off voucher for a hotel or restaurant that is on the path of a requested route–map.
- Newsletters. Although these are more 'email' than 'website', they are often in html and so could carry ads. As with other 'community' oriented communication, the newsletter is likely to be very subject specific and so a good vehicle for targeted advertising – or perhaps better still, sponsorship, which although readers are likely to perceive as advertising, might be more acceptable to them.
- Emails (1). For the likes of Hotmail and Googlemail, this is a business model in its own right – with users getting excellent web–based email facilities in return for their out–going emails carrying ads. Although contextual matching can be effective, users of such services will vouch for any relationship between some ads and email content being ambiguous to say the least.
- Emails (2). Having your own emails carry ads is an option for some organizations, though this must be practiced with care. Having an ad on emails that go out in response to customer inquiries, for example, might work. However, adding an ad to every email that leaves the organization is questionable. How would a supplier, complaining customer, union spokesperson or government official – for example – feel if their business correspondence included an ad for your latest promotion?
- Question and answer (Q&A) websites. The name of these sites rather gives away their purpose, but the questions are both posed and – hopefully – answered by users. As the questions are on a multitude of subjects every page is an excellent host for contextual ads.
- Any other website. A curious category perhaps, but as the major networks now make it a relatively simple task to include ad–script in the HTML of a web page it is possible for your ads to turn up virtually anywhere that there is a contextual match–up between your ad's keywords and the content of the web page.

A further consideration for ad hosting is online gaming. Frequently disregarded because they are not websites per se, the use of ads within the games played online has a number of applications and advantages in reaching certain target markets, and with games being widely predicted to move online (away from consoles) this is a vehicle for online advertising that may increase in the future. The Interactive Advertising Bureau (2007) suggests a number of methods of in–game advertising, including:

- Static in-game – ads that are shown either within the game (on a billboard feature within the game, for example) or on a menu or leader board.
- Dynamic in-game – where displayed ads can be changed depending on location, day of week and time of day.
- Inter-level ads – displayed during natural breaks in gameplay, such as between levels – hence the title.
- Game skinning – sponsorship of display units around the game and/or custom branding integration into the game.
- Product placement – as with its film and TV equivalent, branded products are featured within the game – a mobile phone or car used by a character, for example.
- Sponsorships – where the advertiser 'owns' the game or an aspect of it. This might be sponsorship of a tournament, level or session of gameplay.
- Post-game – ads that appear on screen following completion of the game.
- Pre-game – ads that appear on screen before a game commences, possibly while it is loading.

## RESEARCH SNAPSHOT

**Girls like gaming, apparently.**

For those marketers who might stereotype gamers, the Nielsen Entertainment third annual Active Gamer Benchmark Study (released in Oct 2007) makes interesting reading. It revealed – perhaps surprisingly – that 64% of all online gamers are female. Other information of interest to online marketers includes that:

- In-game ads increased brand familiarity by 64 per cent
- Average brand rating increased by 37 per cent
- Purchase consideration increased by 41 per cent
- Average ad recall increased by 41 per cent

A footnote to this section is that although as online marketers we are concentrating on which sites can carry our ads, we should not forget our own publications for in–site ads. An obvious example is for the front page of an online retailer's site to include ads for specific promotions or products. Less common, however, is consideration of other pages for carrying a promotional message. Suggestions would include the following – but there will be others depending on the objectives of the site.

- Searching page. If the site offers such a feature the process might take a few seconds – so instead of a blank page or a 'please wait' message, why not feature a search or site relevant message. For example, a hotel searcher might be informed that the site also offers travel insurance at a competitive rate.

- Search results page. As with the major search engines, an in–site SERP could include an ad for a product that is related to the search. A search for 'casual shirts', for example, could include an ad for a range of polo shirts that are on promotion.
- Purchase confirmation. When an order is made it is normal practice to show a page confirming the details – why not include a pertinent ad? Admittedly, this comes at the end of a purchase procedure, so instant action is unlikely, but a branding message can be easily embedded on the page.

A caveat is that that to be effective these need to be carefully prepared and presented. Indeed, badly executed they could actually put customers off – the opposite of the hoped–for response. Note that this model uses the same concept as described in section 8.3 – email as medium for marketing messages. A warning with regard to hosting ads on your own website is that unless it is part of your business model, you should never host ads for other companies – it will simply devalue your site and impact on your credibility.

## RESEARCH SNAPSHOT

### Targeting: Must try harder

A survey of web users aged 18 years and older found that the majority of those 45 years and older believe online content is focused on younger age segments – and 83 per cent of respondents 55 years and older feel the focus of online advertising is on younger people.

*Source: BurstMedia, 2008 (www.burstmedia.com)*

## DECISION TIME

Though segmentation and targeting are staples of marketing, it is worth reminding the reader that wherever an ad is run the response rate will be determined by its relevance to the audience of the publication. So it is online. At its most basic, we are talking about women's cosmetics being advertised on a website that attracts women users and car tyres on a site whose visitors are most likely to be car owners – and so on.

An advantage of online advertising is that – like magazines – the content of a web page will determine its viewers, making contextual advertising relatively straightforward – though far from simple. As you will see in later sections of this chapter, both search engine and network marketing are generically contextual in nature. It is very much the case, therefore, that the e–marketer must have identified the target market for the product or service they are advertising before online placement is considered. Once that decision is made then website demographics can be matched with those of the target segment – with those demographics largely dictating the categories of sites that will be most effective as vehicles for the organization's ads.

> " the content of a web page will determine its viewers, making contextual advertising relatively straightforward "

*You Decide*    Advise Howard Johnson on what categories of websites might be most suitable for carrying ads for the Rockridge Museum (case study 1).
Alternatively, conduct the same exercise for your organization or that of your employer.

## 7.4   ONLINE AD FORMATS

The formats available to the e–marketer for online ads are determined by two issues, (1) the objectives of the ad, and (2) where they are to be displayed. The former is a decision that is made by the organization but the second – though there may be a preference – is determined by the publishers of the ad–carrying sites. For example, SERP ads on the big three search engines are text–only – therefore, if you want to advertise there your ads will not include images (note that this was true at the time of writing – mid–2008 – and may well change in the not–too–distant future). Portals, on the other hand, will often insist on banner ads. Ad formats are, therefore, loosely divided into *text only* and those that include images – commonly called *banner* ads. Note, however, that the title banner can be confusing in that a banner could actually present only textual content to the web user – the differentiation is *technical* – describing the type of file used on the web page.

### Text–only ads

**These can be divided into two categories, (1) within textual content, and (2) stand–alone.**

1. Text–link ads. As the name suggests, this kind of ad is one that is 'embedded' within a line of textual content on the web page. The concept stems from the practice of making links out of references to a product within textual content – something that is effective when compared to others methods of on–page advertising. It is, however, problematic for publishers to insert such ads because they can impact on the actual content and distort the natural flow of the narrative. It is common, therefore, that in–text ads are used only on sites where the publisher is also the advertiser – with affiliates being the prime exponents of the craft (affiliate marketing is covered in section 7 of this chapter). For example, a football–related website might include an article on David Beckham – with the name being a hyperlink to the player's autobiography on Amazon. Whilst this might be considered a valid practice on some sites, it would be more dubious in, for example, a match report on a game in which Beckham played.

   It is also the case that the actual content might be *tainted* by the inclusion of an in–text ad. Take my own pages about the city of Athens as an example (there is a screen shot of it in section 6 of this chapter). Essentially, it is simply my thoughts about Athens that might be useful to someone looking to visit the city. I have included textual 'network' ads down the sides of the pages as a demonstration for students (and readers of this book). It is clear that any ad is just that – an advert independent of my content. However, if on my page about hotels, I was to say 'I think the **Residence Georgio** was the best hotel in Athens', with the name of the hotel being a hyperlink to a hotel–booking agency who would pay me for any clickthroughs, then my credibility becomes an issue. The consideration for the reader is; do I trust the author in his advice on the hotel, or is he simply recommending it to get a payment? If such a doubt enters the readers' thoughts, then they may not have confidence in any of the other content. On the other hand, if the recommendation is *genuine* it will generate a higher CTR than other ads because the reader takes it as a sincere recommendation from the writer.

As we have seen in other aspects of this book, some of the terms and phrases related to Internet marketing can be confusingly similar – or even interchangeable, and here we have another example. The basic – and original – concept of *text–link ads* is as I have described above. However, technology has presented an augmented version of the original – dubbed *in–text* advertising. This is where the hyperlinked words do not take the user to a new website, but open a small pop–up ad when scrolled over by a mouse – the reason for them also being known as *rollover*–ads. Depending on your point of view, these are either an excellent source of income or an unwanted annoyance when reading website content. For publishers and content providers this is an additional form of income generation as they can 'sell' words or phrases that are *naturally* included within an article. For readers the usability of the page is compromised by the intrusion of the ads and content writers argue that their credibility is threatened as the ads can intrude on serious articles or content – as with my previous David Beckham example, perhaps.

*Go Online*   Follow the link from the chapter's web page for an example of poor in–text advertising.

2. Stand–alone text ads. These are *probably* the most common type of online ad (sources on the subject differ, and none seems absolute as ad definitions within surveys are mixed) if only because they are used by the search engines and network ad providers (see section 6 of this chapter). Not only do these ads appear on nearly every SERP, but their easy availability to any website publisher has resulted in them being (almost) ubiquitous on any site that is not published as part of the online marketing strategy of a specific company, brand or product. Depending on the network used, the format of these ads will be fixed, though they will normally have a headline, body text and advertiser's name – with each having a character–related limitation.

Also included in this category is the advertorial. A kind of crossover to the in–text ad in that the actual ad is integral to the textual content, advertorials can be used to great effect to reach consumers who switch–off to conventional ads.

# Banner ads

Now commonly re–named *online display ads* – perhaps to avoid the negative perception that many people have about them – banner ads were first used in October 1994 but faded in popularity as their cost–effectiveness was called into question. They have, however, made a comeback as their prices have dropped – and so represent a reasonably–priced online advertising option. Technology has also played a part in the banners' resurgence as they can now carry animation, video and other interactive features that appeal to both advertisers and web users.

It is another example of the lack of assimilation in Internet marketing activities that even the definition of the term 'banner ad' is open to debate. In this book I will use the classification as being any banner–type ad that is presented as an image rather than pure text. However – as previously mentioned – in some circles the term 'banner' has been replaced by 'display', with banner being used to describe a specific ad dimension – 468 × 60 pixels. Traditionally, however, banners come in a number of sizes that are recognized by website designers who can allocate suitable space within ad–hosting pages. These include:

- The aforementioned 468 × 60 – the 'standard', size
- 728 × 90 – 'leaderboards' that go across the top or bottom of a page
- 234 × 60 – the 'half' banner
- 120 × 60 and 125 × 125 – 'button' size
- 120 × 600 and 160 × 600 – 'skyscrapers' that go at the side of a web page
- 300 × 250 and 336 × 280 – medium/large rectangles that can be used within a paragraph of text.

Banner ads can include the following types.

- Static – images with no movement are simply hyperlinked to an advertiser's site or landing page.
- Animated – using GIF or Flash formats there is some movement on the banner – this could range from changing text to any kind of animation seen online. The use of more advanced applications in these ads has resulted in them sometimes being referred to as 'rich media' ads – a description also given to subsequent types of ads in this list.
- Interactive – offer a function to the user, most popular are games (e.g. a simple space invader–type game) or tool (check the current exchange rates, for example). With the latter it is important that the 'tool' is related to the product or service being advertised, in this example overseas holidays would be appropriate.
- Expanding – ads that increase in size when the mouse is run over them or they are clicked on. Subsequent *expanded* ads can present any of the features listed above.
- Video – where a short video is triggered automatically when the host page opens, or it is user-activated. Note that March 2008 saw Google launch video ads in the 'sponsored link' elements of their SERPs. The PPC charges are triggered when someone clicks to play the video in the ad.
- Pop–ups – second only to spam emails when it comes to online irritations, the pop–up ad has largely been made redundant by the 'pop–up

blockers' available on the most popular browsers. Certainly at one time it seemed to be impossible to visit any site without a plethora of tiny ad–bearing windows being automatically opened on every page. However, used judiciously, made easy for the user to close and with a defined purpose for each, the pop-up can be very effective.

- Pop–unders – these follow the same principles as the pop–up, except that they open under the user's browser window – making them visible only when the main window is closed.

## Practical Insight

### The pop–up now leaving from terminal two

I am reminded of the first pop–up I ever saw on a mainstream website – around January 1998. I was looking for flights to Boston on (I think) the American Airways website. Bear in mind this was before online booking was common, effectively you simply looked up the schedule as you would on a paper timetable – and rang the airline to make a booking. At that time there was no scheduled flight from London Heathrow to Boston, but when I was on a page for the Gatwick – Boston flights, a pop–up appeared saying that from June that year the airline was introducing a daily flight from Heathrow. I clicked on the pop–up, which informed me of a special offer for early bookings – of which I took advantage on the telephone later that day. Had the 'new Heathrow routes' been part of the Gatwick page I could easily have missed it, so the pop–up was an effective way of getting the message across. Sadly, marketers were not so sensible with their use and pop–ups soon developed a very poor reputation.

For another example of effective use of a pop–up, follow the link from the chapter's web page.

- Floating ads – a close relative of the pop-up, but more sophisticated, this is the image that 'floats' over the top of a web page's content rather than appearing in a small browser box. Effectively, all the positives and negatives of the pop-up apply to the floating ad – though perhaps with the additional irritant that the 'close' button is often difficult to locate.

*Go Online*    The Interactive Advertising Bureau has a list of guidelines on its website, including recognized a banner ad sizes, pop–up guides and rich media packages. Follow the link from the chapter's web page to see for yourself.

## DECISION TIME

Having decided on the objectives of an online advertising campaign the e–marketer must decide on which sites (or types of sites) the ads will appear. Essentially, the decision on the management of the ads, and the sites on which they will be hosted, will largely determine the type of ad to be used – a Google AdWords networked ad, for example, will be text only.

A constant thread to this book is that there are *some* aspects of online marketing that are best left to experts, and ad design fits into that category. That said, the development of ads to be used online is far more achievable to the 'do–it–yourself' marketer than ads in many other media. Indeed, as banner ads use the same scripting as websites, they can be developed by members of the web–design team. Similarly, if someone is employed to write web page copy they too could be engaged in writing the ad copy. The following points are a guide to what ad developers should consider when working on them.

As is the case for other elements of online advertising covered in this chapter, the objectives of the advertising campaign will determine the actual ad design. For example, an ad that seeks to generate income (e.g. stimulate sales) will need a strong call to action and perhaps a picture of the product. A branding ad, on the other hand, will require livery, name and logo to be prominent. Although the technology used will have an influence, the significant issues will come under one of two headings, aesthetic (how it looks) and textual (what it says).

## *Aesthetic*

 Any ad should grab attention, interest, create desire and invoke action

Any ad should grab attention, interest, create desire and invoke action (AIDA, see section 1.6) – and to do this it should, in some way, stand out from the page. One way to do this is with the visual appeal of the ad – its aesthetics. An important consideration is the size of the file, or files, that make up the ad. As a large file ad will delay the downloading of the page and may cause visitors to leave the site, publishers are likely to impose file size limitations. This is particularly relevant to banners that incorporate new–media applications.

### Practical Insight

**Ads appeal to our basic instincts – apparently**

Usability expert Jakob Nielsen suggests that there are three design elements that are most effective at attracting attention:

- Plain text (i.e. no pictures)
- Faces
- Cleavage and other 'private' body parts

Technically, an ad can be placed anywhere on a web page, though common practice has resulted in there being a number of 'standard' placements:

- The top of the page – above any other content
- To the extreme right or left of any page content
- In the middle of the page between sections of content
- At the bottom of the page – below other content

Note that the 'header-columns-footer' web page design (see section 3.2) lends itself to accommodating ads in any of these placements. Whilst few can agree on which is the best of these options, it is generally recognised that being 'above the fold' – that is, on the screen as the page opens before any scrolling takes place – is the place to be.

*Textual*

Whatever the objective of the campaign, each ad must convey a message to the target audience. This can be a simple communication telling of a promotion, 'the XXXX sale starts on Friday' for example, or something more complex. However, it is rare that a message can be delivered in picture form only. Even Nike's series of branding ads featuring pictures of famous sports stars will carry the tagline 'Just Do It' (and the 'swoosh' logo) – without which the ad is simply a picture of a sportsperson.

Essentially, the textual content of the ad has two primary objectives:

1. Let the audience know what benefit they will gain from purchasing the product (or whatever the objective of the ad is)
2. Make clear the *call to action*. I have considered this in some detail in section 3.2 with regard to website copy, and the same principles also apply to email marketing – but on the online ad it is essential that *something* entices the audience to take some kind of action, normally to click on a link that will start them down the sales funnel. As with websites and emails, the call to action should be specific and hi–lighted within the ad, e.g. featured on a red button.

## Practical Insight

### Advertising has a job to do

The following quote about ad development is from advertiser Alvin Hampel.

'If you remember the joke in my commercial while forgetting my product, the joke is on my client. If my presenter grabs you but you ignore what she's trying to sell you, I've blown it. If you are struck by my cleverness but remain unsold by my ideas, I've bombed as a copywriter ... the very things that are remembered most may contribute least to making the sale.'

I would add that the comment is equally valid with regard to website design.

Web users are canny folk, however, and well used to being advertised *at*. They are also wary of scam–type statements, 'you have won a prize, click here to claim it', for example. Such copy should be avoided by the reputable organization or they too will be perceived as scammers. Similarly, while witty headlines might raise a smile, they seldom help the ad meet its objectives. In his 1985 book, *The Copywriter's Handbook*, Robert Bly suggests that headlines have four functions:

1. Get attention.
2. Select an audience.
3. Deliver a complete message.
4. Draw the reader into the body copy.

Bly (echoing Hampel's sentiments) adds that a copywriter's chief job is not to be creative or amusing – it is to sell. The history of offline advertising is littered with ad campaigns that won awards from the designer's peers, but failed to register the brand in the conscious of the viewing public – making them failures in business terms. The Internet marketer would be well advised to take heed – their ad is, first and foremost, published to achieve the campaign's objectives – not win awards. As with websites, do not allow design to overcome substance.

*You Decide*

Consider the different types of online ad formats and offer Philip Ball advice on which might be most suitable for the Cleethorpes Visitors Association (case study 4).

Alternatively, conduct the same exercise for your organization or that of your employer.

## 7.5 SEARCH ENGINE ADVERTISING

It is important to appreciate that *advertising* on search engines is not the same as being featured in their *organic* results – that element of search engine marketing is covered in chapter 6. In this section we look at the listing on SERPs that are *paid for*. Although most people – if not all – recognize them as adverts, the search engines still avoid the term on their results pages. On their SERPs, Google calls them 'sponsored links', Yahoo! opts for 'sponsor results' and MSN Live 'sponsored sites'. Marketing students in particular might want to point out that there is a difference between 'advertising' and 'sponsorship' – and that the search engines seem to be using a loose interpretation of what *sponsorship* is.

## MINI CASE

### The origins of paid search

The concept is accredited to Bill Gross, who launched the first paid search engine, GoTo.com, in September 1998. At the time, search engines were inundated with spam – particularly from adult websites (it is generally recognized that pornography and gambling sites have always been at the leading edge of any developments in search engine manipulation). Gross thought the only way to combat spam was to have businesses pay to have their sites listed. This would lead to users being more likely to use a spam-free engine and, more importantly for GoTo, far greater income from PPC (pay per click) advertising – which would replace the CPM (cost per thousand impressions) method more common at the time.

Gross realized that the inherent value of intentional traffic was far greater than that of undifferentiated traffic. He also realized that some key words and phrases were more valuable than others, so ad prices were not fixed, they varied depending on demand. Although GoTo's arbitrage–based business model (it purchased links from other sites for a flat rate selection and so are given the default option – the *broad* match. Other options are the *phrase* match, the *exact* match and the *negative* match. Aspects of the four choices are addressed below.

| Type of match | Description | Advantages | Disadvantages |
|---|---|---|---|
| Broad | Ads are shown whenever the keywords appear in any order or combination with other keywords that might be search terms in their own right. For example: "Internet marketing" would appear under 'Internet marketing training' and 'training courses for marketing on the Internet' but not 'training courses for online marketing'. | As this is the default setting it requires least time to set up. The wide coverage might attract keyword matches you had not considered. Can be used for 'brand' advertising where appearing at the top of the ads for a search term is more important than direct sales. | As the keywords are not highly targeted, they may produce traffic that is not really in your target market and so is unlikely to convert. Generic keywords are usually more expensive as they have more competitors for the bids – in this example "Internet marketing" could be targeted by any organization that offers any kind of online marketing services (including the publishers of this book!). |
| Phrase | The same as broad match, but the keywords must be searched in the order they are bid on. "Internet marketing" would get no returns on 'marketing on the Internet', for example. | Can be useful if the phrase order is likely to match what you have on offer, i.e. it is the way your product is described. For example, "football boots" is more likely to be searched on than "boots for playing football in". | As with the broad search, the costs can be higher and the traffic not specific. |
| Exact | The keywords used by searchers must match exactly those bid on. The purchased term "Internet marketing training" for example, would not appear on a search for "Internet marketing". | Produces the most relevant matches and so should result in a higher conversion rate from any clickthroughs. An organization offering Internet marketing training, for example, would be found by a searcher looking for such a service rather than those seeking general information on Internet marketing (students, for example). | Far more time consuming to set up as a number of keyword bids may be needed to cover all aspects of the offering or terms the searcher might use. In the example, a user who searches on "Internet marketing courses" would not see an ad for 'Internet marketing training'. |
| Negative | This stops 'random' matches from a search phrase simply because it includes one of your keywords by making that word a *negative*. For example, a bid on "Internet marketing books" could add 'training' and 'courses' as negatives. | Makes targeting much more specific by preventing potential clickthroughs from users who do not want what you have to offer. Conversion rates should be improved with traffic being better targeted. | As with the exact match, this requires more input by the marketer and so is more resource intensive. |

Naturally, the selection of any of the above will depend on the product or service being advertised, the objectives of the ad campaign, the industry or market and the behaviour of buyers of that product – some of these issues are addressed in the following section.

- The long tail of keywords. This concept is built on the notion that the most popular keywords – those at the *head* of the list are the most expensive because they should have the highest CTR. However, at the other end of the list – the *tail* – are the rarely used, and so inexpensive, keywords. It is also the case that such terms are so unusual that anyone using them should be considered as being better candidates for conversion. Continuing the example used in the "keyword matching options" chart, I might extend "Internet marketing training" to "Internet marketing training Sunderland" or "Internet marketing training North East England". Or I could add "certified" or "validated" to "Internet marketing courses". The more specific the keywords become the fewer the competitors will bid for them – so they will come in at a minimum bid. That said, however, fewer – if any – users will include the keywords in their searches. But if anyone was to use the term "certified Internet marketing training North East England" and you offered such a service in that geographic location then there is a very good chance that searcher will become a customer. And remember, if no one uses the term – and so no one clicks on your ad – then it costs you nothing other than the time it takes to develop the ad and bid on the term.

## MINI CASE

### Search engine advertising as a competitive advantage

The immediacy of search engine advertising can be used effectively by the alert marketer – as demonstrated by dog food company Pedigree in 2007. They responded quickly to a nationwide pet food recall that didn't include their products and bought the keywords "dog food recall". Any user typing that phrase into Google were presented with an ad carrying the message: 'Pedigree dog food: 100% safe-not part of recall.'

The flip side of this example of excellent marketing is one of poor marketing. Those firms that were affected by the recall could also have produced an ad – but this one would have linked worried pet owners to an information page that told them what the problem was, how it was being addressed, what symptoms a pet might show, what care the pet might require … and so on. Sadly (at the time I looked) none had taken the opportunity to show that their company was concerned about the situation and that they were acting responsibly in seeking to alleviate the problem. Such a message with a contact 'hot–line' might well have helped head off any loss of brand reputation caused by the recall.

The concept can be extended to include the "differentiators" that are common in offline marketing environments. If, for example, I offered a budget Internet marketing service (rather than certified) I could bid on "cheap Internet marketing training". Similarly, if I ran courses that addressed different aspects of Internet marketing I might buy "B2B Internet marketing training".

Poor practice in this regard soon spreads around the affiliate community and you will find it hard to find high quality sites to carry your affiliate ads. There are few companies that have the resources to manage their own affiliate programmes, however – but as with advertising, there are agencies (affiliate networks) that will handle your affiliate trading.

## MINI CASE

An example of an agency that will manage your affiliates is AMWSO (www.amwso.co.uk). As with any out–sourcing, the convenience of having someone else do the work must be balanced with how the fee charged impacts on selling prices and gross profit.

**The home page of affiliate marketing company, AMWSO**

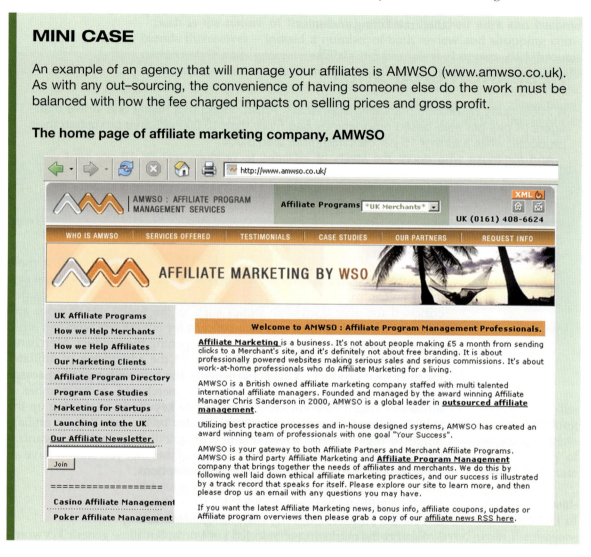

Gaining a good reputation as an affiliate merchant will depend on how you treat your affiliates and the service you offer – as well as your commission rates of course. Issues that need to be addressed include:

- Make incentives realistic. Over and above a set commission additional payments can be made for hitting pre–determined sales targets – e.g. making a sales quota per month. This should be achievable so as to work as a motivation and not a cause for dissatisfaction.

- Offer affiliates a reasonable time frame in which to generate commissions. Amazon, for example, has only a one–day window, so if a referred user purchases something after a couple of days or more the affiliate earns nothing. This is particularly pertinent for products that have a long buying cycle.
- Maintain good communications with affiliates so that they are aware of all news and events regarding the organization, products and the marketplace. Although they are unsalaried, the affiliates are part of your sales force – and should be treated as such.
- Provide superior display (banner) and text ads. Affiliates are not responsible for creating banners – and their quality will have an impact on clickthrough rates. Not only should there be a selection of types of message on the banners, but they should be offered in a range of sizes.
- Develop landing pages that are specific to ad messages. Sending leads to the product or company's site front page will damage the chances of those visitors their converting to customers (see next section for more on landing pages).
- Seek out the best performers and ensure they receive attention worthy of their status. Industry insiders reckon that the 80/20 rule applies in affiliate networks – that is, 80 per cent of sales come from 20 per cent of affiliate practitioners. Losing these 'super-affiliates' to a competing merchant could put a major hole in your business plan.

*Go Online*  **Parasites, copycats and spammers**

Using affiliates is supposed to help generate income – but there are those who will try to defraud you, follow the link from the chapter's web page to see some of the things they might try.

*You Decide*  Advise Robert Terwilliger on the suitability of affiliate marketing for the Modeller's Stand (case study 9).

Alternatively, conduct the same exercise for your organization or that of your employer.

## 7.8  LANDING PAGES

Imagine that you see an ad for a retailer on television that promotes a product in which you were interested. You then saw a similar ad in your local newspaper. These ads include details of a local outlet where the product is available. You drive to the locale and as you near the retailer, billboards repeat the promotional offer. As you pull into the car park signs adorn the shop's windows. Then you enter the store. There is no signage or guides to where in the massive building your sought–after

*Go Online*   For Google's guide to landing page and site quality, plus what business models to avoid, follow the link on the chapter's web page.

## DECISION TIME

As with so many aspects of advertising, both off– and online, the development of a landing page is best assigned to those skilled in its execution. Like ads, the design of the landing page can be handled by web designers, but it is the textual content that will determine whether or not the visitor moves down the sales funnel, or jumps back to the page on which the ad was displayed. It is this text that should be developed by an experienced copy–writer, in essence it is an *extension* of the actual ad. Like all websites, landing pages should be developed with the user in mind, with any copy being written from the buyer's perspective. It is the landing page that is the medium used to communicate the value of whatever you are offering – and how it will meet the needs of the customer.

Given the objective of the landing page – to move customers down the buying funnel – each one requires a number of essential elements, including that the page should:

- Most importantly – facilitate moving the customer onto the next step in making a purchase (or whatever the desired action of the original ad is).
- Have content that is short and to the point.
- Represent the organization – colour, layout, tone etc.
- Be self–contained – is serves no other purpose than to act as an arrival page from an advert. This means that it must contain all relevant information, but at the same time it must focus the visitor on the product being promoted.

The last of these points raises an issue of contention amongst some practitioners – should the landing page carry a navigation system that links the page to other elements of the organization's web presence? There are two schools of thought:

1. The landing page is a stand–alone page and there should be no links to any pages other than those that represents the next stage of the conversion funnel. They might even be hosted on their own promotion–specific domain name and so are not immediately identifiable with the advertising company. Proponents of this stance point out that any other links on the landing page will act as a distraction from the advertiser's desired action.
2. The landing page should be treated as another page in the organization's web presence and so should carry the site's navigation system (i.e. those links found on all web pages). Supporters argue that in order to maintain an online brand image the pages must conform to the criteria laid down for all other pages.

The solution to the issue lies in the objectives of the ads – branding, direct action or lead generation. For the former then a *corporate* web page will best suit the purposes of the ad campaign. For the other two objectives (direct action and lead generation) any additional links from the landing page will not only affect the momentum of customers down the sales funnel, but result in leakage from the funnel as visitors' attraction is taken by the titles of other link–pages.

A final consideration for the landing page is how it is managed after the offer is finished. By their very definition, landing pages are created for a specific ad or campaign – which will have a limited life–span. It is normally the case that once the promotion is over the landing page is removed. This can be a mistake for two reasons:

1. The page may have been indexed by the search engines – and so the link to it remains live, and
2. The ads may still be available on forgotten or ghost websites, and customers may still click on them.

To remedy this, the landing page can be left live indefinitely, though naturally, if the promotion is time specific the actual content will need changing. This could be a simple message explaining that the original offer has now ended and give a link to the site's home page. Better still, the link could go to any similar offers that are available at that time – though that course of action would require constant monitoring.

*You Decide*    Advise the board of the Matthew Humberstone Foundation Hospital (case study 6) on how specific landing pages will help convert 'lookers' into 'buyers'. What issues are particular to the hospital's products with regard to this issue?

Alternatively, conduct the same exercise on your organization or that of your employer.

## CHAPTER EXERCISE

Giving justifications for all your decisions, advise the marketing team at the Gilded Truffle Hotel (case study 3) on all aspects of online advertising covered in this chapter.

Alternatively, conduct the same exercise on your own organization or that of your employer.

## REFERENCES

Association of National Advertisers [with BtoB magazine] (2007). *Harnessing the Power of New Media Platforms*. Available on: www.btobon-line.com

Bly, R.W. (1985). *The Copywriter's Handbook*. Henry Holt & Company.

Borrell Associates (2008). *Online Promotions: The Big Shift*. Available online at http://www.borrellassociates.com

Goldschmidt, S., Junghagen, S. & Harris, U. (2003). *Strategic affiliate Marketing*. Edward Elgar Publishing.

Gregoriadis, L. (2008). *Affiliate Marketing Networks Buyer's Guide 2008*. E-consultancy (www.e-consultancy.com)

Interactive Advertising Bureau October (2007). *Games Advertising Platform Status Report*. Available on http://www.iab.net/resources/games.aspx

Marchex (2008). Perspectives on Local Online Advertising and Content www.marchex.com

Nielsen/NetRatings (2003). *The State of Online Advertising*. Available on www.nielsen-netratings.com

Prospectiv (2008). Social Network Advertising (www.prospectiv.com)

Scott, D.M. (2007). *The New Rules of Marketing & PR*. Wiley.

Seda, C. (2004). *Search Engine Advertising*. New Riders Publishing.

# Permission marketing

> *Men of business must not break their word twice*
> Thomas Fuller

## CHAPTER AT A GLANCE

## 8.1  INTRODUCTION

This chapter considers those elements of Internet marketing that are deemed to be permission based – that is, the recipient of the marketing message has given explicit *permission* for that message to be sent. This is the opposite of interruption marketing where the message interrupts whatever the recipient is doing to present itself – the obvious example is the advertising break in a TV programme.

As with so many elements of Internet marketing, however, there is inconsistency in this definition. This comes about because I – like many others – argue that the Internet itself is permission based. This is built on the premise that every web page must be requested by the user – effectively, therefore, it is given *permission* to show itself on the users computer screen. Indeed, this concept is key to web marketing in that because the user has requested your web page they are exhibiting an interest in your product, brand or organization which is not the case when firing multi–media advertising at them.

That said, in order to both study and practice the subject we must differentiate elements of Internet marketing into distinct sections – and so we have a chapter devoted to more specific permission–based Internet marketing.

It is a common misconception in e-marketing that email can only be used in a direct marketing context – that is, the electronic delivery of a sales message. This is wrong because it ignores the value of *all* email communications as a medium for carrying a marketing message. In the first two sections of this chapter we will consider these two aspects of email marketing separately, starting with direct marketing email and then looking at the use of email in non–sales communication.

## Customer Relationship management (CRM)

As with other elements of the discipline and practice we call *marketing* – the marketing mix and market research, for example – CRM is a subject in its own right and is not exclusive to the Internet. It is for this reason that I have elected to include it only as an element of this section and not address the subject as a whole. That Internet technology saw an advance – and a boom – in CRM practice, is a cloud to the issue that it is not based, or dependent, on the Internet. Although the concept of CRM pre-dates the development of Internet technology, the mid to late 1990s gave light to the concept that intelligence on customers could be managed using those technologies. Thus, the end of the 20th century saw many organizations spending vast sums of money on CRM software and/or systems – many of which were sold as the panacea to all marketing ills. Not only is history littered with empirical evidence of the failings of these systems, but academic research supports the view that they did not achieve their objectives (see Ebnar et al, 2002, for example). The principle problem with CRM (at that time) was that it was perceived as being about IT, and so it was predominantly IT–led. Systems were developed that gathered vast mountains of data simply because the software had the ability to gather it. That few (if any) organizations had staff

> **"** managing relationships with customers is a better description of the objectives behind the concept **"**

with the ability to (a) turn the data into information, (b) interpret that information, and (c) use it in any kind of tactical or strategic planning was almost irrelevant because no one had the time to keep pace with the data being spewed forth on a daily basis.

CRM practice changed fundamentally when IT consulted other departments about their requirements of any system, then developed the software to meet those needs. As this book is about marketing I am bound to say that CRM is a marketing discipline – indeed, I think that *managing relationships* with *customers* is a better description of the objectives behind the concept. This re-wording shifts the emphasis to customers – as it should be – and away from customer relationship *management* where the title suggests the task of managing something that is a burden to the organization – like waste disposal, for example.

Another key element to CRM is that it assumes there is a relationship between the organization or brand and the customer – and that the customer wants a relationship. Marketers, and particularly front line sales staff, recognise this and adapt their actions accordingly. However, the all-encompassing CRM systems of the last century (designed by non-marketers) took no account of this and attempted to 'force' CRM where no relationship existed. The results were the exact opposite of what was intended.

It is also the case that CRM should be practiced wherever there is a touch-point between organization and customer – hence it cannot be confined to the Internet only. It is for this reason that I have decided not to include a section in this book that is devoted to CRM. Pure–online CRM (e–CRM) does exist, but it is encompassed within the other elements of online marketing rather than being isolated as a separate subject. Much of this chapter, for example, is CRM–related in that actions are based on the information held on customers. Similarly, social media marketing relies on *managing* the online relationship between the website publisher and other members of the community. Important to add, however, is that data gathered online can be included within any strategic CRM initiative.

## 8.2   EMAIL AS A MEDIUM FOR DIRECT MARKETING

Although research, such as that from Pew Internet & American Life Project (2007) which found that US teenagers favour social networking sites to connect with friends, supports a common view that email as a marketing tool is now unfashionable, email's demise is far from absolute. The simply reason for this is that it works. According to research carried out by Vertis Communications (2007) 21 per cent of adults have responded to direct mail advertising in the month prior to the interview by visiting a sender's website. The same research suggests that while only one percent of adults read all email advertising available to them, 20 per cent *occasionally* read emails personalized to them. With statistics like these there is no wonder organizations continue to send direct marketing emails as part of their Internet marketing strategy. Note, however, with regard to teenager's diminishing use of email, (1) if they are your target market, think of other methods of communicating with them, and (2) when they move into employment they will use the media of communication embedded in organizations – notably the telephone and email. Only time will tell whether the next generation adapt *their* practice in the workplace – or change the way their employers communicate.

---

## RESEARCH SNAPSHOT

### Email is dead – or is it?

Research published in the McKinsey Quarterly (www.mckinseyquarterly.com) in September 2007 revealed that of the marketing executives surveyed, 83 per cent used email as a marketing tool – ahead of paid search, display ads and online video.

Furthermore, the Center for the Digital Future (2008) found that 99 per cent of Internet users said they used email. The same report found that non–commercial applications of email communication are increasing, with more than half of users reporting that they have used email to contact a teacher or government official.

---

Direct marketing email campaigns can be broken into seven distinct elements, chronologically, they are:

1. Determine objectives of the campaign
2. Development of a mailing list
3. Development of the content
4. Development of the landing page
5. Testing of content and technology
6. Send
7. Measure the results

Let's now consider each of these in more detail.

## Determine objectives of the campaign

A recurring theme of this book is that the setting of objectives for any marketing exercise – off– or online – is essential – and email marketing is no exception. Without an objective (or objectives) none of the following tasks can be completed effectively – and so the campaign will not be successful (with no objectives, how would you know if it were successful anyway?) and will not give a return on any investment. For direct marketing emails, the objectives will normally be to elicit an action from the recipients. Although income generation is likely to be the ultimate aim of the email campaign, that can be too simplistic – not least that the email might start a recipient down the sales funnel, but some other element of marketing (price too high, for example) may stop them making a purchase. It is necessary, therefore, to consider the email campaign as (1) an element of an integrated marketing campaign where it dovetails with other elements of the strategy, or (2) a stand–alone operation. Where the email marketer's objective might be to drive customers to a web page or a bricks and mortar store, after that, it is the responsibility of the website or shop to convert those visitors into customers – effectively, their objectives.

Sales are not the only objectives, however. The email campaign might be looking to increase registrations to a newsletter, encourage membership of a club or promote donations to a charity. In section 1.6 we considered how the AIDA concept can be applied to Internet marketing – and it is also true of direct marketing by email. All of the elements – attention, interest, desire, action – can be achieved using email, indeed a well–constructed message might accomplish all four in a single email. For example, a solicitor might be aware of a new law that will impact on a certain industry. Therefore, a mailing list made up of managers in that industry can be used to contact them. The same message would make them *aware* of the new law, develop *interest* by showing how it will impact on them, create *desire* by spelling out how the impending problem can be averted – and finally promote *action* by directing them to a web page or contact phone number for the solicitor.

## Practical Insight

### Spam – and legal attempts to stop it

Although an absolute definition is difficult, in legal terms spam is email that is sent to a recipient without them giving permission – explicit or implied – to receive it.

Both the European Union and the USA have introduced laws in an attempt to cut down email spam. The EU Directive on Privacy and Electronic Communications (introduced at the end of 2003) is Europe–wide, though how it is interpreted and implemented is up to each member country.

The CAN-SPAM Act of 2003 (Controlling the Assault of Non-Solicited Pornography and Marketing Act) – which has a much higher profile – set requirements for those who send commercial email and gave consumers the right to ask emailers to stop spamming them. The Act covers direct marketing email (where the primary purpose is advertise or promote a commercial product or service) but not those emails that transmit a 'transactional or relationship message' (which update a customer in an existing business relationship, for example).

Whilst both laws were generally welcomed, they were criticised for not going far enough. The principle problem with each is that they apply only to emails sent from within the relevant countries and cannot be applied to entities operating outside those boundaries.

Rather than adding clarity, both of these pieces of legislation manage to further cloud the issue in their definitions of 'spam'. However, Chad White of the Email Experience Council offers a more down–to–earth interpretation, He says an email is spam if it is (1) unsolicited, (2) sent from spoofed addresses, (3) fraudulent, (4) full of objectionable content, (5) likely to contain viruses or malware – or all of the these.

For more details on both the Directive and Act follow the link on the chapter's web page.

## Development of a mailing list

If you are going to send emails, you need email addresses to send them to. However, to simply send an email to any email address you can find is both poor marketing and potentially illegal. Essentially, therefore, the Internet marketer should be looking for the email address of (1) potential customers who are in the target market for whatever is being promoted, and (2) people in that segment that have given permission to receive promotional emails. These mailing lists – as they are called – can be built in two ways, internally or external to the organization. Let's look at these two methods in more detail:

1. Internal. Lists that are developed in–house will always carry the most integrity – and so produce best results. Often an integral element of other marketing initiatives such as CRM or retailing, email addresses can be gathered both off– and online. Offline, practices used for decades to collect postal addresses can be applied to email addresses. These can range from free give–a–ways to competitions to win a free meal if you leave your email address at a restaurant. Online, technology can be used to save any email address that is gathered as part of the organization's online operations – a customer order or an online quotation form, for example.

   No matter what methods of collecting email addresses are used, for reason of good practice and legal requirement, it is important for the online marketer to get permission from recipients to send them emails. There are two ways to get this permission:

   I. *Opt-out* is where the receiver must take an action to opt-out of receiving email messages. For example, the default setting for a message that says 'do you wish to receive email messages' is for there to be a tick in the 'yes' box. The visitor must, therefore, remove the tick if they do not wish to get emails.

   II. *Opt-in* is where the receiver chooses to receive email by taking an action. With a *single* opt-in they could, for example, 'tick' a box on an off- or online form. This is open to abuse, however. Whether for a joke or more malicious purposes, someone might tick to receive email and enter the email address of someone else. Naturally, the receiver is not aware of what has happened and assumes any email from this source is spam. *Double* opt-in, however, requires confirmation by the recipient. After the initial opt-in is made, an email is sent to them giving details of the opt-in agreement. Only when the recipient replies to this email does the opt-in become active. Opt-in reduces take-up rates but produces databases with the most integrity.

      Note that a further use of the *opt-out* facility is that there should be such an option at the bottom of all emails sent to people as the result of them opting to receive emails – in other words, they must be able to change their minds. Although this is a legal requirement in the USA, it should also serve as a warning to keep any email contact relevant and interesting – or you will lose that customer if they elect to opt-out.

## Practical Insight

**Remove barriers to email subscription**

When Travis Falstad joined Hot Topic (www.hottopic.com) he found that the email sign-up process asked for 20 pieces of information. Users were unimpressed by the effort required and Hot Topic's list size was shrinking fast. A simple change got the subscription rate moving up again – the form was reduced to just three elements; email address, confirmation of email address and birth date.

*Source: Travis Falstad, speaking at the Email Evolution Conference. February 2008, San Diego, USA.*

2. External. This option entails the buying–in of a list of email addresses from a third–party supplier – and can be effective if care is taken. There are legitimate brokers who, as a business model, collect email addresses from people who have given their permission – opted–in – to receive emails from organizations with whom they have had no prior communication. These lists are then segmented and sold – or to be more accurate, *rented* – to companies who wish to target specific groups of customers. A car manufacturer that has launched a new model that is particularly suitable for towing caravans might, for example, buy in a list of known caravan owners. For smaller organizations there is an added advantage that some of the brokers, particularly those who value their legitimacy, will also handle the sending of emails on behalf of their clients. Obviously, the purchase cost per email address will depend on how specific the list is, and therein lies the main problem – that of the validity of the list of email addresses. Some – less scrupulous – companies will simple gather email addresses from anywhere they can (often by harvesting them from websites) and sell them on for a few dollars per thousand. As these address owners have not given permission to receive emails, any sent to them are spam. Such lists are to be avoided by legitimate companies who value their reputation.

Unless you are conducting a one–off, never–to–be–repeated email campaign, it is important to treat the mailing list as a living thing that requires constant attention. Not only will new names be added, but addresses will need to be purged – whether by request (opt–out) or because the address has bounced a previous email. Simply conducting a periodic review just prior to a new campaign is not sufficient if the campaign is to be successful.

## Development of the content

The development of the email itself – what the recipient will get in their in–box – has two distinct elements: (1) the technical aspect, and (2) the textual content. Let's now look at these in more detail.

259

1. Technical. The problem with email is that it is not guaranteed to look the same when it is received as when it was sent. This is because different email client systems *read* and present the message in a different way depending on how both the defaults settings of each service provider and how each recipient has set up their own system. A basic example is whether the service provider, by default, presents images (Messenger Express does, Google Mail does not, for example) or whether the user has their default set at 'show images' or not. Obviously, any image–only email sent to a Googlemail account will not be seen by the recipient unless they take action to open the image. Also with regard to images, some browsers present them above any text, others below – and some at the side. Not only is this aesthetically problematic for the email marketer, but it can destroy a sales message within the email. Similarly, recipients might use a preview pane for their incoming email, therefore they see only around a third of any image. So if images do not download in a uniform manner, why not use only plain text? For some, this is an answer – in some circumstances, a short text–only message might be all that is needed to prompt a response. However, text only means there is no corporate image projected, or pictures that might help sell the product are missing – so reducing the potential clickthrough rate. As with all things marketing, the answer lies in giving the recipient (the customer) what best suits them or their needs – even if this means asking them to select 'text only' or 'html' when they opt–in. Note that further technical issues related to delivery are addressed in the next section.

2. Textual content. As with the development of website content (see section 3.4) writing the words for a successful direct marketing email is a specialized job.

   The sender has a few words – and very little time – to impress upon the recipient that (a) the email is not spam, (b) it is relevant to them, and (c) they should take the action it promotes. Not only is the content important, but the subject line is essential in encouraging the receiver to even open the email – or simply click on 'delete'. Get the subject line wrong and any resource spent on the rest of the email campaign is a waste of time because the recipient simply won't open it. In essence, the textual content of the email is sales copy, it is there to elicit an immediate response – and very few people can write it effectively. The days of a subject line that says 'open this for a free gift' being effective have long since passed – if they ever existed in the first place. As with any sales or advertising, the subject line should seek to sell not the product – but the advantages gained by its purchase.

   For example, a subject line that says 'shop for insurance' has no appeal to me – particularly if I have all the insurance that I need. However, a subject of 'are you paying too much for insurance' might well hit a nerve, particularly if I have an insurance policy due for renewal in the near future.

*Go Online*   As mentioned earlier in this section (re spam) the legal aspects of email marketing are complex – in the UK, for example, each direct marketing email should include a company registration number, place of registration and the registered office address of the business in the email footer. For sources of more information on the subject, follow the link from the chapter's web page.

## Development of the landing page

In section 7.8 great emphasis was placed on the importance of landing pages – so much so that I elected to devote a whole section to the subject. As direct marketing emails also seek to elicit a response from the receiver (as do ads) it is equally important to consider carefully the landing page for every email. Rather than covering all the details again here – I will simply advise you to take another look at section 7.8.

## Testing of content and technology

If there is an element of email marketing that is neglected – or even missed out altogether, testing is it. And yet the most successful practitioners will spend as much time on testing as they will on all the other aspects of the campaign put together. As with the development, testing of emails must consider technical issues and the content. Before reaching that stage, however, more 'traditional' direct marketing issues need to be tested – including such things as the target audience (market segment) and the promotion that is being transmitted (e.g. 20 per cent discount or free shipping). You might be surprised how many email campaigns' failure is nothing to do with the medium of communication and everything to do with a promotion that does not appeal to the recipients. A successful clickthrough rate can also be negated by a poor landing page, therefore it too should be tested.

*Go Online*   For more on the technical issues surrounding direct email marketing, follow the link on the chapter's web page.

Technical issues will include the aforementioned browser issue – does the email configure in all browsers and email service provider client system? If images are used, the size of the images must be checked – many client systems (of universities, for example) will block emails that are above a certain file size. Anti–spam facilities – known as spam filters – will also look at elements of the email to assess its validity. Infringe any of their rules and not only will the email not be delivered, but your organization may be branded as a spammer, and have all subsequent emails from your domain blocked. A proactive approach is to have 'authentication tags' embedded into each email to identify the sending organization. These enable receiving ISPs to verify that senders are actually who they say they are, making it virtually impossible for spammers to hide their identities.

## Practical Insight

### Guilty of spam by association

One of the issues with spam is that it is the offending email's Internet protocol (IP) address that is 'blacklisted', not the organization committing the offence. This can be problematic in that most email service providers (ESP) share IPs across a number of customers. This means that in a pooled IP environment the bad practices of one company can spoil the (innocent) reputation of everyone in that pool. The way around this potential problem is to pay the ESP for a dedicated IP address. That is, it is used only for the emails of only one of their clients, therefore the email reputation belongs to that organization, rather than a group of clients. Further reputation security can be achieved by using a dedicated server that hosts only your IP (numerous dedicated IPs can be used on the same server). Naturally the cost increases accordingly, and so this option is only really for *serious* email marketers.

Testing of textual content – as well as images and presentation – most commonly uses A/B testing, where an equal number of test–users are exposed to an email that has been developed in two formats – hence A and B (using more than two options is known as multivariate testing). In the test, equal quantities of each variant are directed to recipients and results recorded to measure which works best. A basic – and obvious – test is to use different subject lines and see which results in more emails being opened. However, professional email marketers will also test everything from the headline through the colour of the text and different images to the size of the 'click here' button. Although this may seem excessive to some, it is very much a task of finding the best option in a numbers game. For example, if a million emails are to be sent and changing one element improves the open rate by a quarter of one per cent, that equates to a significant number of potential customers reading the marketing message. Make another three changes with a similar improvement and the open rate goes up by a full percentage point. Given that a clickthrough rate that is measured in single figures is the norm for many industries – an extra 10 thousand emails being opened is a significant improvement.

## Practical Insight

**Do as we say, not as we do**

This is what can happen if you don't test your emails in all browsers. What's worse, the message was an invite to an OMMA event – the OMMA being a body that represents the business of Online Media, Marketing and Advertising. Oops.

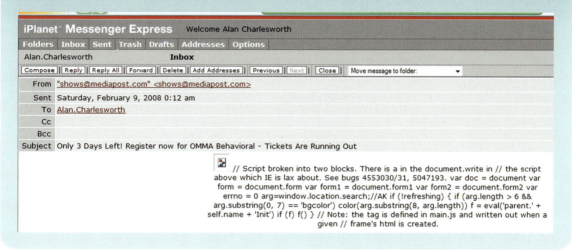

## Send

This is the easiest part of the process, with technology requiring that all is needed is to click on 'send'. However, consideration might need to be given to which day they should be sent or even the time of day they are posted (note that there may also be an issue with time zones). It is also possible that they should be sent in batches to prevent an overload on whatever facility will handle potential responses – for example, if recipients are encouraged to contact a freephone number they do not want to find it permanently engaged.

## Practical Insight

**Today's the day**

Over the years much research – and testing – has been conducted into what day is the best day to send out emails. And the answer, depending on who you ask, is ... Monday. Or Tuesday, or Wednesday, or Thursday, or Friday, or Saturday, or Sunday.

Essentially, unless your offer or message is day specific, then it doesn't really matter – not least that you have no control over when the recipient will actually read the email. It also stands to reason that *if* there were a universal best day to send emails, wouldn't our inboxes fill up on that day, and that day alone?

## Measure the results

One of the main advantages that email direct marketing has over its offline relation is that technology can be used to determine the success – or otherwise – of the campaign.

Like the metrics for websites, those for email campaigns should concur with the objectives of the campaign of which the emails are a part. It is also the case that the ultimate metric is how successful the campaign has been in its primary objective – sales generated, leads created or membership sign–ups, for example. However, there are metrics that can be tracked in order to assess the various stages required in meeting – or otherwise – those objectives. It is, therefore, necessary to identify those aspects of the campaign that can make or break the chances of success, these are commonly known as key performance indicators (KPIs).

Generic email KPIs would include such things as:

- Delivery rate – the percentage of sent emails that reach a 'live' in-box
- Open rate – the percentage of sent emails that are opened by the receiver
- Clickthrough rate – the percentage of sent emails that are opened and then have an embedded link 'clicked'
- Viral rate – how many opened emails are forwarded to another address
- Campaign comparison – any of the above measured against metrics from similar previous campaigns

These metrics – like all useful metrics – not only help measure success, but help to identify elements of the campaign's process that are not as effective as they should be. For example, if the open rate is low that might suggest that the subject line is not sufficiently attractive to the receiver that they feel compelled to open the email and read the full message. Note also that delivery, open and clickthrough rates are grouped as 'response rates' – valuable to branding campaigns because they suggest exposure to a brand message. KPIs for email campaigns with specific objectives might include:

- Sales units
- Sales' value
- Orders
- Average order value
- Total profit
- Downloads
- Leads generated
- Response rates – for both opening and clickthrough

Note that all of the above can be calculated per total emails sent, total delivered, total opened or how many clickthroughs from the email.

Two other useful metrics represent the extremes of results. They are

- The churn rate – the loss of addresses from an email list. This could be because the email is not delivered (e.g. the address no longer exists) or because the receiver decides to unsubscribe from the mailing list.

- List growth – how many people decide to join a mailing list as a result of an off– or online list–building campaign.

It is worthwhile for the email marketer to note that company CEOs, MDs, owners or finance officers prefer metrics that determine how the email campaign is benefiting the organization. For example, 'units sold' is a tangible metric that means something to them, whilst 'delivery rate' is an intangible that is not represented on the profit and loss sheet.

## RESEARCH SNAPSHOT

### Spam by any other name

A survey by online marketing services provider Q Interactive and MarketingSherpa (2008) found that consumers' perceptions of what they consider to be spam does not match 'official' definitions. The report found that 56 per cent of consumers consider marketing messages from known senders to be spam if the message is 'not interesting to me'. Furthermore, 50 per cent think that 'too frequent emails from companies I know' also to be spam. This is problematic for online marketers as most ISPs make readily available a 'report as spam' button on their email browsers – this means innocent companies can find themselves being reported as spammers for sending emails that the receivers have actually requested.

## DECISION TIME

After the initial decision of whether or not direct email marketing might work for the organization (i.e. there are feasible objectives that will give an appropriate return on investment), the next key consideration is how will any objectives be translated into something that the receiver will value – in sales terms, what is the *offer*? The offer can take a number of guises, for example:

- A financial incentive – buy–one–get–one–free or free shipping
- Time specific – offer ends Saturday or one–day–only sale
- No direct–monetary value – a quality upgrade or accumulated purchases rewards.

The next issue to address is how that campaign might be planned and implemented. At this stage, what denotes a *campaign* is open to interpretation. Certainly for the major brands the campaign will involve the sending of thousands, if not millions, of emails at one time. However, for the SME – or even larger company that operates in a number of niche markets, the number of emails sent might not reach three figures. Obviously, the number being sent will impact on (a) whether any campaign is worthwhile, (b) what resources are required, and (c) are those resources available in–house or is it necessary to out–source the operation?

## RESEARCH SNAPSHOT

**Why customers open emails**

The Return Path Third Annual Email Consumer Survey (2007) revealed the key reasons for people to open an email sent to them. Though the first will include personal emails from friends and relations, the others are significant for online marketers in developing direct email campaigns.

| | |
|---|---|
| Know and trust the sender | 56 per cent |
| Previously opened and thought valuable | 51 per cent |
| Subject line | 41 per cent |
| Only open emails I normally read | 32 per cent |
| Discount | 20 per cent |
| Free shipping | 17 per cent |

Following the chronologically order of the seven distinct elements of email marketing listed in the previous section, the next issue is the development – or acquisition – of a mailing list. This issue will depend on the nature of the objectives. If existing customers are to be targeted for increased business then it is likely that their email addresses will already be know. However, if gaining new customers – or generating sales leads – is the objective then an email list will need to be bought in.

## Practical Insight

**Whitelists prevent being blacklisted**

Registered with individual users' Internet service provider (ISP) and overriding any spam filters the ISP might operate, a whitelist is a list of email addresses that an Internet user is always willing to receive email from. Because the practice is seen as building a list of people that it is *safe* to receive email from, whitelists are also known as safelists. For the online marker the aim is to be included on the user's whitelist – which can be achieved by having a clear message on emails and subscription forms asking the subscriber to add the company's email address to their safelist (adding the sender to your address book normally serves the purpose).

Although guides are available, for a successful campaign the content development is best left to experts in the field. This will, however, cost money and should be taken into consideration when setting objectives. For example, a niche business' goal of identifying 20 new customers who might have an average spend of five pounds is not going to give a ROI if the development costs are over a couple of hundred pounds. This being the case, then a DIY approach – even if it not as successful – will at least make a profit. As a budget campaign will have little resource for testing, sending the first draft to friends and family (and monitoring the results) is better than nothing. Results of the campaign should always be measured against its objectives – even if little is achieved, the experience can still be used in the development of any future campaigns.

For the larger entity that has (or can obtain) a significant mailing list, using professionals or the appropriate software in–house is best practice. Sending direct marketing messages on the CC/BCC facility is not good practice – and it makes you look cheap

---

*You Decide*  Advise the marketers at the Gilded Truffle Hotel (case study 3) on appropriate objectives for a direct marketing email campaign. What elements of the process might be particularly troublesome for this particular organization?

Alternatively, conduct the same exercise for your organization or that of your employer.

---

## 8.3 EMAIL AS MEDIUM FOR MARKETING MESSAGES

In this section we look at the use of email for marketing purposes where the email is not a direct marketing message. The inclusion of this subject as a distinct section of this chapter might surprise some. However, it is an extremely important aspect of Internet marketing and it is also one that is too often forgotten by even the most experienced marketers.

Offline, it is common practice that any contact with a customer – via any of the various touch points – is carefully prepared as even the smallest of communiqué will play a part in any relationship building or CRM strategy. Online, however, it is common practice for emails – particularly those that are automated responses, sometimes called *triggered* emails – to be sent to customers with no consideration of how their content might impact on the marketing efforts of the organization. Worse still, many emails are written by non–marketing staff – who might write in such a way that a relationship can actually be damaged by the message's presentation. Furthermore, such emails do not need to be *customer* oriented (i.e. serve a sales, service or marketing purpose often dubbed *transactional* emails) – any email sent by human resources (to a prospective employee, for example), finance (an invoice reminder) or procurement (a purchase order) represent the organization and so can be seen as an element of brand building.

In these latter examples, it is likely that the staff can be trusted to write the content, but email design and presentation should be managed for appearance and deliverability by email marketing experts – with best practice being the provision of email templates. It is also worth noting that communications do not need to be initiated by the organization. As with the examples above, the out–going email might be in response to an

Note that a newsletter developed by a practitioner (e.g. a consultant) risks having its validity diminished by carrying ads.

5. Newsletter content can be included on the organization's website, making it available as an archive – which can be attractive to search engines.

## MINI CASE

### Retail newsletters have ready–made content

Although some might argue that a list of special offers is not really a newsletter – the issue is actually decided by the consumer. If they perceive that an email with details of forthcoming promotions is worth receiving on a regular basis, then it meets the criteria of being a newsletter.

The massive advantage for retailers is that they will often run in–store promotions as part of their marketing strategy – and those offers are obvious content for a regular newsletter. Notice how the one shown below – from Lidl – includes the address of my local store (I had given my postcode in my 'profile').

A Lidl newsletter from April 2008:

**Lidl Newsletter**

Dear newsletter subscriber,

You will find the following offers at your prefered **Lidl store**:

**Ryhope Road**
**SR2 9ST Durham/Grangetown**

····> **Select another store**

**Our special offers**
**Camping Essentials. From 24.04.**

**3 Person Tent**
Made from water-resistant polyester with taped seams and a breathable polyester inner sheet. Zip-up entrance with mosquito net and 2 air vents. Supplied with durable PE groundsheet, lightweight fibreglass poles. Click details for more info...

Further details on this item

29.99*

**Foldable Chair**
Lightweight tubular construction. Folds flat for easy transport and storage. Available in blue or green. Size (cm): 62 x 58 x 87.5. Price per item.

Further details on this item

8.99*

In marketing terms, the RSS feed serves the same objectives as the newsletter in that pertinent information is passed to the recipient. In the case of RSS, however, the content is published on a web page (which could be a blog) and then pushed to recipients as individual elements rather than being included on one website.

However, it is perhaps the *individualized* aspect of RSS that is both its strength and failing when compared to the newsletter. If I, for example, had to be very specific about the online marketing news I requested through RSS feeds then I might – inadvertently – fail to request something that would be of interest. Therefore (at the time of writing) I elect to still receive dozens of email newsletters which I then sift through for articles that might be of interest or useful. To me, the obvious trade–off on my part is between the time taken in rejecting uninteresting content and the chance that I may miss something I would find interesting or valuable.

For both newsletter and RSS feeds the same issue is paramount in their use. If content is king on websites, in newsletters and RSS feeds it is the entire royal family. Whether the content is written for newsletters or is originally published on web pages, that content has to be developed. In much the same way as content for the organization's web presence should be developed *properly* (see section 3.4), so too must that which is to be distributed to interested parties who have requested it. It is for this reason that many well–intentioned campaigns either fail to take off or simply wither on the vine of lack–of–content. For the organization that is sending its own 'our–company' newsletter to customers, developing content is problematic – not only finding interesting subjects, but its writing also. There are only so many 'new starters', 'promotions', 'new product developments' and 'CEO visits China' –type stories that recipients will read before they cancel their subscription. Even if the newsletter is to be little more than a series of links to articles on other sites – with reviews or comments added – those articles must be sourced, read and the comments written, all of which takes time. Ironically, it is blog–writing that makes the RSS feed workable (though a periodic newsletter could simply list the best blog entries). If a blog is to be kept on a regular basis, then recipients can be invited to be *fed* either all entries or just those that relate to a specific subject area.

*You Decide*

Advise Milo and his marketing team at 22 Catches Fish Products (case study 7) on how either a newsletter or RSS feeds could be integrated into their online marketing. Comment on both advantages and disadvantages of undertaking either.

Alternatively, conduct the same exercise on your organization or that of your employer.

## 8.5  PERSONALIZATION

In this section there is yet another issue of how the subject is interpreted in an online scenario. The definitions to be addressed here are those of *personalization* and *customization* – and whether each applies to a tangible a personalized service to be offered at a much lower price, and more conveniently, than it can be offline. If the nature of the product lends itself to being a gift, this gives an obvious opportunity for offering a personalized service in the fulfilment aspect of an online purchase. Instead of parcelling a book (for example) in plain brown card, the book can be wrapped in gift paper with a personal message – supplied by the buyer – attached.

## Practical Insight

### Personalized page – customized product

Williams-Sonoma (williams-sonoma.com) saw conversions increase by 50 per cent when they tested personalization software for some of their products. The online 'store for cooks' offers monogrammed products – so when registered customers surfed product pages they were presented with images that had on them the customer's own name or initials.

*Source: Priscilla Lawrence of Scene7 (www.scene7.com)*

Personalization of a web page will first and foremost be dependent on the how often a customer is likely to visit a site, with the width and depth of the range of products or services offered by a site having an obviously impact on visitor frequency. Tesco, for example, might expect a monthly, or even weekly, visit to their online store. Amazon would hope for multiple visits per year, but not on a regular basis – and so the visits to purchase ratio would be much lower. Both of these companies would look to develop a relationship with the customer – and personalization could have an intrinsic part to play in such a strategy. However, a car manufacturer might not expect people to visit their site on a regular basis – few people renew their car more often than every couple of years, and then they may not stick with the same manufacturer. Similarly, a *used* car sales operation would be best advised to maintain an offline relationship with customers rather than personalizing a website that people might never re–visit after a purchase is made.

However, a car dealership (one franchised to a manufacturer) might not only look to get repeat sales for cars (they do, lifetime value of customers is an important metric to them) but the same customers would be targeted for after–sales and service income. In this case, it might be the customer's car that is the key personalization criteria rather than the customer. Visits to the dealer's website would be personalized to include such content as service–due messages, promotions on accessories suitable to the car or seasonally–related issues like winter safety checks.

Personalization features (widgets) should be considered with care – with frequency of visit being paramount. A flight–booking website, for example, could not be expected to include a permanent display of clocks showing times for all the world's cities. However, if I fly to a couple of time–zones on a regular basis perhaps being able to put clocks set at those times on my home page would be useful. Similarly, local weather forecasts for those places would also add to my on–site satisfaction. Adding such facilities to company websites is not normally a good idea, however. Whilst these might have novelty value, they are unlikely to add to the customer experience – and could well detract from the validity of other content. If things like the local weather is useful for a website (an airport, for example), then it should be a permanent element of the site, not an optional add–on.

---

*You Decide*

Advise Frank at Hill Street Motorist Shops (case study 8) on how the use of web personalized web pages might better satisfy their customers.
Alternatively, conduct the same exercise for your organization or that of your employer.

---

## 8.6 MOBILE MARKETING

The introduction to this section must include the question as to whether or not it belongs in a book on Internet marketing at all. The answer lies in the definition of what the *mobile web* is. For some, it applies to any wireless device. For example, when they conducted research into the demographics of mobile Internet users, the Pew Internet Project (2007) considered a laptop, PDA and cell phone to be the same. However, I disagree with this demarcation. Modern laptops are commonly used to surf the web with no problem. That the screens are (generally) smaller than those of desk–bound PCs is not normally an issue as web pages are either set to be small enough to fit or the site is programmed to adjust to the size of the screen. Wireless broadband is also efficient enough to carry the majority of website content. Indeed, some web users may only ever use 'mobile' Internet access in their own homes or university. For the purposes of this book, therefore, I consider mobile to mean those devices than can be used in the palm of one hand and carried in a pocket or handbag – essentially, a PDA or mobile/cell phone.

---

### Practical Insight

**Snd me a book pls**

Although Europe is ahead of the USA in the adoption of text messaging as a medium for marketing, Amazon has pressed ahead with TextBuyIt – a new service that lets customers use text messages to find and buy products sold on Amazon.com. It complements the already existing mobile offering, including its mobile site and mobile iPhone site. TextBuyIt allows Amazon's customers to shop, compare prices and buy from Amazon.com from virtually anywhere, with any mobile device, using either text messages or their mobile device's web browser. Note that for the time being, *anywhere* refers to anywhere in the USA as TextBuyIt and the mobile sites only work with the .com version of Amazon and for those users with US Zip codes.

Even within this stance on the definition, however, there are still further problems. Indeed, my initial thoughts were that *mobile marketing* is a different subject to *Internet marketing* – with mobile normally being associated with mobile (cell) phones and so is – predominantly – about text messaging, which does not use Internet technology. However, some phones – and other devices such as PDAs and iPhones – can connect to both the web and email, therefore there must be a consideration of them. Certainly, there is a part that text messaging can play in marketing, but its use in direct marketing or advertising is not – in my opinion – part of Internet marketing, and is a specialism in its own right. However, text messaging can be used in conjunction with online marketing to great effect. Passengers booking a flight or train journey, for example, could opt to be informed by text of any delays or cancellations before they start their journey to the airport or station.

## RESEARCH SNAPSHOT

**Be warned**

Results of a survey – published in 2007 – from Nielsen/NetRatings (www.nielsen-netratings .com) and SEM firm Webvisible (www.webvisible.com) of consumer behaviour and attitudes towards online advertising found that 92 per cent of respondents said that receiving local business ads on their mobile phones would be 'irritating'.

Since the launch of the 3G networks at the turn of the century, industry evangelists have predicted great things for the medium that never truly matured. Even as I write this (in May 2008) great things are being predicted on the back of the successful (2007) launch of Apple's iPhone – and its forthcoming updated version – and similar mobile web Initiatives like Google's Open Handset.

The over–riding issue is that of technology, where a wide variety of factors, not least bandwidth availability and the hundreds of different types of devices offered by vendors is hindering progress. The user experience, small screens and different viewing environments (e.g. in sunlight) is also restricting widespread adoption. These factors have forced many mobile applications to reduce visuals and rely on simple text applications (Fitzgerald, 2007).

Put simply, the browsers and standards that allow us to view websites on a PC or laptop are not replicated on mobile devices. Although websites can be designed in mobile–friendly coding (the .mobi domain name was introduced for such sites) this requires a duplication of web content. Furthermore, if users want access to the web on their mobile phone they (normally) pay an increased tariff to the network provider. It is not clear whether users are put off by the (high) cost or simply that they do not want the service – nearly 90 per cent of users in the USA still use mobile devices primarily for talking (M:Metrics, cited by Alice C. Cuneo, 2008). One way that those charges might be lowered is if more marketers used the medium for advertising – but there is something of a catch 22 situation. The users won't access the mobile web unless the price comes down, but the price is unlikely to come down unless ad income is generated – and the advertisers will not buy ad space if no one is accessing it. A further issue raised by advertisers is that in other aspects of 'online' advertising they have become accustomed to a range of metrics with which to judge the effectiveness of any advertising. For mobile, however, such technologies are not available – and unless the network providers can make available accurate analytics advertisers will continue to shy away from mobile. Note that in Europe a number of providers work together to deliver cross-operator metrics to media and ad companies – but this is not the case in America – and it is the USA that [still] drives digital marketing practice. Further complication comes from the fact that the latest hand–held devices – such as the iPhone – facilitate both text and email/web connection. Such is the nature of connection tarifs that texts must be paid for, but if the user is in one of the increasingly popular free wi–fi zones email will cost nothing.

## Practical Insight

### Proximity Marketing

What many might see as another name for mobile marketing, proximity marketing is the name given to the deliver of wireless, location-based promotions to people via their mobile phones or other portable devices such as PDAs. There are three main ways of achieving this:

1. Via mobile phones when they are in a specific location served by a particular transmitter.
2. Via devices that have a global positioning system (GPS) that can identify the location of the device.
3. Via Bluetooth or WiFi enabled devices that are in range of a transmitter.

The concept is that the people in the target market are prompted to visit a retail outlet that is located close to where they are when they get a promotional message.

Mobile phone and GPS messages must be sent by the service operator, but the latter – particularly Bluetooth – can be sent from a local computer. With a range of around 10 metres for mobile phones and 30 metres for laptop/PDAs, the system operates from a small server which scans for Bluetooth targets in its reach, sending messages as people enter the covered area.

The advertising model is that as I walk towards a particular coffee shop, for example, I get a message telling me about current special offers available in that outlet.

While supporters – usually people who have a financial interest in the mobile web – continue to predict that a break through will come soon, others have doubts. To have a successful web based mobile–marketing application there has to be a coming together in the development of handsets, networks and markets. Perhaps – as in the development of all products – if the public demands it, it will happen. To date, the demand for surfing the web on a pocket–sized device is, though expending, still limited.

## DECISION TIME

As with all aspects of marketing the key issue for consideration is whether or not the use of mobile devices for delivery of web pages is a need – or even want – of the organization's target market. If the answer is no, then – at least for the time being – the medium can be ignored. However, even if there is a perceived need, the question of which technology to use still has to be addressed.

If there is a demand, it is most likely to come from the younger generation of customers who are more used to wireless applications. A May 2008 survey by interactive online market research company, Lightspeed Research, suggests that the demand *might* exist – finding that 17 per cent of respondents said that they would be willing to make purchases through their mobile phone. However, it is sellers of intangible products that would seem to be the beneficiaries – with entertainment and travel tickets being the most popular types of products and services respondents said they would buy in this way. This reflects an 'on–the–go' demand – where, for example, rail and theatre tickets might be purchased after the customer has left their home or workplace on their way to the event. This would be in contrast to how the web is used in the purchase process of other – often tangible – products, where research into potential purchases that is likely to be conducted over a period of time and in a situation where the potential customer can either print off web pages or make notes on paper.

*You Decide*    Advise Syd and Charlie at Two Cities Manufacturing Ltd (case study 11) on how they might use the mobile Internet – now or in the future – in their marketing.

Alternatively, conduct the same exercise for your organization or that of your employer.

## CHAPTER EXERCISE

Giving justifications for all your decisions, advise Howard Johnson and his marketers at The Rockridge Museum (case study 1) on all aspects of Internet marketing covered in this chapter. This includes taking a look at the 'dummy' emails that can be found by following the link from the chapter's web page.

Alternatively, conduct the same exercise on your own organization or that of your employer.

# REFERENCES

Allred, C.R., Smith, S.M. & Swinyard, W.R. (2006). E-shopping lovers and fearful conservatives: a market segmentation analysis. Marriott School of Management, Brigham Young University, Provo, Utah, USA.

Center for the Digital Future (2008). Surveying the Digital Future. The University of Southern California's Annenberg School for Communication.

Cuneo, A. C. (2008). *Why '08 Isn't Mobile's Year – Again.* Available on: http://adage.com/digital/article?article_id=125977

Ebnar, M., Hu, A., Levitt, D. & McCrory, J. (2002). How to rescue CRM. *McKinsey Quarterly.* Vol. 4 pp. 49–57. , special edition: Technology issue

Fitzgerald, M. (2007). Mobile web: so far, yet so close, November 25, 2. New York Times.

Lawrence, P. (2008). speaking at the Email Evolution Conference. February 12/13, 2008, San Diego USA.

Nielsen, J. (2008). *What SEO/SEM Professionals Should Know About Website Usability.* Available online at: http://searchengineland.com/080501-115858.php

Pew Internet Project, (2007). *Wireless Internet Access.*

Pew Internet & American Life Project (2007). *Teens and Social Media*

Q Interactive & MarketingSherpa (2008). *Spam Complainers Survey.* www.qinteractive.com/www.marketingsherpa.com.

Vertis Communications (2007). *Customer Focus® Tech Savvy study.* www.vertiscommunications.com

# Social media marketing

> *Social circles spin too fast for me*
>
> Sammy Davis Jnr

## CHAPTER AT A GLANCE

## 9.1 INTRODUCTION

In describing social media, McConnell and Huba (2007) suggest that it is *'the sum total of people who create content online, as well as the people who interact with it or one another'* (it is the element of interaction that gives grounds to the term *conversational marketing*). In more tangible terms, 'social media' is generally applied to sites where users can add their own content but do not have control over the site in the same way as they would their own website. For example, I can have my own FaceBook page on which I can add my own content and a blog on blogger.com where I write my own thoughts and opinions. However, I do not own the domain name, nor do I have any influence over how the site is run. Indeed, at the click of a mouse the host could delete my content – or they could close down the whole site. Social media, therefore, is not normally used to describe any content that is on my own website (there is an exception covered in section 9.3, *cyberbashing* sites). Once again, in the dynamic – and still developing – world of the Internet terms, definitions and practices are not quite as finite as in traditional environments and media.

In order to help readers come to grips with what social media is – or includes – Figure 9.1 shows a matrix that should help. It is based on the original concept of David Bowen (www.bowencraggs.net) who used it as an attempt to describe how 'web 2.0' fitted in to other online applications.

| | | |
|---|---|---|
| **Two way**<br>(Horizontal web) | **Home web 2**<br><br>In this square communication is two–way from the organization to the customer – but is controlled by the organization.<br><br>It is made up of the organization's own blogs and forum. | **Extended web 2**<br><br>Elements of this square are those most often associated with web 2.0.<br><br>These are the sites over which organizations have no control and people talk to one another.<br><br>It includes: individuals' blogs, social network sites, traditional forums or discussion areas, Q and A pages and sites such as Wikipedia. |
| **One way**<br>(Vertical web) | **Home web 1**<br><br>In this quadrant, communication is one–way from the organization, mirroring traditional marketing where the marketing message is controllable.<br><br>The organization's own web site(s) – including images, video, podcasts as well as textual content – makes up this section. | **Extended web 1**<br><br>This square represents the web sites on which the organization can place content, but they do not control.<br><br>This includes consumer and review sites as well as (for example) videos on YouTube, photographs on Flickr and groups the organization has set up or sponsored on social network sites such as Facebook. It also includes ads hosted on other sites. |
| | You control<br>(Home web) | Others control<br>(Extended web) |

**Figure 9.1** Web 2009

Bowen originally deemed it to be 'Web 2007'– and so in deference to him, I've titled this one 'Web 2009'. In essence, the four quadrants of the matrix describe how web content is controlled by the organization through to that content over which it has no control.

In the subsequent sections of this chapter I have divided social media into different elements in order to address the differing ways in which the web user can add their own content to a web presence. The first, consumer generated content, concentrates on reviews and ratings. Second is social networks and online communities followed by virtual worlds before looking at the phenomenon of blogging.

If, therefore, 'social media' can be anyone or everyone who uses the web, before we can delve deeper into the titular subject of this chapter, we need a definition of that subject. In my book, *Key Concepts in e–Commerce* (2007) I describe social media marketing (SMM) as: '*a term used to encompasses any online marketing strategy or tactic which uses social media as the medium for its communication. Although this can include advertising on social media sites, it is more commonly used in the context of either viral marketing or social media optimization. Further use of social media is where the marketer engages in discourse with members of the general public (i.e. potential customers) in virtual communities or submits to elements of consumer generated media.*'

Although I am happy to stand by this definition, social media is perhaps one of the most fluid and dynamic aspects of the Internet – and so this classification might be seen by some as out–dated or open to interpretation. Other authors associate social media with 'Web 2.0' – but this serves only to cloud the issue. Needless to say, this ambiguity continues into the practice of SMM. Like many aspects of online marketing – and, indeed, marketing in general – it is difficult to draw a line where one element ends and another starts. Suppose, for example, that on MySpace (a social networking site) a member receives a message from a 'friend' about an amusing video – and then emails another person (who is not a MySpace member) to tell them of the URL of the video. Does this describe social networking or viral marketing? Similarly, how is social media distinct from online communities? And where does consumer generated content fit in with all other aspects of the concept?

> " social media is perhaps one of the most fluid and dynamic aspects of the Internet "

## RESEARCH SNAPSHOT

A study by the Pew Internet & American Life Project, published in December 2007, suggests that almost two-thirds of American online teens have created something online – mainly on social networking sites such as Facebook and MySpace where on–site tools mean that no technical or design skills are necessary. Delving into the demographics of the report shows that teenage girls blog more than boys, but that teenage boys are twice as likely as girls to upload a video.

Another aspect of SMM that adds to the confusion can be found in its practice. Much of social media itself tends to attract a younger audience – and many marketers and CEOs are not of that generation – and so in many cases they simply don't get it. Research from TNS, TRU & Marketing Evolution (2007) supports this, saying that the brand manager must realise – and it might be difficult for those not in the relevant generation – that social networking is more than just something to do, it's also the venue in which they do it.

In this chapter we will consider all of the relevant aspects of social media marketing in dedicated sections. However, you should bear in mind that the distinctions between some categories are blurred – better that you try to consider the whole chapter as one big subject.

Also worth noting at this point is that in this chapter I have concentrated on the *social* aspect of social media. That is to say, content that is not written in a commercial context – hobby or pastime rather than work. This is not to say that social media has no commercial application – or else why would I have included the subject in this book? As the following sections will show, what the public writes is of interest to organizations. Certainly, sites such as Linkedin (www.linkedin.com) have an element of professional development about them, but they are not commercial networks per se. However, commercial communities do exist, where industry–related subjects – rather than the *social* issues like your favourite rock band – are discussed. I have made the decision to include these in section 5.5 on e-marketplaces – though I do appreciate there can be a blurring of the lines between where some social and commercial networking sites meet.

In studying the subject, it is also worth considering the theory on which social media marketing hangs. With roots in psychology, sociology and economics (in which it is known as the theory of economic behaviour) *social exchange theory* suggests that social behaviour is the result of an exchange process where each party seeks to maximise benefits and minimize costs. In a commercial environment – where benefits and costs can be evaluated in financial terms – this is a relatively straightforward proposal to assess. In a social environment, however, the costs and benefits are far more intangible and will differ from person to person. Nevertheless, whatever the interpretation of costs and benefits, individuals weigh one against the other before deciding if what they will get out of any resulting relationship is offset by what they must put into it. If the risks outweigh the rewards, the relationship will be terminated or abandoned. It is the very nature of the online environment that make both the benefits and costs more easily gained or discarded than in the real world – a click of the mouse being all that is required. Perhaps it is this apparent ease in accepting or rejection that makes social media so appealing to its predominantly young users and such a marketing minefield for those wishing to make commercial gain from it.

## RESEARCH SNAPSHOT

### Social media set to take marketing spend

An interesting study conducted by TWI Surveys on behalf of the Society for New Communications Research and Joseph Jaffe found that – amongst other things – by 2012, 81 per cent of marketers believe that they will be spending as much or more on conversational (social media) marketing as they will on more traditional marketing methods.

*Cited in Jaffe, J. (2007) Join the Conversation. Wiley*

Also from offline sociology is reasoning for the success of viral marketing through social websites, in particular, Mark Granovetter's seminal paper on social networking, The Strength of Weak Ties (1973). In it he argues that while our acquaintances (weak ties) are less likely to be socially involved with one another than our close friends (strong ties), our acquaintances will have their own close friends – and our only link with those people is through our *weak ties* – hence they are important to us. In social networking terms this means that if I have an idea that I pass on to my acquaintances (weak ties) I am reliant on *their* close friends (strong ties) to continue the spread of the idea. Pre Internet it was (a) difficult for me to make contact with weak ties, (b) easy for them to block any contact from me, and (c) have no motivation to pass on the idea, even if they received it. In the online world of social networking the click of a mouse on a 'friends' link means that my message (idea) goes out to all my friends and acquaintances (in an instant) – and not only do subsequent clicks from those people send the message to all of their friends and acquaintances, and so on and so on, but the flexibility of computer-mediated-communication (CMC) easily overcomes the offline communications hurdles of geography and time–zones.

In terms of Granovetter's model, those people who are well down on my 'friends' or mailing list (weak ties) all get my message, as do *their* weak ties – which means that in terms of networking of messages, as much (if not more) communication is conducted via weak ties than strong ones – hence their strength.

**AIDA moves into the Internet age**

In section 1.6 and 3.2 we used the AIDA model to consider buyer behaviour and website development respectively. In the original concept, the action – normally a purchase – is the end of the chain of events. However, when considering the impact of social networking on contemporary marketing perhaps an additional element should be added to make the social media version: Attention, Interest, Desire, Action and *Tell* (AIDAT) where the additional 'T' indicates that the customer should be encouraged to 'tell someone about it'.

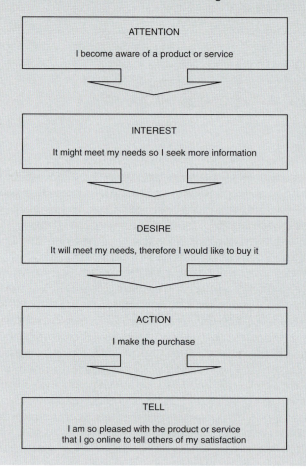

When examining how the marketer can use social media in either strategic or operational planning, there are three further issues to be addressed. They are:

1. Online marketing – and particularly social media – is a reflection of the time in which it developed. In the relationship between marketers and consumers, things were changing, and 'Internet marketing was simply the catalyst for a sea change that had been long coming' (Meadows-Klue 2008).
2. Social media participants do not like to be lied to, or even fooled. They don't even like to be *marketed at* – which makes the issue of how to use the social media in marketing even more problematic.

3. As I write this (in mid-2008) the elements that make up SMM – social networking, viral marketing and virtual worlds, for example – might be perceived as *cool*, but there is a distinct lack of hard data that says they *actually* help sell products. Social media is, after all, for the people by the people – not for the marketer by the marketer.

## RESEARCH SNAPSHOT

A survey investigating consumer preferences in receiving marketing messages revealed that 72 per cent of respondents said they'd prefer to receive opt-in promotional messages via email, while zero per cent (yes, none) prefer them via social networking sites.

*Source: ExactTarget 2008 Channel Preference Survey (www.exacttarget.com)*

These three points lead us to what is the critical impact of social media on contemporary marketing – potentially the most significant change in marketing since the practice was recognised as a discipline in its own right. That impact is that the marketer no longer has control over the brand – a frightening thought for many who practice in the field.

> " the marketer no longer has control over the brand "

Prior to the emergence of the commercial Internet, the marketer had control over any marketing message that reached the public. As US TV executive Don S. Hewitt once famously commented: *'The businessman only wants two things said about his company – what he pays his public relations people to say and what he pays his advertising people to say.'* That age has now passed. Certainly in the past a dissatisfied customer could tell friends and acquaintances of their experiences, they might even submit a letter to a newspaper or magazine (though the chances of any publication including a letter criticising any potential advertiser was questionable), but their sphere of influence was limited. Now, the Internet – by way of social media – allows the single disgruntled customer to reach hundreds, thousands or even millions of people at the click of a mouse. And those recipients can then replicate that message to untold other masses of people.

Whether the marketer – or more accurately, the organization – sees this loss of control as an opportunity or threat may well determine how well that organization will prosper in the new marketing environment. Constantinides & Fountain (2008) make the point that it is essential for marketers to look to Web 2.0 as a challenge rather than as a threat and consider it as a new domain of commercial strategy. Social media marketing is, essentially, all about using the medium to encourage the dissemination of a positive brand, product or organizational message. Marketing students – and practitioners – may also recognise that some elements of SMM could be considered to be part of a *relationship* approach to marketing, with the web being used as another conduit through which the organization can build and develop a relationship with its customers or public. One thing is certain, consumers are interacting with brands and participating in marketing on a scale that wasn't conceived by most marketers just a decade ago (Compete Inc, 2006b).

## Practical Insight

### SEO vs SMO

As with search engine optimization (SEO), social media optimization (SMO) is all about driving traffic to your site. However, whereas SEO traffic tends to be fairly steady, SMO traffic is more likely to be a series of peaks and troughs. This is because it reacts to specific articles or events that can be optimized on a social network. This isn't to say that SMO results are instantaneous, like SEO some preparatory work is necessary. In the case of SMO a network of friends is necessary to pass on the message that will drive visitors to the website – and any network will take time to build. The main difference between SEO and SMO, however, lies in to whom they appeal. With SEO it is the search engine algorithms that are pampered to using code and content that help match keywords to searches. For SMO, the appeal is to humans, for it is humans who – albeit using technology – will pass on the message and so drive traffic to your site. It is essential, therefore, that the content appeals to people – including its visual presentation. Think of SMO as front of house performance, with SEO the backstage support.

## 9.2 CONSUMER GENERATED CONTENT

As is the case with other topics covered in this book, consumer generated content (CGC) is yet to have a finite definition. Indeed, in my own book *Key Concepts in e–Commerce* (2007 – published only 18 months before this one) I favoured the term consumer generated *media* (CGM). I made the differentiation to represent the wider entity in which CGC is hosted (the media) rather than the actual content presented in that media. However, as that media has now merged – and arguably the medium was always the Internet in its entirety – the emphasis is now more on the *content* than the media on which it sits.

A further complication comes from other popular terminology that are used in the same context as CGC and CGM – that being where, in both terms, the word *consumer* is replaced by *user* (i.e. user generated content). Whilst we could get pedantic and examine any possible differentiation of these terms, in reality there is little – with their application being down to individual preference or practice. This being the case, this section will use the abbreviation CGC to cover the concept.

Although the issues surrounding the media/content and consumer/user issues can be considered one of semantics, another phrase often used in the same context has a distinctly different meaning. This is citizen journalism – or journalist – though *citizen* can be replaced by *civilian*. It is taken that this term refers to an amateur (i.e. not trained as a journalist) who plays an active role in collection, analysis, reporting and dissemination of news and information. Although the content may include statements, comments or stories about products, organizations or brands it is not intended as some kind of review. With CGC, on the other hand, the content suggests that the writer has experienced the product, organization or service and wishes to pass that experience on to others.

Which brings us to another term that appears in social media – citizen marketers. In their book on the subject, McConnell & Huba (2007)

# MINI CASE

## Citizen marketers help SoaP clean up

It is not unusual for films to generate cult followings – the Star Trek franchise springs readily to mind, as does the low–budget *Blair Witch Project*, which owed much to the Internet for its success – but the 2006 film *Snakes on a Plane* turned the concept on its head.

For some reason, the title itself created a spark with movie–goers and a *buzz* began to spread across the online community. Flickr had hundreds of images posted, Technorati had over 20,000 blog entries about the movie – by this time abbreviated to *SoaP* by its fans. Those same fans created their own SoaP merchandise, with T–shirts being available featuring quotes from the film's star, Samuel L. Jackson. Trailers and posters also appeared for purchase on the web.

But there is a twist. This all happened *before* the film was ever released. The images, trailers and posters were all *invented* by the fans. They made up their own visions of what the film was about – and with that title, there was little room for doubt as to its story line.

The film studio (New Line Cinema) played along with the viral community. No law suites about copyright infringement were issued – but most importantly, whilst endorsing the buzz they did not attempt to control, or even get involved with it. This was key. Had the SoaP–citizens perceived that they were being *used* by the movie makers they would not only have abandoned their campaigns, but more than likely turned against the film and its makers. Furthermore,

New Line – extending what is common practice in Hollywood – listened to what selected pre–release audiences had to say. And those audience's comments were based on the buzz–fuelled perceptions they had before they saw the film. The result was the re–shooting of some scenes in the movie with more violence, more nudity, more deaths, more snakes – and more swearing from the lead character played by Jackson. The latter only served to add more muscle to the film's pre–release buzz on two counts. Firstly, the makers had to up the parental guidance (PG) age rating – creating news in its own right – but secondly, one particular line of profanity spoken by Jackson's character became a catch phrase that appeared not only on T–shirts, but late–night TV chat shows.

On its eventual release, the film was a commercial success. Would it have been without the citizen marketing – who can tell? Will we ever see anything similar again? Doubtful – it was just the right title in the right place at the right time. Could a studio reproduce the effect? No, those people upon who the viral buzz would depend would shun the commercialism of their medium. Lessons learned? Listen to your public. If a viral buzz is happening, let it happen – don't try to control or manipulate – then sit back and count the profit.

Note that I gathered details of this case study from various sources at the time that the events were taking place. However Ben McConnell and Jackie Huba give an excellent narrative of the SoaP phenomenon in their 2007 book *Citizen Marketers* (pp.162–169).

However, doubts are beginning to creep in about the authenticity of some reviews. Sir Tim Berners-Lee, the British inventor of the world wide web, commented in November 2006 (at the launch of a degree in web science) that there is a great danger that it becomes a place where untruths start to spread more than truths. Research by MarketingSherpa and Prospectiv (2007) revealed that five per cent of respondents said that they don't trust consumer reviews. As reports of organizations 'doctoring' reviews spread, web users may become more sceptical and perhaps this five per cent will rise. Worse still is another issue – the false review. Some industries are more susceptible to this than others, but the phenomenon is particularly problematic in the travel industry, where numerous websites invite customers to give feedback on hotels in which they have stayed. The problem is twofold; hotel owners and management leave (1) exceedingly positive reviews for their own establishments, or (2) negative comments about competitors' hotels.

*Go Online*    To read stories on the problem of false reviews in the hotel industry, follow the links on the chapter's web page.

## DECISION TIME

For the professional marketer the dilemma is not only *how* to best utilize consumer, user or citizen input, but *can* they utilize it at all?

In the case of the writings of a citizen marketer it is something that happens and it is doubtful if the marketer can influence it, but they can monitor and react to it. McConnell & Huba (2007) cite the case of singer Fiona Apple whose 'rejected' third album was picked up by an evangelistic citizen marketer who was so successful in promoting it himself that Sony eventually released the recordings. However, no matter how doubtful it is that either the artist or Sony could have influenced the individual concerned, the more cynical amongst us might still wonder if that evangelist was not a 'plant' from the marketing department of the recording company which was covertly working with, and supporting financially, the citizen marketer. Whilst there was no suggestion that this is the case with the Fiona Apple story, it is worth noting that in a number of cases of citizen marketing the amateur has actually been revealed as being a *front* for a professional marketing campaign. Needless to say, once discovered (and they usually are) the effect on the product or brand is the opposite of that hoped for.

When considering consumer generated content, the online marketer has the choice of being passive or proactive. Most are passive, simply tracking comments made by consumers as they appear online. For many it is a case of using the reviews as market research and little more (see also section 2.6 where social media sites are considered as a source of market research). However, in some circumstances it is feasible for an organization to be proactive by joining in with online comments or responding to them. Although some organizations choose to conduct this covertly – adding comments as another reviewer responding to previous comments. This is a risky practice, however. Not only would discovery result in lost credibility for the organization, brand or product – but under the Consumer Protection from Unfair Trading Regulations (2008) in Europe the practice is likely to be deemed an offence. Overt comments made in response to criticism, on the other hand, can have the opposite effect – with the public reacting positively to companies that are honest and up-front with regard to their failings.

There is a further consideration for the online marketer with regard to CGC that has its routes in traditional marketing. Marketers have long been aware that in order for a new product to be successfully launched they must win over those members of society that influence others in their purchase decision making. These early adopters in the product life cycle were traditionally difficult to both identify and reach, but the advent of the Internet – social media in particular – has resulted in members of this influential segment actually identifying themselves. Not only that, but online marketers can actually assess their influence by monitoring the blogs, reviews and websites created by what are becoming known as e–fluencers. Potential customers are most effectively persuaded by e-fluencers who carry some credibility in their online presence by becoming experts in a specific area of interest. Pre–Internet, such people were found only on TV, radio or in print – making them a kind of elite. In the Internet era, however, anyone can get online and fulfil this roll, as Chris Anderson points out in his influential book, *The Long Tail* (2006), the new tastemakers aren't a super-elite of people cooler than us; they are *us*.

*Go Online*  For an excellent article on the role and power of influencers, follow the link on the chapter's web page to *'Is the Tipping Point Toast*?' by Duncan Watts.

> *Go Online*    For examples of public relations disaster associated with cyberbashing sites, follow the links from the chapter's web page.

## DECISION TIME

There are three models that the commercial organization can use in adopting online communities or the social media for strategic purposes, they are: facilitating, employing and joining. Let's consider each in more detail.

### Facilitate

This is where the organization provides a system where users can create profiles and interact with other members of a community. A business model in its own right (MySpace and Bebo, for example), it is expensive to develop and operate as an income source in its own right. However, it can be part of a wider online strategy – a 'club' as part of a web presence, perhaps. An excellent example of this is LEGO.

**The home page of LEGO's community site.**

©2008 The LEGO Group

Far from being simply a 'toy' for kids to practice hand-eye coordination and develop dexterity skills, LEGO has another significant market in the enthusiasts who use the bricks to build anything they can think of. It is at these aficionados that the social media element of a company's website is mainly targeted. With less than 10 per cent of LEGO's product range available in offline stores, the online store – along with catalogues – is the place to get the other 90 per cent. But the site is not simply a shop – it is a destination for the LEGO community. Model swapping and collaborative building projects are encouraged, as is a user-generated database of what packs contain the elements necessary to build the various models. There is even downloadable software that allows builders to design their own models, upload the design to the LEGO site and take delivery of the custom-made kit of parts necessary to make the self-designed model – complete with a box featuring a picture of the completed model on the lid.

### Employ

This tactic is to use social media as a channel for recognized promotional activities. There are two fundamental methods:

* Sponsorship – as with its offline application, online sponsorship is chiefly used as part of a wider branding exercise. The organization simply seeks to sponsor a community site where the majority of the participants are in the target market segment for the organization, brand or product. It is particularly useful for niche communities where the concentration of demographics is better, but still relatively inexpensive because overall member numbers are small.
* Advertising (for selling) aimed at the demographic represented by users, for example. As covered in detail in chapter 7, social media and community sites provide excellent opportunities for targeted advertising – though as noted in that chapter, clickthrough rates are poor.

Note that with both of these methods there may be a good opportunity to *join* the network – as described in the next element of this section. This is particularly the case if the members of the community use the advertised/sponsoring product or service in their activity subject.

## MINI CASE

### Call Centres 0 : YouTube 1

In November 2007, after six months trying to contact BT's customer services over a billing query, frustrated customer Patrick Askins made a video of himself talking about the issue and the problems he was having getting it resolved. He then posted the clip on YouTube. His plight soon became news, with newspapers the *Telegraph*, *Sun* and *Mail* covering the story as well the BBC and CNN featuring it on TV.

It would appear that his innovative method of complaint did the trick, two days after his comments went live on YouTube, Mr Askins received a letter from the telecoms giant acknowledging the problems.

### Join

Perhaps the most common use of social media sites by marketers because of its convenience (and perceived ease), this is where the organization actively engages in publishing on social media sites by entering into exchanges and interacting with the community. Writing a blog would be included in this method. Note that any of these practices should be conducted with overt disclosure of the brand or organization being represented.

The key decision for organizations in this element of e–marketing is not simply whether or not to be proactive in adopting it as part of their online activities, but also whether or not you are going to be reactive in response to any comments on social media sites that may be applicable to the organization.

Weber (2007) suggests that there are seven steps to this method of marketing on the social web:

1. Observe – who is talking about whom, and where are they doing it?
2. Recruit – a core group that will shape a community is essential.
3. Evaluate platforms – what will work best? Blogs or e–communities, for example.
4. Engage – the development of content that will get people coming, talking and responding.
5. Measure – what are the most relevant metrics?
6. Promote – 'build it and they will come' rarely works (if ever).
7. Improve – always look to improve what is on offer.

## MINI CASE

### Pop goes social networking

Following a path already trodden by artists such as Kylie Minogue and the Pussycat Dolls, 2008 saw rap artist 50 Cent launch his own social media site – thisis50.com. Although the rapper has a popular site on MySpace, transferring his networking presence to his own site gives the artist's management greater control over any marketing *on* (e.g. on–page advertising) or *from* (e.g. the email database) the site.

One aspect of business where social media can be used to good effect is in either a niche market or where the promoted product is a person – a consultant, for example. In these cases, the name – the brand – of the seller can be raised in a specific market place by engaging in a small number of influential blogs or communities. Online marketer and blogger, Chris Winfield (www.10e20.com), offers a guide to this practice, including that to be effective you should:

- Connect – add two contacts per week on to sites such as Linkedin or FaceBook.
- Master a forum – find one active forum in your niche and create a real profile there.
- Cut down and move up – focus on a handful in your industry that are viewed as highly influential.
- Meet a digger a day – spend 15 minutes per day contacting a new person from Digg via instant message and forging a bond.
- Focus – stay away from the over-hyped, all-purpose social networks that don't drive traffic or influence people.
- Join the conversation – once per day, use a blog–search tool to search for your name and your company. See where people are talking about you and join in on the conversation.

## Practical Insight

**Students beware – on the Internet, there's no place to hide**

Employers are now looking for job applicants online – so you've registered with the online jobs agency. Great – but what about your own social media pages?
Some SM sites are geared towards finding work – but not all of them. What about:

- That picture of you mooning/flashing passing cars
- That story about you being so drunk/drugged–up after the party you were too ill to go to work?
- Your blog that lists all the lectures you haven't been to?

Employers might think they are hilarious – but they are unlikely to offer you a job. So remember:
Make sure there's nothing on the web that you wouldn't want everyone to see, because online, there's no place to hide.

Practitioner and writer on the subject, Glen Allsopp, is more strategic in his advice, suggesting that there are 15 *'fundamental truths about social media marketing'*. They are:

1. You must get involved in the top social media sites to understand them thoroughly.
2. You must be a real user.
3. Not everything you try will work.

4. Digg failure doesn't mean campaign failure.
5. Results can't be guaranteed.
6. Going niche is often better.
7. Don't try to game the systems.
8. Respect client brands in the process.
9. Go light on selling or promotional messaging.
10. Engage in communities.
11. Offer people value.
12. Create something that is honest.
13. Understand the benefits.
14. Keep track of what is going on.
15. Social media marketing is only one strategy.

---

*Go Online*    To read more on both Chris Winfield and Glen Allsopp's guides follow the link on the chapter's web page.

---

Although I would endorse both of these guides, I would raise a point that is relevant to all and yet ignored by many – be they individual or corporation – and that is this. Whilst some elements of social media marketing can be tactical, to practice it effectively is a strategic decision in that it is long–term in nature. A common reason for failure of SMM initiatives is that they are incorrectly perceived as being both easy and a quick fit. Although a limited number of ad hoc campaigns have had some successful – those which really help organizations meet their strategic online marketing objectives are not only well researched, planned and instigated, they are expensive.

---

*Go Online*    For some of the secrets behind successful social media marketing, follow the link from the chapter's website to read the controversial article 'The Secret Strategies Behind Many "Viral" Videos'.

---

*You Decide*    Advise the marketing department at Huxley University (case study 10) on how they might best use either social networks and/or online communities in their online marketing efforts.
    Alternatively, conduct the same exercise on your organization or that of your employer.

---

## 9.4  VIRTUAL WORLDS

In this section we will look specifically at virtual worlds. However, it should be noted that some virtual worlds exist *within* social networking sites – so emphasising that social media should be considered to be one entity rather than a number of distinct subgroups.

Although serious participants might disagree, virtual worlds are essentially online games played in 3–D environments in which players create virtual characters – avatars – for themselves and use them to inhabit the virtual world and interact with other residents. Perhaps the most famous – and most visited – is Second Life (www.secondlife.com) which opened to the public in 2003 as a futuristic version of Earth – albeit one that has sections that resemble ancient Japan and a virtual Amsterdam, complete with canals. Becoming a *basic* resident of Second Life is free – you simply register, download some software and then create an avatar, give it a name and choose its physical appearance. After spending some time in a training area where you are shown the fundamentals including how your avatar walks or uses any of the various methods of transport available in the virtual world, your virtual life is your own. Once there you – or the virtual you – can wander around, read the Second Life newspaper, watch the Second Life TV station or visit museums and cinemas. Paying a subscription – which start at $10 a month – allows you to spend the local currency (Linden dollars) at shopping malls – or you can buy accommodation, a car or designer clothes for your character. Chatting to other residents is facilitated by a dialogue box at the bottom of the screen. There are even tech-savvy residents who are virtual entrepreneurs – making real money by selling land or items they've created to other residents. The virtual dollars are converted to real dollars where they can be spent in the real world – once the real tax has been paid on it.

**The home page of Second Life**

## DECISION TIME

Although there is evidence of some successful use of virtual worlds as a medium for a marketing message, the opportunities would seem to be limited. As with social networking sites, the major brands have struggled to define a model whereby virtual worlds can be used successfully to – ultimately – generate increased sales. Also like social networking, organizations have the choice of either joining an existing virtual world, or setting up their own. Although a number of global brands – Dell, Adidas and Gap, for example – have joined Second Life, critics of this model point out that when people set up avatars they are not receptive to ads in their virtual worlds – indeed, they have created the online persona to 'escape' everyday life – including its advertising. This online anonymity adds to the problems of marketers – how can you target an audience if they are pretending to be something they are not? Those brands that have found virtual world success are the ones that have set up their own virtual communities. These include MTV and Coca–Cola, who (in December 2007) closed down its YouTube-like social networking channel, 'The Coke Show', and replaced it with CC Metro which allows users to create music mashups and play games, but more importantly, create an avatar which can then shop and dance at the Coca-Cola diner, visit a cinema or fly on a hover–board around a virtual island that is shaped like a Coke bottle.

## MINI CASE

### Virtual bank – real customers

One company that has successfully developed its own virtual environment and seen it integrate effectively into its overall marketing strategy is Wells Fargo. After participating in a third party's environment for around two years the US bank decided to host its own virtual world – with the result that email addresses of thousands of potential (offline) customers have been collected. In addition, the members of the gaming community – called Stagecoach Island – have been subject to brand messages from the bank. That the virtual world had extensive offline promotion at colleges and universities prior to its launch betrays the bank's intention of gaining brand recognition in the 16-to-24-year-old demographic so valuable to financial institutions.

The most successful branded virtual worlds, however, are those targeted at children – which may bode well for the future popularity of virtual worlds. As well as fashion doll-makers Barbie (www.barbiegirls.com) and Bratz (www.be-bratz.com) – who both opened virtual worlds for girls in the summer of 2007 – two of the most popular are Disney's Club Penguin (www. clubpenguin.com) and Webkinz (www.webkinz.com), both of which are free from ads – with users paying for premium content, either by subscription (Club Penguin) or by buying a stuffed toy which comes with a code to the site (Webkinz). One of the oldest virtual worlds, Neopets (www.neopets. com) is reversing the offline–goes–online model by extending its characters to books, toys and TV broadcasts through its parent company – MTV.

*You Decide*  Advise Martha and her marketers at Phelps Online Department Store (case study 13) on how they might use virtual worlds as part of their online marketing efforts.

Alternatively, conduct the same exercise on your organization or that of your employer.

## 9.5  BLOGGING

Although the term *weblog* was first used in 1997, with the *blog* being introduced in 1999, the practice dates back to the early 1990s when individuals who surfed the web and listed (or *logged*) websites that they found interesting, often with their own review of the sites (Charlesworth, 2007). Since that time, online blogs have developed through being online personal journals to mini websites based around the thoughts or interests of the writer. The advent of 'blogging' sites (e.g. blogger.com) that facilitate their easy development saw an explosion of blogs in 2006/07.

> **"** not only are blogs quick and free to set up, they are listed immediately by the search engines **"**

In recent years David Sifry, CEO and founder of blog search engine Technorati (www.technorati.com), has regularly posted his 'State of the Blogosphere' in which he provides blog–related information. In the latest available at the time of writing (April 2007) he says there are 70 million blogs – with Japanese (37 per cent) and English (36 per cent) the most popular languages. However, the majority of these blogs have been created by individuals and are rarely read by anyone other than the writer's close friends – and untold millions are abandoned soon after their creators realise that it can be a chore thinking of content on a regular basis. Research from Jacob Nielsen (2006) suggests that only 0.1 per cent of bloggers contribute [to blogs] on a regular basis. There is, however, a greater problem that is a scourge of the medium – blog spam. Indeed, some commentators suggest that a large percentage of new blogs are set up for this purpose. As we covered in section 6.5, incoming links play an important part in search engine optimization – and so developing as many disingenuous links as possible is a temptation for unscrupulous operators. Prior to the easy–to–set–up blog pages, the so–called black–hat optimizers had to buy domain names and set up web pages on them with the links embedded. More seriously, they had to wait until the sites were indexed by the search engines before those links gained credit. However, not only are blogs quick and free to set up, they are listed immediately by the search engines – particularly blogger.com which is part of the Google empire. Content for these erroneous blogs are often gleaned by harvesting pertinent content from other sites, which although looks OK at first glance, is often nonsense when read in detail.

## MINI CASE

### Dell Hell demonstrates the power of the blogger

When Dell computers gave Jeff Jarvis poor quality goods and even worse quality after–sales service, they didn't realise the publicity that could be generated by someone who is (amongst other things) a former television critic, Sunday editor of the *New York Daily News*, journalism professor at the City University of New York – and keen blogger.

Jeff's blog post – 'Dell lies. Dell sucks' – snowballed in size as readers added their own tales of 'Dell Hell' and dozens of bloggers added links to the page from their own sites. Despite Jarvis emailing Dell advising them to read his comments and the blog appearing high in the search engine returns for searches on "Dell", Jarvis only heard from the computer company when he sent an email to the company's chief marketing officer. By this time, however, the story had been picked up by mainstream media around the globe, Jarvis had become a celebrity and 'Dell Hell' was a pseudonym for bad service. Not a good brand endorsement.

Another way that links can be created is by adding comments to other people's blogs – where membership of that blogging community will sometimes automatically add a link to your own website. Whilst genuine blog–commenters (myself included) will only take the time to leave comments on blogs they feel strongly about (e.g. very good or ill–informed), blog–spammers have the single purpose of gaining an incoming link to their site and add nothing relevant to the subject of the original blog – often spamming a comment like 'I couldn't understand some parts of this article, but found it interesting anyway' on thousands of blogs. Obviously, this adds nothing to the content of the host blog.

A page from my own blog, which I use to hi-light good and bad practice in online marketing, in this case blog spamming.

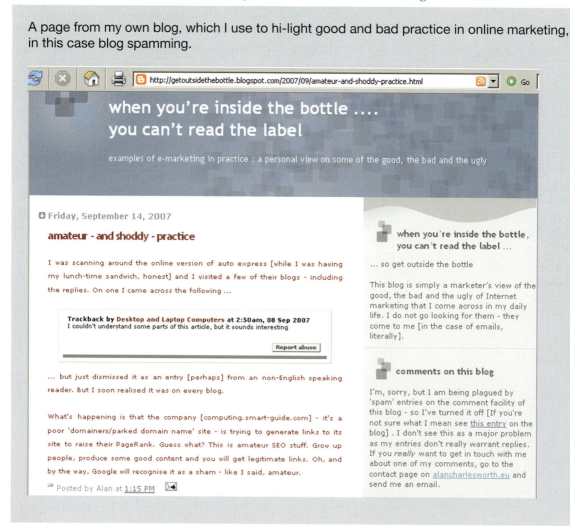

In commercial terms, blogs are normally used as a voice of an organization, an individual within an organization or as an outlet for people who are promoting themselves (e.g. their consulting services). With all of these, the writer is looking to exhibit their skills and experience within the topic on which they are writing and so develop an affinity between the brand and reader. It is not surprising that many 'experts' in e-marketing have become recognized – or more extensively recognized – in their field by developing blog sites that are widely read. Similarly, the blog-commenter can also raise their profile by responding to comments in well-read blogs. Obviously this requires some knowledge in the subject area, and no little time, but my own limited experience shows that when I add a pertinent comment to a blog the visitor numbers to my website will rise for a day or so.

Bloggers are also a valuable tool in viral marketing – which we cover in more detail in the next section – in that they may read content on your own blog (or website, or offline publication) and make their own observations on it. Such is the nature of the web that those observations may, in turn, be commented on in other blogs – so extending the readership of your original content. Indeed, it is not unusual for individual's blogs to become the debating chambers for online arguments.

## Practical Insight

### Socially unacceptable

It is not uncommon for promotional companies to act as go-betweens for advertisers and bloggers – arranging fees for each time a blogger 'promotes' a product or brand. For example, within her daily content, a 'rewarded' female teen blogger might rave about a new movie she has just seen and suggest her online friends go and watch it. The practice becomes even more dubious if the blogger has a reputation as an expert within a certain subject area. Having an expert blogger tell of a website she finds useful – and why – is what social media is all about and so her being paid to do so raises moral questions about the blogger and betrays the concept that is social media. However, it is to the credit of social media and its users that 'phoney' bloggers are soon rumbled and so lose their appeal, readers and income. It is, however, acceptable for genuine bloggers to accept payments if they declare their interests. In the blogosphere, honesty goes a long way. Note that popular bloggers are often the e–influencers I mentioned in section 2 of this chapter.

## DECISION TIME

For many marketers – if not most – blogs are something that might cause a blip on their online radar occasionally, but in the main they simply ignore them as a medium for a marketing message. If you are to employ them, however, Scott (2007) suggests there are three ways to use blogs:

1. Monitor other blogs (see also *online public relations* and *reputation management* in chapter 10)

- If you do relate to an original blog – make sure you (1) quote it correctly, and (2) get your facts right – i.e. make sure you appreciate the point that is being made.

---

*Go Online*   The Word of Mouth Marketing Association (WOMMA) offers marketers a list of 10 Principles for Ethical Contact with bloggers – follow the link from the chapter's web page to read them.

---

*You Decide*   Advise Lindsey Naegle (case study 12) on how she might use blogs as an element of the online marketing of her consulting service.

Alternatively, conduct the same exercise for your organization or that of your employer.

---

## 9.6  VIRAL MARKETING

It is worth starting this section by explaining why I have included it in a chapter on social media marketing. The reason is quite simple. Although it is an online marketing concept in its own right, if it is to be successful, any viral campaign relies heavily – perhaps totally – on people using the various elements of social media in order to forward the message. Indeed, an extensive review of social networking by TNS, TRU & Marketing Evolution (2007) found that whilst advertising still has some effect, over half of the impact of social network marketing comes from 'the momentum effect' that occurs when one consumer passes along the information to their 'friends'. Also worth mentioning is that – like many aspects of SMM – effective viral marketing is strategic, and not something to be left to individuals to conduct on an ad hoc basis. The merging of social media and viral is exemplified in the contemporary marketing of movies. Earlier in the chapter I used the film *Snakes on a Plane* as an example of citizen marketing, where the movie's marketers had little to do with its social media success. Leading up to the summer blockbusters for 2008, however, the film makers looked to kick–start SMM with viral campaigns. Warner Brothers, for example, developed more than 30 websites in the 12 months running up to the July release of the latest Batman movie – Dark Knight. The sites provided clues to where the pre–release screening would take place – though solving clues apparently left by Batman character *the Joker* was far from simple. It would be hard to argue that the studio's social media campaign was not a significant element in the film's takings for pre-view screenings, opening night and the three-day opening all breaking box office records.

The concept of viral marketing is based on the centuries-old practice of word-of-mouth marketing – an oral, person-to-person communication between a receiver and a communicator (whom the receiver perceives as non-commercial) regarding a brand, a product or a service (Arndt, 1967). The contribution made by the Internet – as was the case with the printing press, the telephone, radio and television – is that once the word is out, it can get around faster than ever before. However, rather being used simply to represent online word–of–mouth, the term *viral marketing* has been somewhat hijacked by what social web expert Larry Weber (2007), describes as 'silly virals'. He uses Burger King's 'Subservient Chicken' (www.subservientchicken.com) promotion as an example of this phenomenon and goes on to suggest that true online word-of-mouth is about content–based *virality*. In other words, it is something about the product, brand or organization that the marketer wishes to be passed on by – hopefully satisfied – customers. To be employed successfully, it is the marketing message that should be communicated by the consumers. In his book *Unleashing the Ideavirus* (2001) author and acknowledged expert on the subject, Seth Godin, expands on the word-of-mouth origins of viral marketing by making the point that a viral message (his *ideavirus*) gains momentum by spreading across multiple media, so helping it reach more people. His point is well made – many online virals only move away from a niche audience when they are featured in offline media.

*Go Online* **Walking the viral walk**

Note that Seth Godin doesn't just talk the talk when he eulogises viral marketing. *Unleashing the Idea Virus*, can be purchased as a hardcover book from a shop – but he also gives it away as an e–book. Follow the link on the chapter's web page for your free copy.

Indeed, the truly global virals – the ones that get featured in books like this one – depend on an aspect of both the off- and online exposure that is essential if the campaign is to be successful. Whilst viral marketing is built around consumers communicating with consumers (and the use of social media obviously enhances this) the main conduit for a successful viral campaign is often the TV, radio, and the printed press. Reporters pick up the message and release the viral message through their own media – and for a short while this has the effect of a virtuous circle. People see the story on TV, radio or in a newspaper (often as a news story, which means it meets the criteria of public relations when compared to advertising) and so seek out the viral message online. They then forward it to their friends and colleagues and so the virus spreads even faster. The reverse can also be practiced by the astute marketer. Cadbury's, for example, released clips of their 'drumming gorilla' advert onto the web long before the ad was ever aired on television – making the impact even greater when it was seen by a 'new' TV audience. The virtuous circle continues into search engine listings – the more that websites and blogs talk about a viral, the more link popularity it gains and so it rises to the top of listings – where it is available to an even wider audience.

## Practical Insight

**Us? No we would never do such a thing.**

Some of the most successful viral campaigns have been those with a sense of controversy. Although there will always be a line that should not be crossed, sometimes controversy itself is part of the viral strategy. In order to court public outcry without damaging the brand, companies sometimes use so-called 'sub virals' – often spoofs deliberately released by advertisers mocking their own ads. Naturally, they deny all knowledge of the spoofs, though enough doubt is left in the public domain to increase debate – and so develop the viral campaign even more.

See the chapter's web page for links to one of the most controversial – and so successful – sub viral campaign, Ford's Ka 'eviltwin' story as well as an excellent article about some campaigns that were too risqué to include in this book.

Most viral campaigns depend either on something that can be transmitted online – a joke, image or game, for example – or they are in response to an event or happening (for examples, see the minicase 'Add sweet to soda and take cover' in this section and the *Snakes on a Plane* example in the section 9.2). There is, however, a third option – the *manufactured* event. In this case the viral elements will need a kick start from (1) the event being in some way amusing or interesting, and (2) there being offline coverage through news and/or PR. Successful proponents of this tactic is the online casino, GoldenPalace.com. Perhaps their most notable 'event' was when they bought TV star William Shatner's kidney stone for some $25,000. Expensive, you may think – but not when you consider the amount of times the story was featured on TV and how many bloggers commented on the story. And every one of those blogs included the term 'goldenpalace.com' and usually a link to that site. In both branding and search engine link terms this represents a kind of marketing nirvana – and cheap at the price.

## MINI CASE

**Add candy to soda and take cover**

Although pranksters had apparently been doing it for a number of years, it wasn't until the result of putting a Mentos sweet (candy) into a bottle of Diet Coke – a geyser of foam up to ten feet high – appeared in an online video that it became a world–wide phenomenon. After Fritz Grobe and Stephen Voltz featured the basic experiment on their website, the viral buzz went into overdrive when they combined 200 litres of Diet Coke and over 500 Mentos mints. The pair gained even more notoriety as the mainstream press caught on – including them appearing on popular late night chat shows. Mentos also rode the free–publicity bandwagon, joining in with the fun and raising their credibility – and sales – in a demographic they could never hope to reach with traditional promotional efforts. Coca Cola, on the other hand, adopted a more formal approach, originally shunning the publicity and distancing themselves from the whole thing – and got berated by bloggers for failing to show a sense of humour.

> many would argue that the 'manufactured' viral is more like *advertising*, and betrays the basic ethos of the concept

Viral marketing does not have to be a complex undertaking, however. As with Weber's comment (re 'silly virals') the custom–made event, video clip or campaign that – ultimately – promotes the organization is often perceived as what viral marketing is all about. This is not the case – and many would argue that the 'manufactured' viral is more like *advertising*, and betrays the basic ethos of the concept, which is to encourage, aid or prompt satis-fied customers in spreading a good word about – or recommen-dation for – the product, service, brand or organization. An email signature line that encourages users to click through the link to a web page, for example, would be considered as viral. Similarly, a website or email link that prompts readers to 'forward this to a friend' helps transmit the message beyond the original recipient. Perhaps the classic example of online viral marketing is Hotmail (www.hotmail.com), which went from launch to twelve million users spending less than $500K on marketing, advertising and promotion. The Hotmail concept was simple, develop a quality product, then give it away – but on every 'prod-uct' (email) include a message advising readers on how to sign up for the same free service. The users did the rest (Gay et al, 2007). Although he never claimed to have invented the concept, Steve Jurvetson – the venture capital-ist behind Hotmail – was the first to coin the phrase 'viral marketing'.

Essentially, the success of any viral marketing depends on three funda-mental issues, they are that:

1. The originator of the message must benefit from its propagation – there-fore there should be a specific objective behind any viral campaign.
2. The sender – that is, anyone who passes the message on to others – is actively seeking, or at least willing to receive, any kudos that comes from forwarding the message.
3. The receiver must perceive value in the message. For example if it is a joke they should find it funny.

A fourth element might be added here – one that relates to the time that the viral is in the public domain and is consistent with another offline model – the product life cycle (PLC). In its early days, the viral add will be worth more kudos to the sender in that it is new – these people are the early adopters in the PLC. They are proactive in seeking new virals and are seen as influencers in the marketplace (see also e-fluencers, section 9.2). As time goes by – the life cycle of the viral, if you will – the early adop-ters will distance themselves from the campaign as the mainstream and (eventually) laggards take in the viral. In the longer time frame this notion becomes detrimental to the campaign itself. If anyone has already received the message when the media-fed user sends it out, then:

• The esteem in which the sender is held is reduced – and so they are unwilling to risk their reputation by forwarding 'old news'.
• If they have seen it before, the receiver perceives no value in the com-munication, and so
• The originator receives no benefit – and such is the nature of some campaigns being seen as 'leading edge', that they may experience an 'unfashionable' backlash if the campaigns goes on for too long.

This last point brings us to what is the major drawback in viral marketing, that of control – or lack thereof – once the message is 'launched'. As indicated above, time is the first issue in this respect. A viral campaign has no closing date – as there would be in an advertising campaign, for example, where all ads can be withdrawn before a set date. The second – equally important – issue is that of keeping the message within the sphere of the target audience. Viral messages are normally targeted at a particular segment of the market who (hopefully) will find them relevant, amusing or useful. Although getting the message outside of this 'safe' environment might be the intention of a viral marketer who wants an element of controversy, generally having a message arrive in the email in–box or social media home page of another group of customers who find them to be offensive is to be avoided.

## MINI CASE

**Beauty is in the eye of the beholder**

The Cannes Lions Grand Prix winner in 2007 was Dove's 'Evolution' that relied on people to socially, or *virally*, spread the message. The short – it lasts just over a minute – time-lapse film depicts a young woman's transformation from ordinary girl to beautiful billboard model. It has the objective of promoting 'Dove Self-Esteem' workshops by revealing how everything from the lighting, hair styling, make-up and even the photoshop-stretching of neck and impossible widening of eyes is used to produce the 'model' in the ad. The end–message of 'no wonder our perception of beauty is distorted' emphasises the message. Naturally enough, it is an easy target for parody – links to the original and 'slob evolution' can both be found on the chapter's web page.

## DECISION TIME

With the exception of the basic aspects of what is recognized as viral marketing ('forward this to a friend', for example), the concept is not for all – indeed, some would argue it is suitable for very few organizations.

Even those basic elements should be considered carefully. It is not unknown for organizations to have the IT department set up a 'footer' that is appended to every email sent by every member of staff. Such messages are marketing–related, but sadly they are not suitable for all communications. Something like 'see our special offers on our website' (with an associated link) might be OK for new customers – but not so for email messages to suppliers, potential employees or even dissatisfied customers. Even the excellent concept of a 'forward to a friend' facility should be carefully considered before being put into practice. I have come across such services that required me to complete a form with my name, address, phone number (and more) before I could forward the page. The email address of the sender and recipient plus either a fixed message (your friend at this email address thought you would find this useful) or a space for a personalized message should be enough.

## Practical Insight

### Pepsi reward evangelists

Speaking at the Email Evolution Conference, (Feb 2008, San Diego, USA), Pepsi's senior marketing manager, Lawrence DiCapua, commented that the company identifies customers who forward email messages and rewards them with a special VIP programme within the Pepsi Extras loyalty program.

If viral is to be used beyond these basic elements, however, there are a number of criteria that any successful viral campaign requires, not least that:

- The message is worth forwarding – peer status rises or falls depending on quality the messages forwarded. Good news, or that which makes the receiver feel happy, is more likely to be forwarded repeatedly (Lin et al, 2006). Adding something tangible – a quiz, video or joke, for example – adds to the chances of a message being passed on.
- It must be easy to forward – good usability techniques should make it simple for the receiver to pass the message on to others. A prominent, easy to use (e.g. no detailed form to complete) 'forward to a friend' button is essential.
- The right audience is targeted – though, by the very nature of viral marketing, this is problematic. The difficulty is that although the targeting of the original message is controlled by the organization – that control is lost once the message is released. The original recipients cannot be relied on to forward the message to those who will appreciate it, particularly if 'group' or 'all friends' lists are used to pass it on.
- The message is placed where it can be seen – rather than targeting a mailing list, for example, the original message can be placed on an appropriate website, message board or blog.

# MINI CASE

### Check the date of this offer

In the UK, April 1st is 'April Fools' day – where anyone falling for a trick is deemed to be an 'April Fool'. In 2008, fast food restaurant Pizza Hut joined in the fun with a spoof email offering household services with pizza deliveries. Following the 'click for details' link revealed the prank. Naturally, anyone caught out by the prank–email forwarded it on to friends and colleagues in an attempt to fool them also.

The April the first email message from Pizza Hut

The trick is revealed on the website

As with so many elements of online marketing, specialist help is best engaged in instigating a viral marketing campaign. Although the original idea of – for example – a spoof video can come from in–house, the technical aspects of developing both the video and the way in which it will be communicated is not something the staff (marketing and technical) of most organizations will be able to do themselves. And do not be fooled by those 'amateur' viral videos that are often successful (though very rare exceptions exist) they too are the result of skilled crafts people who recognise that the facade of amateurism serves the objective better than a more 'professional' appearance.

## Practical Insight

### Forgotten, but not gone

Viral campaigns have no time frame so any page locations-URLs – should be permanent. For example, a blog might say 'take a look at this useful article' (with a link), and though most visitors might arrive within days of the blog being written, users could be clicking on the link for years to come. If the campaign has become out-dated then the content on the URL can be amended appropriately.

As a footnote, it is worth noting that the online marketer must have appropriate objectives for any viral campaign they instigate. As with the online presence, where few businesses can expect thousands of visitors every day, then *success* for a campaign does not necessarily mean it has been featured on CNN and the BBC and has become a catchphrase for comedians. For a small B2B organization having your industry-related viral game played by most of your customers and a few of their social contacts is as much as you can expect. And as with all marketing – off- and online – there must be a return on any investment made, so paying out £10,000 for a personalized game for 20 customers who have an annual invoice value of a few hundred pounds each is simply not going to pay its dues. Similarly, like some TV adverts, any virals should not succeed in form over substance – it is no good having a novelty video that everyone is talking about if no one can remember the brand behind the promotion.

*You Decide*  Advise Phil and his marketers at the Cleethorpes Visitors Association (case study 4) on how they might use viral marketing to their advantage.
   Alternatively, conduct the same exercise for your organization or that of your employer.

## 9.7   ONLINE PUBLIC RELATIONS AND REPUTATION MANAGEMENT

Before getting into the detail of this section it is worth pointing out why I decided to include it in this chapter. The Collins English Dictionary describes 'public relations' as; *'the practice of creating, promoting or maintaining goodwill and a favourable image among the public towards an institution, public body etc'* – with the same term being used to describe *'the methods and techniques employed'* in that practice. As you will see in the following pages – with the exception of the content of the organization's own website – online, those 'methods and techniques' invariably use social media sites – the examples I use in the section on viral marketing are evidence of this. It is also the case that in the 21st century, public relations (PR) goes beyond promoting goodwill and has responsibility for responding to – or defending – that goodwill from events, actions or stories that might damage its reputation or brand. It is also worth mentioning that I do appreciate that *public* and *press* relations are not the same thing. However, such is the nature of public relations that any relationship with the press is an important element of its practice – therefore an element of press relations is integral to this section.

Also significant is the increase in the quantity of media outlets brought about by the *digital* age. Up until the last decade of the last century newspapers and TV and radio channels were limited in number. This meant that journalists held a position of some power in that they were the gatekeepers to a limited number of media outlets. With the proliferation of media outlets, however, the power has switched somewhat. Now, rather than the PR operative seeking out a small number of influential journalists, it is becoming the case that it is the reporter who is the one seeking the information – and in a very competitive marketplace. Internet technology and its use have led to PR being made available to marketers beyond the close-knit society that is (was?) offline public and press relations. It has also diluted PR's role as the 'gatekeepers of access' that representatives of offline media had over the dissemination of information. Prior to the Internet, the organization's PR staff or agents would have a list of journalists to whom they could pass (by post, fax or 'wire') their carefully prepared releases. If the journalist (a) received the release, (b) read it, (c) liked the content, and (d) had space in their column or publication, then the release was published in a place where the general public might read it. Nowadays, however, the release can be made immediately available to the general public – which includes citizen journalists. Obviously, having any press release be featured on a popular or influential website will undoubtedly help spread the message further and faster. To this end, the online PR team should get the attention of those publishers and bloggers that are prominent in the marketplace or environment relevant to the story being propagated.

> " It has also diluted PR's role as the 'gatekeepers of access' that representatives of offline media had over the dissemination of information "

## Link development and public relations

As we discovered in section 6.5, having links into your website can increase its search engine ranking – and it didn't take search engine optimizers long to realise that all online press releases include a (legitimate) link to the organization's website. This meant that if any reputable online news sites featured the story a *quality* link would be a by–product.

### MINI CASE

#### Expensive music download – cut-price marketing

Creating your own story – and then publicizing it online can be considered good online PR. An excellent example came following the 'Radiohead name–your–price download' event in October 2007 (see the link on the chapter's web page). Ohio based button–makers – we call them *badges* in the UK – 'Pure Buttons' showed their support for the band by paying $1,000. However, rather than keeping it their little secret, they not only issued a press release, but submitted a link targeting the press release on the social media site, Digg (www.digg.com).

That I have perpetuated the publicity by using the event as a case study simply confirms how good an idea it was.

However, for some organizations this *by–product* was soon to become equally important – and for many, the primary motive for extensive PR campaigns. Indeed, there is a reasonable argument that to a certain degree the *traditional* purposes of a press release have been hi–jacked by SEOs and used simply as a means of creating inbound links. Consider, for example, PRWeb (www.prweb.com), the leading online distributor of press releases – on its website, at the top of a list of 'exclusive benefits' is the statement: 'boost your website traffic and SEO'. 'Send your news to top journalists' comes in at number four. Supporting this argument is research by non–profit think tank the Society for New Communications Research (2008). According to the study, less than a third of press releases have their primary objective as conveying information to the press – their traditional purpose. Their value in search engine optimization was the chief objective.

Purists argue that it is this practice that has diluted both the reputation and the quality of the press release. An example would be the 'manufactured event'. Whilst traditional PR is normally concerned with getting the best leverage from events that take place as part of an organization's operations, for link development – as with some aspects of viral marketing with which online PR has a strong relationship – events are staged with no other objective other than to create a newsworthy story.

Whatever the primary objective of the press release, however, it is still the case that in the majority of cases it is the standing of the releasing organization that dictates its proliferation. Whilst a story about a factory extension that will create 20 new jobs might make the local news, it carries little or no interest outside the region in which that factory is located. Similarly, the announcement of a new product in a specific industry will interest only those who will benefit from that product's development. Although both of these examples will generate limited publicity – and so inbound links – they cannot compare with the PR of major organizations or brands. A Google press release, for example, might be of interest to (1) anyone who uses search engines (everyone who uses the Internet), (2) those who work in that industry, and (3) the financial institutions that monitor the value of Google's stock. Ultimately, as with all marketing, effective press–release practice requires the targeting of segments that are receptive of the message you are sending. Get that right and you will benefit from both the PR exercise and in–coming links to your website.

## PR meets SEO

An optimized press release can increase an organization's online visibility. This 'infographic' demonstrates how – from a search perspective – you can gain in-bound links and an industry buzz.

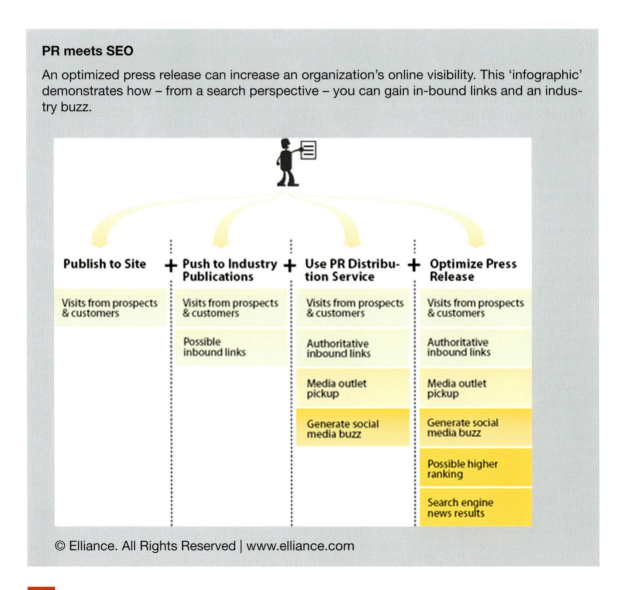

| Publish to Site | + Push to Industry Publications | + Use PR Distribution Service | + Optimize Press Release |
|---|---|---|---|
| Visits from prospects & customers | Visits from prospects & customers | Visits from prospects & customers | Visits from prospects & customers |
| | Possible inbound links | Authoritative inbound links | Authoritative inbound links |
| | | Media outlet pickup | Media outlet pickup |
| | | Generate social media buzz | Generate social media buzz |
| | | | Possible higher ranking |
| | | | Search engine news results |

# Reputation management

Although we considered in section 9.3 how the online marketer might use social networks and online communities as part of an integrated strategy, the issue of reputation management is a more specific element of that strategy, and it would normally fall under the remit of the public relations department (though it could also be an facet of market intelligence). It has long been common practice for an organization to keep track of how it – and its brands or products – are depicted in the media. Prior to the Internet this would amount to perusing national or significant local newspapers and tracking TV and radio news and current affairs programmes. However, as we have seen in earlier sections of this chapter, there are now more media channels and even more websites that are accessible for the 'person in the street' to comment on products, brands and organizations. Negative reputation issues might arise online in a number of types of website, including:

- Detrimental feedback on forums or review sites
- Cyberbashing sites
- Negative blog posts – or damaging comments added to posts that originally take a neutral or positive stance
- Logo Infringement – bids on trademarked terms in pay per click advertising, for example
- Negative social network groups – not all groups set out to support products or organizations.

Fortunately, software is available to help the PR professional to track what is being said online. As with many aspect of marketing – both off– and online – the process can be carried out in–house out out–sourced to a specialist firm. Either way, an effective reputation management process would include:

- The collection of data – this could be from such online presences as; blogs, forums, review sites and message boards for user generated content, plus news and magazine sites as well as PR newswires for that of professional journalists.
- In the processing stage useless data (duplicated content that is common in blogs, for example) or irrelevant (perhaps a similar brand or organizational name) is discarded. Useful data is then processed into logical groups for analysis.
- The data analysis phase normally sees the first human action, where staff can review that data deemed important by the digital investigation. Such analysis would grade each article or comment based on criteria that might include: its relevance (potential effect on sales or marketing) and spread (how popular is the website on which it appears) as well as the influence of its author and/or the web presence that hosts it. Reports are then developed that can be made available to decision makers.
- Action. Although the nature of the problem and structure of the organization will determine the responsibility for taking action to address any

issues, it is at this stage that many reputation management programmes fail. By their very nature, online problems need to be addressed immediately – even an hour's delay in responding to negative comments from an influential blogger might be long enough for the story to catch the imagination of the fellow bloggers and spread around the web. Preferably, the reputation management team will have the authority to react themselves (a good reason for it to be part of PR) or have immediate access to decision makers if the issue is more serious. Having the report sit in an in–tray or in–box of a senior manager is not the way to manage your reputation online.

## Practical Insight

### Negative search–term tracking

Google has a (free) faculty that informs you whenever a searcher uses specific keywords in a Google search – plus the site they go to from the SERP (narcissistically, I track searches on my own name). By adding some negative terms such as 'sucks' or 'problems' to your brand, product or organization's name you will get an early warning of potential problems. Commercial software is available that will widen the hunt beyond Google searches.

A final consideration for those responsible for online reputation management is that of disaster recovery. Although any contingency planning to address potential disasters that might strike the organization is a strategic business decision – it is the PR department that will be the public face of that plan – and online has a part to play. No matter what the size of the organization, or its dependency on the Internet for its income, any contingency plan should include pre–prepared web content, be that in the form of PR releases, blog content, email messages or mini–sites complete with contact details, FAQ pages and a media newsroom. Not that it ever was, but particularly in the digital age, burying your head in the sand when something goes wrong is not an option.

## DECISION TIME

Although this section includes the term 'online public relations' in its title it is unlikely that any organization will conduct purely online PR – even online–only traders need to address PR offline. It is the case, therefore, that the online element will be just part of the overall PR strategy. This being so, as with other aspects of marketing covered in this book, the online ingredients of the PR mix will take their lead from the offline strategy and so I will not spend time attempting to cover the entire subject of PR (a book in its own right) – but simply address the web–based aspects.

The first issue to address is what do we tell folk about? We'll ignore the manufactured events covered earlier as features of other aspects of online marketing (SEO and viral, for example) and concentrate on *natural* events. David Meerman Scott (2007) suggests that news releases should be a frequent occurrence and not just for 'big news' – and he is right, although too many minor stories may overload recipients and cause major events to pass without notice within the volume. Careful consideration over segmentation can help here. The appointment of a new sales director might interest industry insiders, for example, but be of little interest to a product–oriented blogger. The second issue to address is where can releases be published online? Possibilities include:

- Your own website – preferably on a dedicated press or news page
- Trade associations – spreading news about their members' activities is normally part of any association's objectives
- Local business networks – as with trade associations, these networks, many of them government sponsored, actively seek to promote releases from local businesses as part of their remit
- Online magazines and journals
- Newspapers – particularly those local to your organization, they all have an online edition
- Blogs – always do your research on the relevant blogs to see how, or if, they accept releases. Attempting to sneak them in as comments or feedback is not good practice
- Online press services – websites where you can upload press releases so that they are available to be searched by a global audience
- Press release distributors – who, for a fee, will handle the online distribution of your release. For those organizations that lack the in-house resources this might be the best option
- PR agencies – the full-service option, these undertake your entire PR requirements from research through writing to publishing and distribution of releases.

Note that for all except your own website, time should be spent in identifying which person or department you need to send your release to before its submission. It is also the case that a release can be tweaked to best suit a particular publication's readers. Both of these time-consuming exercises would be part of a PR agency's commission – usually making the fee worth paying. It should go without saying that any release – press or public – should be professionally written. Like any corporate communication, the message and its presentation is a symbol of the sending organization – and as with all web content cost–cutting in this regard is an error. Two important issues to note with regard to the content development are that (1) releases can benefit the SEO of the organization, therefore they should also be written with key word inclusion as a priority, and (2) as highlight by Scott (2007), because the public is just as likely to read the publications in which the releases appear, they should appeal to buyers, not just journalists. This second point is emphasized in section 5.2, where mention was made (in a research snapshot) of what B2B buyers look at

# MINI CASE

## Enter the social–media newsroom

Although a number of organizations have made full use of what the web can offer in their PR efforts (notably Cisco – see www.newsroom.cisco.com), one of the first to apply social media–friendly applications to its press and public relations efforts was General Motors. GM's social–media newsroom includes:

- News releases to which journalists can add their own comments in blog style – with a trackback facility to follow subsequent comments
- Cool photos – not old 'stock' pictures – in an online album hosted on photo-sharing site Flickr.
- Similarly fashionable videos in a library hosted on YouTube.
- Links to facilitate all news releases being saved or shared via social media sites like del.icio.us and dig.
- Content that is represented by a keyword cloud – allowing visitors to organize the content to their own purposes

GM's innovative approach was also rewarded from an unexpected quarter in that their adventurous social media newsroom became the talk of that very media in their own columns and blogs – not only making the newsroom into news, but scoring high in search engine indexes.

The GM Europe Social Media Newsroom:

online. Not only was the top reason for going online to keep up to date with news in their sector – which would obviously include content that originates in press releases – but the other purposes (noted in the research) included: to review/analyze competitor activity, research and inform business decisions, review products and suppliers, and research and inform purchasing decisions. The astute PR manager could include information pertinent to all of these in any PR material.

## Practical Insight

### Online, timing isn't the same as it is offline

Press releases delivered in traditional media are immediate, and by tomorrow – they are history. Therefore, when putting release online – where it may sit for years – it is worth 'doctoring' it for an online audience. For example, the prose of the release will be that it is breaking news – it will use 'today' in its description of events, not something that makes sense if read on a website several months later. Similarly, it will include a description of the key players and even the organization itself – none of which are necessary if the release is being read on that organization's website.

With regard to reputation management the key decisions are:

1. Is it worthwhile – that is, will the cost out-weigh any potential damage?
2. To what extent do we need to monitor the web?
3. In-house or outsource – do we have the resources within the organization, or do we use a specialist company?

Let's consider those issues in turn. Although this chapter (and others) cover in detail the role of the web in buying decisions, there are still markets and industries that are not Internet-dependent. Someone commenting on an obscure blog that they think a certain employee in a local restaurant somewhere in downtown Smallsville is bad at their job is not going to cause that business to close down. The truth of the matter is that no one except the blogger's friends will ever read the comments – and the blogger will already have told them about the restaurant anyway. However, if you are global entity or you trade in a market that is greatly influenced by the web then ignoring negative comments – whether they are valid or not – could lead to lost sales. These two extremes can be carried over into the consideration of the depth you go to in monitoring what is being said about you. For the one-off restaurant simply tracking the use of your trading name using basic software (blog-monitoring tools, for example) will normally be sufficient. Even cheaper is to simply get into the habit of putting your business name into a search engine on a regular basis – if you don't find any adverse comments neither will anyone else. As with other aspects of Internet marketing, the medium's technology can actually come to your aid here. Outside agencies will set up and host reputation management systems that meet your requirements and simply send you the reports – though you will need to facilitate the appropriate action being taken when necessary. A good rule of thumb would be that if your organization is big enough to have a dedicated PR department then their duties should include in-house reputation management. If you outsource your PR operations, go external for reputation management also.

## MINI CASE

### Telecoms company appoint a 'Twitter–monitor'

Comcast, America's largest provider of cable services, doesn't enjoy a good reputation with many of its customers – there is even a cyberbashing site called 'comcastmustdie.com'. However, 2008 saw it add to its customer service provision by tracking customer comments in the social media environment.

The development of the new facility came about rather serendipitously when an influential blogger wrote about his Comcast system failing, the blog entry (on Twitter) was spotted by a Comcast employee – and a tech team was dispatched to his home to fix his Internet connection. His subsequent comments on Twitter describing the incident soon spread around the blogosphere. The Comcast employee, one Frank Eliason, had long held a view that monitoring Twitter would help the organization to provide a better service for customers – and this event was the prompt his bosses needed to agree to him become the company's official 'Twitter guy'.

A final point worth mentioning is that it is not only your own brand or organization's online reputation that is worth tracking – what people are saying about your competitors' reputations is worth watching too. It may not be very sporting, but if one of your competitors does something to damage its public standing, if you are on the ball – and creative with your marketing – you might be able to take advantage of their slip. An example comes from mobile phone makers, Nokia. Although industry reviewers rated their 'Nseries' superior to the Apple 'iPhone', it was the iPhone that hogged the press limelight. However, soon after the iPhone launch it became clear that Apple product could only be used on specified networks (e.g. $O_2$ in the UK and AT&T in the US) and also had download restrictions. As the blogs exploded with comments from disgruntled iPhone buyers, Nokia quickly launched a campaign tagged, *'open to anything'*. At the time, the Nokia website carried the comment that the Nseries (iPhone's direct competitor) was: *'Open to applications. Open to widgets. Open to anything. So go ahead and load it up. What it does is up to you.'* Sporting? No, but it was excellent marketing – business is not a game.

## MINI CASE

### Managing away bad reputations on the SERPs

As part of their job, reputation managers will aim to keep websites that have anything negative to say about their clients away from the top of the search engine results pages. They know, however, that it is impossible to close down these sites – some of them may be reputable publications reporting true stories. What the reputation manager does, therefore, is make sure the SERP has plenty of *positive* sites ahead of those with damaging content. Using SEO tactics (see chapter 6), alternative sites – some of which the clients may have influence over – are optimized to appear at the top of the rankings. If none exist then sites with suitable content are developed to serve the purpose. For obvious reasons such search engine management is not made public, but a little time spent searching for famous – or infamous – celebrities can produce some interesting results.

For an example follow the link on the chapter's web page.

*You Decide*    Advise the marketing team at Hill Street Motorist Shops (case study 8) on whether or not they should undertake a strategy of online reputation management – and what might be the consequences of not doing so.

Alternatively, conduct the same exercise for your organization or that of your employer.

## CHAPTER EXERCISE

Giving justifications for all your decisions, advise the board of the Matthew Humberstone Foundation Hospital (case study 6) on all aspects of social media marketing covered in this chapter. This includes taking a look at the 'dummy' blog that can be found by following the link from the chapter's web page.

Alternatively, conduct the same exercise for your organization or that of your employer.

## REFERENCES

Ahn, R., Ryu, S. & Han, I. (2004). The impact of the online and offline features on the user acceptance of Internet shopping malls. *Electronic Commerce Research and Applications*. Vol. 3, No. 4, pp. 405–420.

Anderson, C. (2006). *The Long Tail*. Hyperion Books.

Arndt, J. (1967). Word of Mouth Advertising: A Review of the Literature. Advertising Research Foundation, New York.

Charlesworth, A. (2007). *Key Concepts in e–Commerce*. Palgrave MacMillan.

CompleteInc (2006a). *S–Commerce: Beyond MySpace and YouTube*. Available on www.competeinc.com/research/spark

Compete inc. (2006b). *Embracing Consumer Buzz Creates Measurement Challenges for Marketers*. Available on wwwcompete.com.

comScore, Inc./The Kelsey Group, November 2007. *Online Review Influence on Purchase Decision*. Available online at www.comscore.com/press/release.asp?press = 1928

ComScore Inc with Procter & Gamble (2007). The Digital Shelf: the Opportunity for Search Marketing in Consumer Packaged Goods. ComScore, Inc.

Constantinides, E. & Fountain, S.J. (2008). Web 2.0: Conceptual foundations and marketing issues. *Journal of Direct, Data and Digital Marketing Practice.* Vol. 9.3 pp. 231–244.

Deloitte (2007). *State of the Media Democracy*. Deloitte Development LLC.

Deloitte Consumer Product Group (2007). *The View from the Glass House: Competing in a Transparent Marketplace*. www.deloitte.com

Euroblog2007: (2007). *Social Software – A Revolution for Communication? Implications and Challenges for Communication Management and PR*. Available on www.euroblog2007.organization

Freedman, L. (2008). *Merchant and Customer Perspectives On Customer Reviews and User-Generated Content*. PowerReviews/the e–tailing group. Available on http://www.powerreviews.com/social-shopping/news/press_white_02122008.html

Gay, R., Charlesworth, A. & Esen, R. (2007). Online Marketing – A Customer-Led Approach. University Press, Oxford.

Gilly, M.C., Graham, J.L., Wolfinbanger, M.F. & Yale, L.J. (1998). A dyadic study of interpersonal information search. *Journal of the Academy of Marketing Science.* Vol. 26 pp. 83–100.

Godin, S. (2001). Unleashing the Ideavirus. Do You Zoom Inc.

Goetzinger, L., Park, J.K. & Widdows, R. (2006). E-customers' third party complaining and complimenting behaviour. *International Journal of Service Industry Management.* Vol. 17, No. 2, pp. 193–206.

Granovetter, M. (1973). The Strength of Weak Ties. *American Journal of Sociology.* Vol. 78, No. 6, pp. 1360–1380.

Hitwise (2007). Presentation of findings by Bill Tancer at web 2.0 Expo, San Francisco April 2007.

Keegan, V. (2007). Amateurs can be good and bad news. *The Guardian*, 5 July 2007.

Keen, A. (2007). *The Cult of the Amateur: How Today's Internet is Killing our Culture*. Doubleday/Random House, New York.

Keller Fay Group (2007). *WOM Marketing* www.kellerfay.com

Kim, W.G., Lee, C. & Hiemstra, S.J. (2004). Effects of an online virtual community on customer loyalty and travel product purchases. *Tourism management.* Vol. 25, No. 2, pp. 343–355.

Lin, H-F. (2007). The role of online and offline features in sustaining virtual communities: an empirical study. *Internet Research.* Vol. 17, No. 2, pp. 119–138.

Lin, T.M.Y., Wu, H-H., Liao, C-W. & Liu, T-H. (2006). Why are some emails forwarded and others not?. *Internet Research*. Vol. 16, No. 1, pp. 81–93.

Luo, X. (2002). Trust production and privacy concerns on the Internet: a framework based on relationship marketing and social exchange theory. *Industrial Marketing Management*. Vol. 31, pp. 111–118.

MarketingSherpa and Prospectiv (2007). *Online Shopping and Email Relationships*. Available on www.marketingsherpa.com/article. html?ident = 29968. Accessed May 2007.

McConnell, B. & Huba, J. (2007). Citizen Marketers. Kaplan.

Meadows-Klue, D. (2008). Falling in Love 2.0: Relationship marketing for the Facebook generation. *Journal of Direct, Data and Digital Marketing Practice*. Vol. 9.3, pp. 245–250.

Nelson, M.R. & Otnes, C.C. (2005). Exploring cross-culture ambivalence, a netnography of intercultural wedding boards. *Journal of Business Research*. Vol. 58, No. 1.

Nielsen, J. (2006). *Participation equality: encouraging more users to contribute*. Available online at: www.useit.com/alertbox/participation_inequality. html

Opinion Research Corporation (2008). Online Consumer Reviews Significantly Impact Consumer Purchasing Decisions. Opinionresearch. com

Pew Internet & American Life Project (2007). *Teens and Social Media*.

Pitta, D.A. & Fowler, D. (2005). Online consumer communities and their value to new product developers. *Journal of Product and Brand management*. Vol. 14, No. 5.

RapLeaf (2008) Press release on research conducted into gender issues in Internet use.www.rapleaf.com

Scott, D.M. (2007). *The New Rules of Marketing & PR*. Wiley.

Tamar (2007). The 2007 Social Media for Brands Report. www.tamar.com

The etailing group inc. (2007). *Social Shopping Study*. www.e-tailing.com

TNS, TRU & Marketing Evolution (2007). Never Ending Friending – *a Journey into Social Networking*. Fox Interactive Media Inc.

Universal McCann (2008). *Power to the people-Social Media Tracker Wave 3*. www.universalmccann.com

Weber, L. (2007). *Marketing to the Social Web*. Wiley.

# The Internet as part of an integrated marketing strategy

> *The questions are the same, but this year the answers are different*
> Albert Einstein

## CHAPTER AT A GLANCE

## 10.1 INTRODUCTION

This chapter differs from all those that have gone before in that it has only one section – and rather than examining a specific element of online marketing it takes a more holistic approach and considers the role of the Internet in contemporary marketing strategy. In essence, it is a review of how all the other chapters' subjects must come together for any Internet marketing to be effective.

> the marketer that will excel at integrating all elements of marketing is the one who puts the needs of the customer first

It is vital, however, that before embarking on any kind of integrated strategy, the online marketer remembers the foundation stone of all effective marketing: the *customer comes first*. Certainly, the eventual strategy should take into account the relative strengths and weaknesses of the various media – and any marketing message must be consistent across those channels, but the marketer that will excel at integrating *all* elements of marketing is the one who puts the needs of the customer first. Any channel decisions, must, therefore, depend foremost on what the customer expects from the selling organization. It is also the case that – as with true market orientation – any integration should go beyond those deemed responsible for the marketing function. The customer cares little for the hierarchical structure of your organization, if they are dissatisfied with *any* element of the integrated strategy – and integration must be strategic – they are dissatisfied with the organization: full stop.

## 10.2 INTEGRATED ONLINE MARKETING

In chapter 1, I made reference to not only how any online objectives must fit with the wider (offline) objectives of the organization – but also that it is increasingly the case that the web is having a growing influence on consumer purchase behaviour. In a very short space of time, so ingrained has the Internet become in the lives of many consumers and businesses that some (including me) would argue that Internet marketing is now an essential, integral part of any contemporary marketing – be that strategic or operational. Indeed, there is an argument that books such as this one will soon be redundant because online marketing will be integrated into all generic marketing texts (though I would argue there will always be a need for Internet marketing *specialists*). While some organizations have acknowledged the Internet as an element of their marketing efforts, others seem more reluctant – despite bodies such as the US Direct Marketing Association (2008) making the point that if businesses are to be successful they must merge and synchronize all channels in terms of consistent brand message, timing, creativity of promotions, loyalty programs and fulfilment. It is also the case that many organizations that have included 'online' as an element of their marketing strategy still use the Internet as an independent aspect of that marketing – rather than integrating it with other *traditional* elements of the marketing mix. Of particular concern is the way in which so many companies use the Internet to drive web users to offline facilities (an acceptable online objective) but fail to consider the reverse – retailers moving customers from in–store to online, for example. There is also a reluctance demonstrated by many offline–only businesses to recognise the value of the Internet in encouraging customers to visit their premises – how many restaurants use email to drive customers to their premises, for example? However, this situation is likely to change if the search engines continue their development of local search.

## RESEARCH SNAPSHOT

### Welcome to the offline-online-offline shuffle

Shoppers are increasingly combining off- and online in their buying decision and purchase behaviour, with 71 per cent of respondents in research for paper – Surveying the Digital Future (University of Southern California's Annenberg School for Communication, 2008) – saying that they browse in retail outlets and either buy online or then research further on the web before returning offline to make a purchase. More specific are the results of a Nielsen survey (May 2008) which found that 80 per cent of people who had bought a consumer electronics product in a bricks and mortar store made that purchase from a store whose website they visited first, and research by Rawnet (Sept 2008) revealed that 86 per cent of UK consumers say they have researched a company online before choosing whether or not to use them. Furthermore – and this stresses the importance of the website's content – the Nielsen survey found that 53 per cent purchased from the retailer on whose site they had spent the most time, and Rawnet that 78 per cent have been put off from dealing with a company offline because of poor usability on its website.

*Source: University of Southern California's Annenberg School for Communication.*

 all aspects of online marketing are inextricably linked - and in many cases *interdependent*

Also worth noting (or reminding) is that like offline marketing, all aspects of online marketing are inextricably linked – and in many cases *interdependent*. Therefore none of the elements of Internet marketing should stand in isolation. The website will never be visited if there are no links to it, viral marketing requires email or social media websites to communicate the message and search engines are useless without websites to link to. So it is that in any Internet marketing strategy all components must dovetail together.

An example of how different elements of Internet marketing are combined to meet an online objective, the 'infographic' below illustrates how the astute marketer can use SEO, search engine advertising and social media marketing – including PR – in a branding exercise.

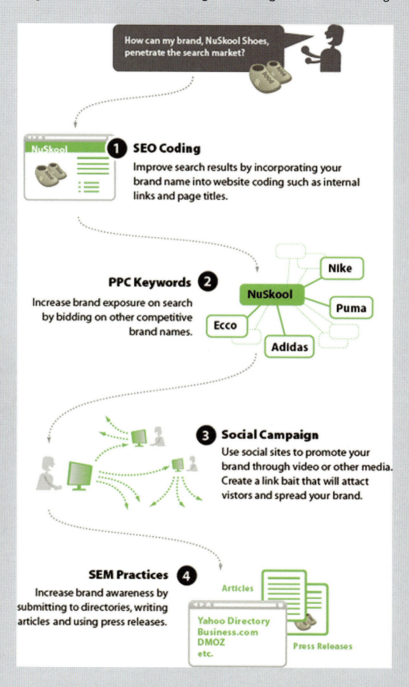

## The use of Internet in buyer behaviour

In section 1.6 we considered online buying behaviour from a theoretical standpoint (*why* it happens), in this section it is worth considering the ways in which that theory is acted out in practice (*how* it happens). In the book written with Richard Gay & Rita Esen (2007), I introduced a *purchase behaviour matrix* to indicate how many options are available to the contemporary retail customer in making a purchase. Figure 10.1 shows a small section of that matrix. The fuller version also makes the point that the purchase does not necessarily take place from the organization that supplies research information.

| Research conducted | Purchase made | Fulfilment method |
|---|---|---|
| Online | Online | Customer collects |
| Online | Online | Online |
| Online | Online | Delivered |
| Online | Offline | Delivered |
| Online | Offline | Customer collects |
| Online | Offline | Online |
| Offline | Online | Delivered |
| Offline | Online | Customer collects |
| Offline | Online | Online |

**Figure 10.1** Elements of the purchase behaviour matrix.

If we were to attempt to develop a matrix that included all the *potential* elements of the various offline media that might have an influence on the contemporary buyer – TV, radio, printed literature, telephone and physical stores, for example – as well as the different elements of online marketing (e.g. company website, retailers' sites, blogs, user generated content, search engines) we would need a matrix the size of a tennis court. Although it is fair to say that not all products will use all elements of such a matrix, marketers must take care that they have addressed every element within *their* matrix as any 'blank' might end a potential buyer's purchase path – and send them into the arms of a competitor who has met those information, purchase or fulfilment needs. Obviously, not only does the marketer need to make sure that they have covered each entry on their product's purchase behaviour matrix, but they should look to optimize the impact of each element on target customers. It is by considering the ways in which consumers go about their buying process that the marketer can make decisions on where their marketing efforts are most effectively concentrated – and for the contemporary marketer, this is rarely on one media.

343

messaging online. Significantly, a third of those multitasking viewers said that they discussed at least one of the commercials aired during the game as they were texting or messaging. The Blinkx study also revealed that opportunities are available to marketers in the targeting the double-dippers. For example, 25 per cent go online for information specific to the programme they are currently viewing on TV. Whilst this can include researching details of the show such as actors' profiles, it also includes some 40 per cent who are looking for products or services that appear in the programme or were advertised during its transmission. So if you know a film that features the main character wearing, driving, flying with or otherwise using your product (or service) is to be broadcast on network TV on a certain evening then perhaps your search engine and network advertising should be optimized for that time – with the ad text being tailored to the circumstances (e.g. 'did you like the resort where George Clooney's character met his future wife? – we have hotels there'). Furthermore, research by Arbitron and Edison Media Research (2008) revealed that 63 per cent of those who listen to the radio online have a profile on a social networking website such as MySpace, Facebook or Linkedin – suggesting that ads might be integrated between online radio and social media sites.

## RESEARCH SNAPSHOT

### Print newspaper ads drive online traffic – and purchases

According to consumer research on internet-using newspaper readers conducted by Clark, Martire & Bartolomeo Inc (published in 2008, and commissioned by Google), among people who research products and services after seeing them advertised in a newspaper, 67 per cent use the Internet to find more information – with nearly 70 per cent of them going on to make a purchase. Furthermore, 48 per cent of respondents said that seeing a product in the newspaper *after* seeing it online would make them trust the product more and so be more likely to purchase.

## B2B buyer behaviour

Although this chapter concentrates on B2C marketing, its elements are equally applicable to B2B environments. Much of this subject has been covered in previous sections of this book, most notably in section 1.4 – the Internet's impact on business. In particular there is a section on 'the business as the buyer' in which the point is made that 'firms make use of the Internet in their purchasing as a source of information' and that 'online research is used in 85 per cent of B2B purchase decision–making'. Section 5.2 also addresses the issue of B2B buyer behaviour, giving an example of an example of a B2B buying process (Figure 5.1). The role of the decision making unit (DMU) is also discussed in that section.

## RESEARCH SNAPSHOT

**What do B2B buyers look at online?**

A 2005 UK Association of Online Publishers (AOP) survey found that 82 per cent of B2B decision makers use the Internet as part of their workday, with more than 45 per cent spending up to five hours a day online for work purposes.

Respondents said they used the Internet 'every time' or 'sometimes' for the following activities:

| Activity | every time | sometimes |
|---|---|---|
| Keep up to date with news in their sector | 44% | 31% |
| Technical reference source | 33% | 38% |
| Review/analyze competitor activity | 25% | 36% |
| Research and inform business decisions | 22% | 41% |
| Review products and suppliers | 22% | 40% |
| Research and inform purchasing decisions | 19% | 36% |

An important message for marketers in a B2B environment is that those people responsible for procurement – your customers – are currently using the web in their personal shopping, and they are transferring their B2C buying expectations to their business practice. Sending out a few pamphlets in response to a telephone inquiry or advertising in obscure trade magazines may have been enough 15 years ago, but it is not the case now. Organizational buying decision makers now expect information to be readily available on a website – long before any formal contact is made with the seller.

## Online and offline integration

Having got this far in the book much of this section should be self–evident – indeed, the sections in which these subject appear take into account the relationship between the off– and online strategies and operations. However, sadly, it is still the case that far too often the Internet's (potential) contribution to any marketing strategy is marginalized – or even ignored. For those like myself who are on the outside and looking in on such campaigns, this is even more frustrating when the offline campaign actually lends itself to (a) directing potential customers to a website for more information, or (b) the nature of the marketing communication is such that the content is fleeting – and so viewers/listeners/readers go online to seek more details. Some integration issues that should be addressed with regard to elements of the online marketing mix include the following:

- Advertising – any multi–media campaign should include online as an element. This is particularly true of branding ads where repeated impressions are necessary to get the message across. The more opportunities

> *… on TV, viewers cannot click on the ad and so take the next step in the buying process*

there are for the target market to see the message the better. The widespread uptake of broadband has also paved the way for video ads to be used online – effectively, the same as users see on TV. Of course, the 'TV' ad that is shown online has a massive advantage over the TV–aired version – on TV, viewers cannot click on the ad and so take the next step in the buying process. Promotional websites set up on campaign–specific domain names can add to the impact in these circumstances. Furthermore, for those who (still) think that online advertising is only effective for online sales, a survey by Yahoo! Research (2007) found that 88 per cent of sales revenue generated from online advertising is derived from consumers who have seen an ad on the Internet but then make their purchase in a bricks and mortar store.

## MINI CASE

### Stand to attention when you access this website

This example of integrated marketing comes from an unexpected source – recruitment ads for the British Army. The campaign starts on TV, with a series of ads which feature hand-held-camera 'action' videos that stop at a critical moment – e.g. a bomb exploding. Viewers are then directed to the website to see how the event turns out. On the website the potential recruit [customer] can watch the full version of the videos that show subsequent events after the TV ad stopped. Follow the link on the chapter's web page to see the army jobs homepage.

- Permission marketing – rather like online advertising, there is an assumption that email marketing is useful only for driving people to websites, but they can be used to good effect in offering inducements to visit retail outlets in much the same way as direct mail has done for years. This is particularly true in the US, where discount coupons are a way of life – and coupons can be delivered electronically and printed by the recipients. Remarkably, many proprietary CRM systems are not designed to connect seamlessly with online–sourced data – that collected on an e–commerce site, for example. This situation means that in many cases the online CRM and the offline CRM are not connected – and so the very benefits that are hoped to be gained by installing the systems in the first place are lost. In my experience financial institutions seem to be particularly guilty of this oversight.
- Social media marketing – perhaps the element of Internet marketing that is proving to be the hardest to integrate with offline marketing. Given that it is the newest of the online marketing applications, this is perhaps not surprising. However, it must be noted that many of those in a position to make strategic marketing decisions do not understand the medium – or even try to do so. The fact that the (very) few social media

>  such is the power of the search engines that *Internet* marketing is – effectively – *search engine* marketing

success stories are highly publicised, does not help – with too many marketers perceiving the medium as being easy – 'you just put a funny video on YouTube and wait for the money to role in'. Naturally, there is also the issue of how the social media is dominated by user generated content – something that cannot be controlled by organizations, though an astute marketing team can use them to their advantage both operationally and strategically. Even blogs developed on behalf of, or by, the organization – where control is complete – can be problematic.

In a survey (Euroblog2007, 2007) of public relations professionals from 24 European countries, 88 per cent of the respondents said that integrating blogs into an organization's communication strategy was the biggest challenge in using blogs.

However, when addressing the subject of this chapter – integrated marketing – it is with search engines that that the overwhelming emphasis must rest. As I suggested in the introduction to chapter 6 (on search engine optimization), there is an argument to support the notion that such is the power of the search engines that *Internet* marketing is – effectively – *search engine* marketing. Although the other elements of the Internet all have a part to play in online marketing, it is the ubiquity of the search engines that sees them as the authority in any e–marketing efforts. Essentially, the search engines are the gateway to website content – and as such they hold the key to integrated marketing strategies and operations.

## RESEARCH SNAPSHOT

### Online business, traditional sales methods

A 2008 report released by Shop.org of a survey conducted by Forrester Research showed that nearly half of online retailers send out print catalogues to customers.

## Online search – offline purchase

Typical of research that emphasises the influence of search engines on Internet marketing is one from DoubleClick Performics (2007) which targeted American 'moms' – of whom 89 per cent used the web daily. The survey found that:

- 70 per cent use search engines before making any online purchase – with 92 per cent saying that they were helpful in providing valuable information prior to purchasing.
- 57 per cent use search engines to gather information before making any offline purchase – 79 per cent said search engines were helpful in this regard.
- 64 per cent use search engines to find out where to purchase products offline (the *local* issue raised in the previous section).

## MINI CASE

### Off– and online partnership works for cereal advertisers

For their Christmas 2006 Special K *healthier eating* TV ad campaign, Kelloggs teamed up with Yahoo!. Instead of the viewers being referred to a specific URL, they were directed to Yahoo!'s search facility. Anyone typing Special K into the search engine was presented with a co-branded customized search result page providing targeted routes for users – with one path being a forum for users to get help and ask questions related to their health. The content – and the co-branding – helped make the web pages appear less like ads and more like a social media site that helped visitors in their endeavours in achieving a healthier lifestyle.

Although the search engines do provide the facility of online search, they are only part of the overall product search. Often, search engines are given the full credit for helping customers find a product – or information that will help them reach a buying decision. However, in many situations the search engine might well be the last step in the search, but it is not necessarily the first. Any contact with the product, whether that be physical (seeing a new model of car in the street), as a result of promotional activity (seeing an ad for the car on the side of a passing bus), in another media (a review of the car in a newspaper or magazine) or online (a blogger commenting on the car) – might prompt the user to go to a search engine. Marketers should remember this, and factor in the benefits – and costs – of other marketing efforts before they heap the laurels on either SEO or search advertising.

*Go Online*

For an example of how a major European car manufacturer missed a 'search plus' trick when launching a new model, follow the link on the chapter's web page.

Two pieces of extensive research on the same subject – but a year apart – suggest that online search is increasingly prompted by offline influences. According to research conducted by iProspect (2007), two-thirds of search engine searches are prompted by offline influences – an equal split between TV ads and word of mouth from friends or acquaintances. They also found that when searching in response to an offline influence, over two-thirds used either the company or product name as a keyword – so called 'branded' keywords. For the contemporary marketer the importance of integration between off- and online is magnified by further findings that of the two-thirds of searches prompted by offline influences, 39 per cent resulted in a purchase. A more recent survey conducted on behalf of Krillion and the E-Tailing Group (Freedman, L. 2008) asked what leading media and other influencers typically trigger a search for product information online. The results are shown in Table 10.1 with the results of the

**Table 10.1** A comparison of events that trigger online search

| Offline influences on web search | IProspect 2007 | Freedman 2008 |
|---|---|---|
| Television | 37 (%) | 50 (%) |
| Word of mouth | 36 (%) | 56 (%) |
| Visit to a store | 20 (%) | 49 (%) |
| Magazine or newspaper | 30 (%) | 44 (%) |

**Table 10.2** Offline influences on online search

| IProspect 2007 | Freedman 2008 |
|---|---|
| Radio ad – 17% | To solve an immediate need – 58% |
| Billboard/other signage – 9% | Catalogues/Direct mail – 44% |
| Ad/name on corp. vehicle – 7% | Article about the product – 42% |
| Ad on train, taxi, bus – 3% | Newspaper circulars – 38% |
|  | Consumer Reports Magazine – 38% |

earlier iProspect research alongside. Table 10.2 lists some of the other offline events that trigger the use of an online search engine.

To consider how off- and online marketing can be integrated to good effect it is worth considering the concept of 'search plus'. Although people may use a search engine to seek further information on a product, brand or organization that they have come across in an offline environment, this concept relies on the marketer being proactive in either building search engine optimization or buying relevant key word advertising for terms that are associated with offline marketing efforts for the period that they run. For example, a TV ad campaign might feature a memorable tagline – in which case the tagline would be purchased as a key word so that when the phrase is entered into a search engine the top listing (organic, sponsored or both) is for the advertised product. Other search plus applications include:

- Search plus television – where ads and product placement can cause search spikes for relevant key phrases e.g. 'Keira Knightley dress' during an Oscar ceremony.
- Search plus outdoor – both pedestrians and commuters often get only a fleeting glance at an outdoor ad, and so may search for details online when they reach their home or work.
- Search plus word of mouth – in this instance, *word of mouth* refers to both the off- and online application (viral). Search advertising can be used to reinforce the positive, and respond to the negative, word of mouth message.
- Search plus public relations – this can be proactive or reactive. Paid placement can be arranged in advanced of a co-ordinated PR event, or pertinent key words can be purchased to provide a reaction to bad news.
- Search plus direct mail – where direct mailings – both off- and online – promote a product or service, key words can be purchased so that

if potential customers go online to seek further information on the promoted product the brand message is reinforced by it appearing high on the SERP.

Note that this section is based on my description of 'search plus' in my book, *Key Concepts in e–Commerce* (2007).

### Building trust through search engine marketing

Even within limited online marketing objectives, different aspects of the discipline must be integrated if there is to be a successful outcome. The 'infographic' below illustrates how search engine marketing can be used to develop the trust of a potential customer. The diagram shows how a search on a single keyword can take the user to a number of different *types* of website – each of which will have an influence on the customer, and all should be part of the Internet marketer's portfolio.

Building trust through search engine marketing:

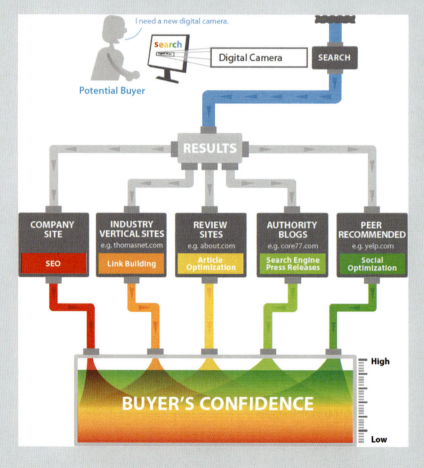

## Decision time

Marketers are now plying their trade in an environment of complex consumer purchase behaviour in which the Internet can sit at the beginning, middle or end of a process that includes traditional media and other influences. Although there is a reasonable argument that in *some* industries, for *some* products, the Internet offers little to the marketer, whether this is the case or not, it is a foolish marketer who does not even *consider* how online might add to their marketing armoury. It is still the case that the potential of online marketing is too often either wasted or disregarded. Even in markets that one would assume were prime targets for Internet marketing, many brands ignore the benefits that digital marketing channels offer them – particularly in the valuable youth market where the young are confronted with *'patronising, ill-conceived, generic attempts to engage them'* (Spero and Stone 2004).

> **"** the potential of online marketing is too often either wasted or disregarded **"**

---

## RESEARCH SNAPSHOT

### Lost online sales is an integrated problem

At the eMetrics Summit in San Francisco in May 2008 online experience specialists iPerceptions gave some early results gleaned from their [then] new 4Q online research facility (http://4q.iperceptions.com). This included that when going to a website 39 per cent of visitors went to learn about products and 27 per cent went to buy – of that 27 per cent, around two-thirds actually completed the task.

Reasons for not purchasing included:

- Better product selection sought −31 per cent
- Better shipping options desired −24 per cent
- Problems with the online shopping cart −17 per cent
- Prices were too high −14 per cent

Why have I included these statistics in this chapter? Take another look at the four complaints listed. Only one – shopping cart problems – is a pure 'online' issue. Price is well beyond online's control, as is stock selection (unless online has chosen not to list all products available offline). Shipping options are part of fulfilment – a part of, but not solely a responsibility of, online.

---

The appreciation that it is rarely one channel in isolation that delivers sales – with customers being likely to have been exposed to multiple marketing channels before making a purchase – brings with it another complexity for the marketer. That is, what are the separate impacts of the various channels on the purchase decision? For example, a customer's journey from first interaction to purchase might include them being exposed to the organization's marketing efforts by:

- Reading about the product in print media as part of pre–launch public relations
- Reading blogs on the new product's capabilities
- Seeing the ad released on social media (e.g. YouTube) as part of pre–launch
- Seeing the ad on TV
- Searching on the product tag line on Google (organic listing)
- Receiving direct email
- Seeing the ad in print media
- Reading consumer generated reviews on social media sites
- Visiting websites to check applicability to their needs
- Telephone call to query suitability – routed through a call centre
- Searching on Google for local availability (sponsored ad listing)
- Visiting a physical outlet to view, touch and feel product
- Using online shopping comparison sites to find cheapest price
- Visiting a physical retailer to make the purchase

When a customer – or potential customer – makes contact with any of the organization's touch–points, one of two things will result:

1. The immediate or eventual result may or may not be a sale.
2. The reputation of the organization, brand or product may be enhanced or damaged.

Not only will any gap in the organization's marketing efforts risk potential failure of the process (the sales funnel), but for the integrated marketer the development of some kind of multi-attribution model is necessary to best apportion credit (or blame) to the various elements and determine budgets for any future marketing efforts.

*You Decide*

Develop a purchase behaviour matrix for either Huxley University or if you are a student – your own university or college. Then identify the key online elements and comment on how they might be part of an integrated marketing strategy.

Alternatively, conduct the same exercise on your own organization or that of your employer.

## CHAPTER EXERCISE

Giving justifications for all your decisions, choose any of the case studies and advise the owners/managers on all aspects of how Internet marketing should be integrated into their overall marketing strategy.

Alternatively, conduct the same exercise on your organization or that of your employer.

# REFERENCES

Arbitron and Edison Media Research (2008). *Infinite Dial 2008: Radio's Digital Platforms*. www.arbitron.com

Association of National Advertisers [with BtoB magazine] (2007). *Harnessing the power of New Media Platforms*.

Blinkx (2008). *Survey of TV and Online Video Habits*. Conducted by Harris Interactive. www.blinkx.com

Clark, Martire & Bartolomeo Inc *Survey, Oct 2007* (published in 2008, and commissioned by Google)

Direct Marketing Association (2008). *Channel Integration and Benchmarks in the Retail Industry*. www.dma.org.uk

DoubleClick Performics (2007). *Searcher Moms – A Search Behavior and Usage Study*. www.performics.com

Euroblog2007 (2007). *Social Software-A Revolution for Communication? Implications and Challenges for Communication Management and PR*. Available on www.euroblog2007.org

Freedman, L. (2008). The Web/Store Cross-Channel Shopping Survey. Krillion and the E-Tailing Group.

Gay, R., Charlesworth, A. & Esen, R. (2007). Online Marketing-Customer-Led Approach. University Press, Oxford.

iProspect (2007). *Offline Channel influence on Online Search behaviour Study* www.iProspect.com.

Nielsen Online (2008). Consumer Electronics Survey. www.nielsen-netratings.com

Rawnet (2008). Online Conversion Report. www.rawnet.com

Shankar, V., Smith, A. & Rangaswamy, R. (2003). Customer satisfaction and loyalty in online and offline environments. *International Journal of Research in marketing*. Vol. 20 pp. 153–175.

Solutions Research Group (2007). *Multitasking Sorts Viewers Engaged with Advertising*. Available online at www.srgnet.com

University of Southern California's Annenberg School for Communications Center for the Digital Future (2008). *Surveying the Digital Future*. www.digitalcenter.org

Yahoo! Research (2007). *Research Online, Buy Offline*.

# Index